CONTEXTS
FOR LEARNING
TO WRITE

Writing Research

Multidisciplinary Inquiries into the Nature of Writing

edited by Marcia Farr, University of Illinois at Chicago

IN PREPARATION

Marcia Farr (ed.), *ADVANCES IN WRITING RESEARCH, VOLUME ONE CHILDREN'S EARLY WRITING DEVELOPMENT*

Lester Faigley, Roger Cherry, David Joliffe, and Anna Skinner, *ASSESSING WRITERS' KNOWLEDGE AND PROCESSES OF COMPOSING*

FORTHCOMING

Martha L. King and Victor Rentel, *The Development of Meaning in Writing: Children 5–10*

Stephen Witte, Keith Walters, Mary Trachsel, Roger Cherry, and Paul Meyer, *Literacy and Writing Assessment: Issues, Traditions, Directions*

Sarah W. Freedman (ed.), *The Acquisition of Written Language: Revision and Response*

William Teale and Elizabeth Sulzby (eds.), *Emergent Literacy: Writing and Reading*

Judith Langer, *Children Reading and Writing: Structures and Strategies*

Anthony Petrosky (ed.), *Reading and Writing: Theory and Research*

Jana Staton, *Interactive Writing in Dialogue Journals: Linguistic, Social, and Cognitive Views*

Elizabeth Sulzby, *A Longitudinal Study of Emergent Writing and Reading in 5–6 Year Olds*

David Smith, *Explorations in the Culture of Literacy*

Robert Gundlach, *Children and Writing in American Education*

Carole Edelsky, *Había Una Vez: Writing in a Bilingual Program*

Leo Ruth and Sandra Murphy, *Designing Writing Tasks for the Assessment of Writing*

Contexts for Learning to Write:
Studies of Secondary School Instruction

Arthur N. Applebee
Stanford University

with contributions by

Judith A. Langer
University of California, Berkeley

Russel K. Durst
Kay Butler-Nalin
James D. Marshall
George E. Newell
Stanford University

ABLEX Publishing Corporation
Norwood, New Jersey 07648

Printed in the United States of America.

Library of Congress Cataloging in Publication Data

Applebee, Arthur N.
  Contexts for learning to write.

  Includes bibliographical references and indexes.
  1. English language—Composition and exercises—
Addresses, essays, lectures. 2. English language—Study
and teaching (Secondary)—Addresses, essays, lectures.
I. Langer, Judith A. II. Title.
LB1631.A59 1984   808'.042'0712   84-6428
ISBN 0-89391-225-5
ISBN 0-89391-283-2 (pbk.)

Ablex Publishing Corporation
355 Chestnut Street
Norwood, New Jersey 07648

Contents

List of Tables

List of Figures

Acknowledgments

Many people have contributed to the success of the project reported in this volume. The most important are those who allowed themselves to become the subjects of our study, including the students whose learning we examined and the schools and teachers who provided the context for those students' work. Without their cooperation, there would have been no study. We hope that the results will be sufficiently interesting to justify their faith that our work was worth the inconveniences we sometimes caused them.

Judith A. Langer was interested in our project from the beginning, and shared her comments and criticisms as the work unfolded. Her involvement developed from consultant and interested colleague, to a full collaborator in the research effort. The project was much the better for her participation, and she rarely grumbled about how much time it ultimately claimed.

From the start, we were lucky to have an enthusiastic and talented group of research assistants. Their expertise in a variety of academic disciplines as well as the years of teaching experience they had behind them were both important to the success of the project. Russel Durst, James Marshall, Kay Butler-Nalin, and George Newell were involved for most of the project, and shared the challenge of reporting our results. Many others made substantial contributions to the project, including David Bergin, Zeph Davis, Arthur Hall, Anne Katz, Marguerite McInnes, Bracha Rubinek, Deborah Swanson-Owens, and William Sweigert. Eve Dimon and Jennie Phillips provided secretarial support.

Funding was provided by a grant from the National Institute of Education to Stanford University, and support staff of both institutions have insured that arrangements for carrying the project through have moved smoothly.

The material in this publication was prepared with support in part by grant number NIE–G–80–0156 from the National Institute of Education, Department of Education. Grantees undertaking such projects under government sponsorship are encouraged to express freely their judgment in professional and technical matters. The opinions expressed in this publication do not necessarily reflect the position or policy of the National Institute of Education, and no official endorsement should be inferred.

Writing Research

Multidisciplinary Inquiries into the Nature of Writing

Marcia Farr, series editor
University of Illinois at Chicago

PREFACE

This series of volumes presents the results of recent scholarly inquiry into the nature of writing. The research presented comes from a mix of disciplines, those which have emerged as significant within the last decade or so in the burgeoning field of writing research. These primarily include English education, linguistics, psychology, anthropology, and rhetoric. A note here on the distinction between field and discipline might be useful: a field can be a multidisciplinary entity focused on a set of significant questions about a central concern (e.g., American Studies), while a discipline usually shares theoretical and methodological approaches which may have a substantial tradition behind them. Writing research, then, is a field, if not yet a discipline.

The history of this particular field is unique. Much of the recent work in this field, and much that is being reported in this series, has been conceptualized and funded by the National Institute of Education. Following a planning conference in June 1977, a program of basic research on the teaching and learning of writing was developed and funded annually. The initial research funded under this program is now coming to fruition, providing both implications for educational improvement and directions for future research. This series is intended as one important outlet for these results.

Chapter 1
Background to the Study

Arthur N. Applebee

INTRODUCTION

Learning to write is a complex and ongoing process. It begins early, with a child's first scribbles on the nearest table or wall, and continues (at least for the academically inclined) through the dissertation and beyond. For most of us, writing remains a difficult process, avoided at some length, and enjoyed most (if at all) only in the completion.

The present volume examines a cross section of the process of learning to write, concentrating on the high-school years, grades 9 through 12. These are the years during which students begin to learn the specialized registers of a variety of academic disciplines, from the intricacies of literary criticism to the abstractions of geometry. These are also years during which most students begin to undertake new and more complicated tasks in their writing, moving beyond initial strategies for reporting and summarizing to more complex techniques of analysis and argument.

The National Study of Writing in the Secondary School, supported for 3 ½ years by grants from the National Institute of Education, has sought to describe in detail the problems students face in learning to write during these years, as well as the instruction that they currently receive. In turn, we hope this account will provide a basis for sensible reform of the secondary school curriculum.

THE CURRENT STATE OF WRITING INSTRUCTION: THE FIRST PHASE OF THE NATIONAL STUDY

The first phase of the National Study (reported in Applebee, 1981) explored the writing instruction and writing experiences provided in various high school subject areas. Project staff members spent a full academic year in an intensive study of writing experiences in two high schools in the midwest. We focussed on ninth and eleventh grade classes, in all subject areas (including academic courses such as English and math, and nonacademic courses such as physical education and home economics). The case studies were designed to examine the variation in writing experiences across grade levels, subject areas, ability levels, and school settings; as a result, the two schools were selected to be as different from one another as possible, rather than to illustrate "typical" practice. One was a small, highly selective, academically-oriented school associated with a major midwestern university; the other was a large, urban high school serving a diverse student population with courses ranging from advanced placement to classes for the educable mentally handicapped. Some 85% of the teachers at the selected grade levels agreed to let us study their classes, 68 teachers in all. During the course of the year, we observed some 13,293 minutes of classroom instruction, interviewed the teachers, and interviewed their pupils.

During the spring of the case study year, we designed a national survey to place the results from our two case-study schools in a more generalizable context. For the survey, we constructed a stratified random sample of some 200 schools, and solicited the principals' help in identifying "good, experienced" teachers in six content areas: English, foreign languages, social science, science, mathematics, and business education. Each of these teachers was in turn asked to report on writing and related activities for a single class (chosen randomly by project staff from the teacher's current teaching assignments), and to provide samples of student writing from a recent assignment completed by the target class.

Results from the case-study schools and the national survey provide a good overview of the present state of writing instruction (see Applebee, 1981, for a detailed presentation of results). In general, there was widespread agreement among teachers in our samples that writing activities should have an important place in a variety of subject areas, not just in the English class. At the same time, however, there was equally widespread confusion about the roles that writing might play in the curriculum, and about the implications of one or another approach for the skills that students would learn.

It has become a commonplace to say that in order to learn to write better, students should be asked to write more often. In one sense, our results support this notion. We found that students were spending only about 3% of their school time—in class or for homework—on writing of paragraph length or longer. On the other hand, students were engaged in a variety of related activities that involved writing but not composing: fill-in-the-blank exercises, worksheets requiring only short responses, translation from one language to another, and the like.

Even in those contexts where students were being asked to write at some length, the writing often served merely as a vehicle to test knowledge of specific content, with the teacher functioning primarily as an examiner. Although this is a traditional and legitimate use of writing in schools, its relationship to the learning of new writing skills must be at best tenuous. In our studies, we have found that the teacher-as-examiner can be a very undemanding audience, one willing to interpret what the student meant to say. Teachers are able to do this because they already know what should have been said, and are looking for hints that at least some of the desired material is present. When the appropriate "evidence" is presented, the teacher, rather than the student, may construct the "argument" that holds the essay together.

In general, we found an imbalance in the kinds of instruction and practice that students were receiving. Although a high proportion of class time in all subject areas emphasized writing skills at the word and sentence levels, students were seldom asked to employ these skills at greater length—rarely even to construct a paragraph, let alone an essay or longer report. Indeed, most school activities had separated the problems of constructing coherent arguments and explanations from those of remembering subject information and concepts. Teachers were taking over the difficulties inherent in using language appropriate to a subject area—including much of the specialized vocabulary and rules of procedure embedded in the text—leaving the student only the task of mechanically "slotting in" missing information.

This "slotting in" took two forms. In the most obvious, "writing tasks" were restricted to the relatively mechanical activities mentioned earlier—fill-in-the-blank exercises, multiple-choice responses, direct translation from one language to another, and the like. Less obviously, even when students were asked to write an essay, the essays were treated as tests of previous learning. The task for the students was one of repeating information that had already been organized by the teacher or textbook, rather than of extending and integrating new learning for themselves.

This emphasis on writing to evaluate previous learning had many direct instructional consequences. Prewriting activities were minimal, usually no more than an explanation of the "topic" and instructions as to length and form; help during the writing task was rarely provided; and reactions to completed work focussed on "accuracy" and "correctness," rather than on the development of ideas.

Such approaches are, however, reasonable when the body of relevant information has been presented and synthesized through lectures and textbooks. In such a situation (if the students have done their work) it should be enough simply to state an essay topic. The topic will cue the relevant information, which students will repeat from memory. If the information has been well learned, the performance will be routine, "writing" should pose little problem, and the teacher's role can be minimal.

In looking at samples of student writing gathered from our national sample, the topic in fact proved to be a good index to this view of writing. In many cases, students were asked to write on topics that were, in a real sense, impossible; the following example is one of our favorites, but it is typical of many that we observed:

> Western Europe on the eve of Reformation was a civilization going through great changes. In a well-written essay describe the political, economic, social, and cultural changes Europe was going through at the time of the Reformation. (23 points)
>
> —9th-grade Social Studies

Books could be written in response to such a question; it becomes a possible topic for school writing only because it serves to index bodies of previously presented information.

Such tasks are highly efficient for some purposes, but the knowledge required can remain isolated and detached. There is little need for students to relate new information to other aspects of their experience, or even to integrate the learning that has taken place within a particular subject area. Though helping students toward such an integration may be one of the most important reasons for asking them to write, it is an approach that is widely neglected.

EXPLORING CONTEXTS FOR LEARNING TO WRITE

Our initial studies provided a rich portrait of the state of writing instruction, by focussing on teachers and classrooms as a whole. In the second phase of our work, reported in this volume, we have shifted our focus toward the development of individual students' writing skills, and have begun to examine the changes that occur when teachers emphasize writing as a tool for exploring new ideas rather than as a way to test previous learning. We believe that such a shift in emphasis, though sometimes difficult to achieve, will be a necessary part of any meaningful reform of the secondary-school curriculum.

In addition to further analysis of data gathered during the national survey and the school studies, we have gathered several additional sets of data. Chapter 2 describes this additional data in detail: a study of textbooks in a variety of secondary school subject areas and a longitudinal study of the writing development of 15 students over a 16-month period. It also describes our system for analyzing student writing in terms of the audience addressed and the function or use the writing serves. Chapter 3 reports the results from our study of the writing activities suggested in popular textbooks. Chapter 4 introduces the case-study students and the writing they undertook during the 16 months we were working with them. Chapters 5 and 6 examine this writing in more detail, focussing on the organizational patterns students are mastering. Chapters 7 and 8 concentrate on the varying approaches our students took to their writing tasks, first as reported in their meetings with us, then as reflected in the evolution of their drafts. Chapters 9 and 10 address two special issues: the link between the problems students have in writing and their knowledge of the topic under consideration, and the role of writing as an aid to learning in content-area classrooms. Chapter 11 steps back from the interpretation of data, to develop in more detail the notion of instructional scaffolding and its usefulness in improving writing instruction. Finally, Chapter 12 highlights the findings that seem to us of most interest, and suggests some questions that need to be addressed in future studies.

Chapter 2
Procedures

Arthur N. Applebee

INTRODUCTION

The studies reported in this volume build upon the work summarized in Chapter 1. Data-gathering began in October 1980, continuing through May 1982. This chapter describes general procedures for the textbook studies, for the longitudinal studies of writing development, and for analyzing writing across all strands of data; results will be presented in the chapters which follow.

TEXTBOOK STUDIES

Sample Selection

Teachers surveyed as part of the National Study of Writing in the Secondary School (Applebee, 1981) were asked whether they regularly used a textbook in the classes being studied, and if so, which textbooks were used. Some 91% of the teachers responding reported regularly using textbooks; each provided us with one or more specific titles. Responses were compiled to generate a list of the three most popular textbooks in each subject, at each of the grade levels surveyed (ninth and eleventh). Because English classes regularly used two textbooks, separate lists were compiled for literature and composition texts. For foreign language texts, we focussed on Spanish, because it is the most widely taught foreign language (Osterdorf, 1975). As a check on our results, education editors at two large publishers of secondary school textbooks were asked to list the textbooks they believed to be most widely used, in each of the target subjects (composition/grammar, literature, Spanish, social science, science, mathematics, and business education).

The editors' reports verified the survey results, leaving us with a target sample containing 42 textbooks, 3 each in 7 subjects at 2 grade levels. Publishers of the

Table 2.1   Textbook sample

| | Number Analyzed | | | | | | Years Since: | |
| | Main Text | | Teacher's Manual | | Supplementary Materials | | First Edition | Edition Studied |
	Gr. 9	Gr. 11	Gr. 9	Gr. 11	Gr. 9	Gr. 11		
Composition/ Grammar	3	3	2	3	1	2	13.3	2.7
Literature	3	3	2	2	1	1	8.7	1.0
Foreign Language	3	3	0	0	2	1	10.8	1.5
Social Science	3	3	2	3	2	2	7.2	2.3
Science	3	3	1	2	2	0	7.6	3.8
Math	3	3	3	2	0	0	11.0	1.7
Business	3	3	2	1	3	3	11.0	1.2
Totals:	21	21	12	13	11	9	9.9	2.0

texts were asked to provide review copies for our analyses, and most did so. Six texts not provided by the publisher were purchased to complete the sample. Because many of the textbooks were part of a larger program, we asked publishers to send us copies of any supplementary materials and teachers manuals designed for use with the target text. Separate manuals were available for 25 of the texts in our sample; supplementary texts or workbooks were available for 20. Table 2.1 summarizes the final sample of material, including the average number of years since publication. (The year of the national survey—1980—is used as the base year for these computations.)

Analyses

The textbook sample was used for two main purposes. In one set of analyses, reported in Chapter 3, we examined the kinds of writing activities provided for students to complete. In a second set of analyses, presented in Chapter 5, we treated textbook writing as one of the major models of expert writing provided to students in various disciplines.

LONGITUDINAL STUDIES OF WRITING DEVELOPMENT

Sample Selection

A second strand of data came from a series of case studies of the development of writing skills in individual students over a 16-month period (March 1981–June 1982). Because our primary interest was in tracing patterns of growth (rather than in documenting failures in instruction), we selected the students from a single academically oriented high school with a strong English department, stable and well trained staff, and supportive community. This school was located in the San Francisco Bay area.

Students were selected for the study on the basis of recommendations from the English department and from the director of English as a Second Language (ESL). Students were initially categorized by grade level (ninth, eleventh), status as a writer (teachers' nominations: more successful, less successful, English as a second language), and sex.

At the beginning of the case study, prospective participants met individually with project staff to discuss the study. Those who met the selection criteria were asked to sign a permission form expressing their willingness to participate; similar permission letters were obtained from their parents.

The initial briefing sessions were followed by background interviews with 21 students chosen to participate in the study; these interviews dealt with writing

Table 2.2   The case-study students

The Fifteen Case-Study Students	Category of Writer	Beginning Grade Level	Months in Study
Bill	More successful	9	16
Sherri	More successful	9	16
Jan	Less successful	9	13
Elaine	Less successful	9	16
Larry	Less successful	9	13
Li	ESL (Chinese)	9	16
Margery	More successful	11	16
Donna	More successful	11	16
Sandy	More successful	11	16
Mark	Less successful	11	16
Terri	Less successful	11	16
Emily	Less successful	11	16
Michael	ESL (Chinese)	11	16
Lynn	ESL (Chinese)	11	16
Tai	ESL (Chinese)	11	16
Students Who Withdrew in Second Year			
Sam	More successful	9	4
Maria	ESL (Spanish)	9	4
Rosa	ESL (Spanish)	9	4
Wayne	More successful	11	4
Randy	Less successful	11	4
Students Who Withdrew in First Year			
Jerry	More successful	9	1
Barry	Less successful	9	2
Fred	More successful	11	3

history, current courses, and general attitudes toward writing. Three of the initial group of students withdrew and were replaced with 2 additional students during the first 7 weeks of the study. Of the 20 students remaining at the beginning of the next academic year, 15 continued to participate throughout the 16-month period. Table 2.2 summarizes the distribution of students in the final sample, as well as those who withdrew before the end of the 16 months.

Case Study Procedures

The success of the case studies depended upon establishing a comfortable relationship between each student and the research team. To foster this, each student worked directly with one team member, with a second team member serving as a backup when scheduling became difficult. This worked well, in spite of some shifts that were necessary because of changes in research staff or in students' schedules.

Participating students were asked to save all writing of at least paragraph length, and to share it with project staff. Each student was given a special file at the school, and was encouraged to leave all papers in that file at the end of each school day. Project staff members checked the files regularly and photocopied all writing, returning the originals to the students. Students were also encouraged to share with us any papers they had saved from earlier years.

All interview sessions were tape recorded, to allow later amplification of notes taken during the sessions. Follow up interviews were scheduled every 2 weeks with each student, to discuss current writing and to insure that completed writing was being shared through the student files. (Some students waited until these meetings to bring in their papers; others preferred the daily school file. We concentrated on collecting as complete a sample as possible, using whichever procedure worked best for a particular student.)

Each interview session began with a series of standard questions about on-going writing projects, followed by discussion of particular assignments. In general, we tried to discuss one piece of completed writing in detail at each session, and to inventory the full range of activities currently underway. In choosing specific assignments to discuss in detail, we focussed on major assignments rather than brief pieces, whenever a choice was available. Even with this focus, 64% of the assignments we discussed at greater length were expected to be completed within one day (usually, within one class period).

The interview sessions provided us with a check on the comprehensiveness of our sample of the students' writing. Overall, we collected 84.5% of the school writing of paragraph length or better completed by our students during the case-study period. We also collected 90.1% of the self-sponsored writing which they discussed with us, though it is likely that some self-sponsored writing activities (e.g., letters and diaries) were not reported to us. In general, the students were most likely to remember to share writing from contexts in which they wrote regularly. Thus collection rates were highest for English and social science classes (85 and 86%, respectively) and lowest in mathematics and foreign languages (67 and 75%, respectively).

Collection rates were essentially identical for the three groups of students: 82.2% for the better writers, 84.0% for the weaker writers, and 86.0% for the students for whom English was a second language.

Throughout this book, in presenting samples of student comments and student writing we have preserved the form in which it was shared with us, including the vocabulary, syntax, and spelling of the original.

Analysis of Interview Data

Data from the case studies were synthesized in a variety of ways. At the end of each interview, researchers prepared a summary of student comments and of issues that had arisen; these provided a first synthesis of the data, as well as a reminder of topics to pursue at the next meeting. At the end of the first academic year (after approximately 3 months of data collection), the results from the biweekly interviews were combined with those from the background interview in a series of portraits of the 20 students then in the study. These portraits provided a reference point for the work in the second year of the study, during which they were elaborated and expanded. A final portrait, confirming or revising the initial commentary, was completed at the end of the second year.

In addition to these qualitative syntheses, tallies of current writing activities were kept throughout the study, to provide estimates of the amount of writing actually being completed and of the completeness of our sample of student writing. A coding of all topics discussed in the biweekly interviews was also completed at the end of the study, during a final review of the tapes from the sessions. This coding was organized around a number of general areas of discussion, allowing us to look first at the topics that were discussed most frequently (e.g., the composing process, marking and evaluation, the nature of the assignment), and then, within each topic, at the particular comments the students had made.

Topics Discussed

The final coding of the tape recorded biweekly interviews was based on 294 separate discussions of individual papers or of the writing process in general. The specific topics addressed in each interview reflected a mixture of (a) our concerns as a research team, and (b) the students' concerns as they shared their writing with us. Table 2.3 summarizes the most frequent topics of discussion, separately for the more successful writers, the less successful writers, and the students for whom English was a second language. In general, there were few differences in the topics discussed with the three groups of students (though as we will see in later chapters, their comments on most topics differed considerably).

Table 2.3   Topics discussed most frequently during interviews

Topic	Total	Better Writers	Poorer Writers	ESL Students
		Mean Percent of Discussions		
Writing process	81.4	66.8	71.8	89.0
Knowledge base	72.7	77.0	68.3	73.8
Choice of topic	66.9	66.6	66.7	67.4
Time for writing	58.3	67.4	58.1	47.4
Preparation before writing	58.6	60.9	50.3	68.1
Audience	51.3	51.2	37.9	71.3
Interest in assignment	51.0	61.9	48.3	41.5
Writing problems	44.8	48.4	32.2	59.4
Nature of revisions	39.9	40.2	31.8	51.5
Teacher's response to the paper	33.1	39.4	19.1	46.2
n of interviews	294	97	116	81
n of students	15	5	6	4

Case-Study Statistics

Our case-study data are characterized by relatively large numbers of observations for relatively small numbers of students. To insure that group results are representative of the full group of case-study students, rather than biased toward those who talked or wrote the most, the data presented throughout this book represent means across students, rather than across observations. Thus to arrive at the estimates in Table 2.3, we first calculated the percent of each individual student's discussions that touched on each of the topics, and then averaged these percents across the 15 students. (The difference between this calculation and simply averaging across the 294 interviews turned out to be small; in Table 2.3, the alternative calculation would change the reported values by no more than 3 percentage points.)

ANALYZING WRITING ACTIVITIES

School writing activities differ from one another in many ways. Some activities are relatively informal, involving notes or observations written down primarily for the student's own later use. Others are more formal, requiring adherence to the conventions of the 5-paragraph theme, the science laboratory report, or the analysis of a literary text. Some require polished "first draft" writing (often as a test of what has been learned); others allow extensive drafting and revising. Some are perfunctory; some playful; some demanding; some involved.

Throughout the work reported in this volume, we have classified writing samples and writing activities along two dimensions that seem fundamental: (a) the audience to whom the student has decided to write, and (b) the function or purpose that gives the piece its shape and direction (e.g., as story or report). Both systems of analysis are based on the work of Britton et al. (1975), as extended and refined in Applebee (1981). The sections that follow provide a brief overview of the major distinctions, as well as a summary of the modifications that we made in order to increase the reliability of the analyses and to extend their scope to include assignments as well as completed writing samples.

Audience

Audience is a complex concept, involving considerations of genre, content, tone, style, and the reader's previous experience with the topic. The system which we chose to use is a relatively simple one that focusses on the relationship which the writer assumes to exist between writer and reader. Four categories were distinguished:

1. Self. Writing that is meant primarily for the writer's own use. Common forms include personal journals and diaries, lists and notes of things to do, and problem-solving notes or jottings used to react to or explore new problems or ideas.
2. Teacher: as part of an instructional dialogue. Writing directed toward the teacher, as part of an ongoing instructional dialogue rather than as a test of skills already learned. Such writing is usually embedded in the context of a particular instructional sequence and assumes that the teacher will respond with help in solving the problem, or with reactions to the ideas expressed.
3. Teacher: in the role of examiner. Writing used to demonstrate learning of information or skills. The writer assumes that the main response will be an evaluation of performance. Usually, the writer assumes that there is one correct answer to give or form to follow, and that the major task is to provide that answer or to follow that form.
4. Wider audience. The writer assumes that he or she has something to say that is of interest to others. With younger students, this often takes the form of writing addressed to a specific person or group (e.g., a letter to a friend; a story to be shared with classmates). With older students, it may take the form of writing to a more general, unknown other (e.g., the readership of a particular magazine) and usually involves the assumption of expertise in a particular subject or genre (e.g., in storytelling).

In the present series of studies, we found that the audience categories used in our earlier work (Britton et al., 1975; Applebee, 1981) extended directly to our analyses of textbook assignments as well as to the new writing samples we collected. We did, however, introduce a number of refinements and elaborations of coding instructions, to reduce ambiguity and improve interrater reliability.

The final version of our coding instructions is included in Appendix 1. Modifications include further rules for distinguishing teacher-as-examiner from teacher-as-trusted adult; elaboration of the rules for coding letters, where there is a tension between an explicit audience (the addressee) and the implicit teacher-as-audience; and additional emphasis upon the need to ignore writing quality in coding audience (to reduce a tendency to rate better writing "up" the scale toward wider audience, and poorer papers "down" the scale).

Analyses of audience in student writing were based on ratings by two independent raters, with a third rating to reconcile disagreements; analyses of textbook assignments were based on a single rating, with a subsample of 277 exercises rated twice to provide estimates of interrater agreement. Textbook assignments were scored in one series of scoring sessions; student writing samples from all of the various strands of our work were scored in another series. Interrater agreement for audience ranged from .97 for the 15,279 textbook samples to .92 for analyses of 1,519 student writing samples. These compare with interrater agreement of .71 for the earlier ratings (Applebee, 1981).

Function

The analysis of writing function distinguished among four general uses of writing, each with a variety of subcategories.

1. Writing without composing. Tasks which require written responses but that do not require the writer to organize text segments of paragraph length. Such tasks range from multiple-choice and fill-in-the-blank exercises to extensive translations from one language to another (where the original text provides the overall organization, allowing the student to focus on sentence-level problems).
2. Informational writing. Writing which focusses on the sharing of information or opinions with others. This includes the wide variety of forms of expository writing, ranging from simple reports about specific events to highly abstract, theoretical arguments. It also includes writing where the attempt to persuade overrides all other purposes (as in advertisements or propaganda), and regulative writing (e.g., laws or school rules).
3. Personal writing. Writing that is embedded within a context of shared, familiar concerns. The audience for such writing is usually the self or a very close friend; the function is to explore new ideas and experiences simply to sort them out, rather than to make a specific point. Gossip in spoken language illustrates the general category; in school writing, this use occurs mostly in journals or "learning logs" where new ideas are explored for the writer's own benefit.
4. Imaginative writing. Writing within any of the various literary genres.

Figure 2.1   Uses of School Writing

Writing without composing (mechanical uses of writing)
- Multiple-choice exercises
- Fill-in-the-blank exercises (answered with less than a sentence)
- Short-answer exercises (brief, one or two sentences per question)
- Math calculations
- Transcription from written material (copying)
- Transcription from oral sources (dictation)
- Translation
- Other mechanical uses

Informational uses of writing
- Note-taking
- Record, of on-going experience (This is what is happening)
- Report. Retrospective account of particular events or series of events. (This is what happened.)
- Summary. Generalized narrative or description of a recurrent pattern of events or steps in a procedure. (This is what happens; this is the way it is done.)
- Analysis. Generalization and classification related to a situation, problem, or theme, with logical or hierarchical relationships among generalizations implicit or explicit.
- Theory. Building and defending at a theoretical level, including implicit or explicit recognition that there are alternative perspectives. Hypotheses and deductions from them.
- Persuasive or regulative uses of writing. (Any instances in which the attempt to convince overrides other functions or in which rules are given and compliance assumed.)
- Other informational uses

Personal uses of writing
- Journal or diary writing, for own use
- Personal letters or notes, where main purpose is "keeping in touch"
- Other personal uses

Imaginative uses of writing
- Stories
- Poems
- Play scripts
- Other imaginative uses

Figure 2.1 summarizes the full set of function categories and subcategories. As with the audience categories, the scoring system was refined to increase interrater agreement. Specific changes included rewriting the rules for coding personal writing to make it clear that personal experience can be the basis for writing in any of the function categories; emphasizing that long pieces should be coded to reflect the highest level of abstraction, rather than the level that may make up the bulk of the supporting detail; pointing out that comparisons among different procedures should be coded as analysis (unlike descriptions of a procedure, which are coded as summary); elaboration of the rules for coding business letters to more fully specify the function category for common types of letters; and modification of the instructions to reduce the tendency to rate better written papers "up" the scale of abstraction and poorer papers "down" the scale. The revised coding manual is included as Appendix 2.

Procedures for coding function were identical to those for coding audience. Samples of student writing were rated by two raters working independently; disagreements were reconciled by a third rater. Textbook assignments were scored by a single rater, with a subsample of 277 exercises scored twice to provide an estimate of interrater reliability. Interrater agreements for the present study ranged from .82 for the textbook samples to .94 for the student-writing samples. This campares with agreement of .67 obtained in analyses using the earlier version of the coding system (Applebee, 1981).

SPECIAL STUDIES

In addition to textbook analyses and the case studies of individual students (both of which extended across the full project period), two special studies were also undertaken. One of these, reported in Chapter 9, explored the relationships between students' knowledge of the topic being written about and the quality of the writing that they produced. The other, reported in Chapter 10, explored the interactions among patterns of instruction, student attitudes, and the writing process in two classrooms where the teachers were making a special effort to emphasize writing activities as an aid to learning of content material.

Chapter 3
Writing Activities in High School Textbooks: An Analysis of Audience and Function

Arthur N. Applebee

INTRODUCTION

Whenever educators have looked directly at instruction, they have found that textbooks play a shaping role. The National Survey and Assessment of Instructional Materials conducted by the Educational Products Information Exchange Institute (EPIE) during the 1974–76 school years, for example, found that some 65% of class time in math, science, social studies, and reading was spent using print materials, for the most part textbooks and their accompanying exercise books (EPIE, no date). Similarly, the National Survey of Science, Mathematics, and Social Studies Education (Helgeson, Blosser, & Howe, 1977; Suydam & Osborne, 1977; Weiss, 1978; Wiley & Race, 1977) found that above grade 3 all but a few classes were using published textbooks as a basis for their programs, and in the majority of cases only one such textbook series. In our own national sampling of secondary school teachers, 91% reported regularly using a textbook with the classes we were studying.

Most analyses of textbooks have been concerned with the sequencing and selection of subject knowledge, rather than with the kinds of tasks that students are asked to do in conjunction with their reading (e.g., Yost, 1973; Zimet et al., 1971). This has been true even within the field of English, where studies of literature anthologies and language textbooks have concentrated on the material included and its relationship to contemporary scholarship. (See Applebee [1974] for discussion of the major studies in this area.) Yet though the results of such studies are interesting and important, they ignore the role of the textbook as a source of activities to be completed as well as of specific content to be covered.

The analyses discussed in this chapter grew out of a concern with such activities. As we saw briefly in Chapter 1, our earlier studies of classroom instruction found that assignments in most classrooms were narrow in scope and limited in the kinds of skills that students were expected to develop. In particular, most assignments seemed to serve an assessment function, testing whether students had learned new material rather than helping them extend and elaborate upon new learning. A high proportion of the writing activities involved writing without composing; that is, the exercise material provided the structure for the text as a whole, and students were left to fill in missing information (e.g., in short-answer or multiple-choice formats).

ANALYSES

To study the extent to which textbooks reflected similar emphases, we analyzed the assignments and activities suggested in our sample of popular textbooks. As we saw in Chapter 2, this sample included the three most popular 9th- and 11th-grade textbooks in seven subjects. Though a number of the textbooks had gone through several editions, the group averaged 2.0 years since publication of the most recent edition (taking 1980 as the base year).

To allow comparisons within as well as between textbooks, two staff members separately divided each book into 8 segments of equal length. Segment boundaries were then adjusted to the nearest natural break in the textbook (e.g., a unit or chapter boundary). Agreement between raters was high: They agreed exactly on segment boundaries for 92.4% of the segments, with an overall rate of disagreement of 0.8 pages/segment. Disagreements were reconciled by a third rater. The first, third, sixth, and eighth segments of each textbook were selected for detailed analysis, allowing us to examine differences in activities over time, as well as any differences between material in the middle of the course and the activities that are used to introduce or conclude a year of study.

To provide comparable units of analysis across disparate textbooks, scoring focussed on whole exercises, where an exercise was defined as a set of related items that would ordinarily be assigned and completed as a set. Thus an essay writing task together with any lead-in activities would be scored as a single exercise; so would a set of 15 practice sentences following a lesson on identifying nouns and verbs.

In all, we analyzed 90,485 individual items representing 15,279 separate exercises distributed through 13,561 pages of textbook material.

Scoring Categories

Each exercise was scored for the intended audience and function of any writing that would be produced, using the coding systems described in Chapter 2. Inter-rater agreement was .97 for audience and .82 for function. In addition to audience and function, 3 other sets of scores were recorded:

1. Recommended/optional: whether the exercise was directed at all students

using the textbook, or marked (in the textbook or the teacher's manual) as optional or supplementary. (Interrater agreement = .99)

2. Writing explicit/implicit: whether the exercise explicitly required a written response, or could be used as a "study" or discussion topic at the teacher's discretion. (Interrater agreement = .94)

3. Number of separate items comprising the exercise. (Interrater agreement = .99)

Scoring Procedures

Ten raters not otherwise involved in the study were trained to score the textbook exercises. Before the rating began, the entire corpus was segmented as outlined above, and the resulting textbook segments put into random order. Scoring involved: (a) identifying and numbering exercises consecutively as they occurred in the textbook segment being analyzed; exercises which did not call for any written response were omitted at this stage (e.g., assignments of the form "reread pages 17–47" or "choose a partner and discuss the significance of President Jackson's decision"); (b) scoring each exercise for audience, function, explicit/implicit, recommended/optional, and number of items. The randomized set of textbook segments included a subsample of 277 exercises that were scored twice for reliability estimates.

Exercise scores were cumulated within textbook segments to yield average scores per textbook segment for statistical analyses. Because the textbooks varied in length and number of exercises, scores were also calculated as a percent of the total number of exercises within each textbook segment. For ease of interpretation, unless otherwise noted, tabled means are estimates of totals for each textbook as a whole.

Multivariate repeated measures analyses of variance were used to estimate main effects and interactions for grade level, subject, and textbook segment. Linear contrasts were used to test differences between categories within each factor.

GENERAL CHARACTERISTICS OF THE TEXTBOOKS

Table 3.1 summarizes the number of pages/textbook, exercises/textbook, exercises/page, items/exercise, and items/page for the textbooks studied. In general, textbooks in literature and the social sciences tended to be longer than those in the other subject areas, devoting much of that length to presenting material for the students to read. Textbooks for composition/grammar courses, foreign languages, and math, on the other hand, emphasized highly structured student activities, producing high ratios of items/exercise and items/page.

Measures of the number of exercises/page produced erratic results, because of

Table 3.1   Characteristics of popular textbooks

		Means per Textbook			
	Pages	Exercises	Exercises/ Page	Items/ Exercise	Items/ Page
Composition/Grammar	508.3	383.7	0.80	12.6	9.8
Literature	760.3	828.3	1.13	1.7	1.8
Foreign Language	325.0	323.7	1.01	8.9	8.8
Social Science	712.3	850.0	1.19	2.2	2.6
Science	482.7	407.3	1.04	4.9	3.8
Math	560.7	462.3	0.83	13.7	11.2
Business	423.7	536.3	1.46	5.4	5.9

N = 42 textbooks.
Significant Multivariate Effects. Subject: $F(24;88) = 7.35, p < .001$

the radically different formats in the subjects examined. In literature textbooks, for example, a reading selection is typically followed by a list of discussion or essay questions, each requiring extensive student response (and hence each categorized as a separate exercise); this pattern elevates the exercise/page ratio, even though the majority of textbook pages contain no exercises at all. In a typical mathematics textbook, on the other hand, exercises are interspersed throughout a unit; each exercise typically consists of a number of related items, however, and often extends over one or more pages. This pattern tends to decrease the exercises/page ratio, even though the majority of pages may in fact contain exercise material.

A multivariate analysis of variance indicated a significant effect for subject but not for grade level, for textbook segment, or for any of the interactions for the measures displayed in Table 3.1.

TYPES OF WRITING TASKS

The analyses of the uses of writing suggested by the various textbooks allow us to address two questions: (a) the balance between activities which require students to write at least a few sentences and those which allow a shorter written response; and (b) the nature of the extended writing that is required.

Table 3.2 summarizes the mean number of restricted and extended exercises for each subject area. Restricted writing activities play a large role in each of the subject areas examined, providing a base of from 286 to 454 exercises/textbook. The variation between subject areas in the number of restricted exercises is relatively small compared with the variation in the number of extended writing activities that are also suggested. Means for extended writing activities range

**Table 3.2   Textbook exercises requiring restricted
or extended writing**

	Mean Number of Exercises per Textbook	
	Restricted Writing	Extended Writing
Composition/Grammar	337.0	46.7
Literature	286.0	542.3
Foreign Language	308.0	15.7
Social Science	295.0	555.0
Science	349.0	58.3
Math	454.0	8.3
Business	452.0	84.3

N = 42 textbooks.
Significant Multivariate Effects. Subject: $F(12;54)$ = 8.62,
$p < .001$.

from a low of 8 in the mathematics textbooks studied to a high of 555 in the social science textbooks. This variation in turn means that the total number of exercises per textbook varies widely too. Figure 3.1 graphs the data from Table 3.2, highlighting the extent to which extended writing activities seem to build upon a base of more restricted work in each of the subject areas examined.

In the multivariate analysis of these data, there was a significant main effect for subject; effects for grade level, textbook segment, and interactions were not significant. Univariate analyses indicated that the multivariate subject effect was due largely to the variation in extended writing activities; the differences among subjects in the number of restricted activities were not statistically significant.

Table 3.3 provides a further breakdown of extended writing activities, here expressed as a percent of total activities. In this analysis, subject differences are again highly significant, and there is a small but significant effect for the subject by textbook segment interaction. These data are displayed in Figure 3.2.

If we examine the results in Figure 3.2, it is clear that literature and social science textbooks place a similarly high emphasis on extended writing activities; science and business education textbooks contain a moderate proportion of such exercises; and foreign language and mathematics textbooks place almost no emphasis on extended writing. Composition/grammar textbooks display an erratic pattern, with almost no extended writing activities in the early segments of these textbooks but considerably more emphasis on such activities later in the course. This reflects the still common pattern of beginning with word and sentence level skills and building from them toward longer units of writing.

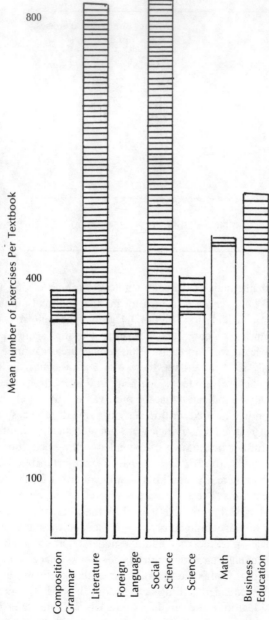

Figure 3.1 Frequency of Restricted and of Extended Writing Activities

Mean number of Exercises Per Textbook

800

400

100

Composition
Grammar

Literature

Foreign
Language

Social
Science

Science

Math

Business
Education

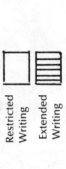

Restricted
Writing

Extended
Writing

Table 3.3 Mean percent of textbook exercises requiring extended writing

| | \multicolumn{4}{c}{Textbook Segment} | |
	1	3	6	8	Overall
Composition/Grammar	3.3	13.5	26.8	6.7	11.7
Literature	70.9	56.3	62.1	83.2	65.5
Foreign Language	2.1	4.3	5.7	5.7	4.6
Social Science	54.3	68.3	66.0	70.0	65.0
Math	4.2	0.2	0.0	0.0	1.8
Science	17.0	18.9	13.2	17.1	16.6
Business	15.4	12.0	19.9	12.0	14.8

N = 42 textbooks.
Significant Multivariate Effects. Subject: F (6;28) = 50.11, $p < .001$.
Textbook Segment × Subject: F (18; 84) = 1.89, $p < .05$.

Figure 3.2 Percent of Extended Writing Activities

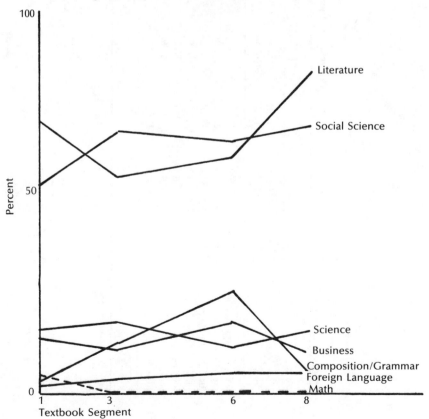

Table 3.4 Types of restricted writing activities

	Multiple Choice	Fill in the Blank	Short Answer	Math Calculation	Recording Data	Copying	Dictation	Translation	Other
					Mean Number of Exercises per Textbook				
Composition/Grammar	58.4	27.4	128.4	0.0	0.0	14.6	3.2	20.4	84.6
Literature	10.6	2.4	259.6	0.0	0.0	1.0	0.0	2.6	9.6
Foreign Language	18.4	34.4	117.4	0.6	0.0	10.0	1.0	19.4	107.0
Social Science	4.4	0.8	261.4	0.0	0.0	0.0	0.0	0.0	27.6
Science	18.6	18.0	159.4	88.6	16.6	0.0	0.0	0.4	49.4
Math	4.2	10.4	22.6	351.6	0.0	5.0	0.0	0.0	60.0
Business	9.0	0.6	117.0	53.0	1.6	182.6	1.0	0.0	86.4

N = 42 textbooks.

Types of Restricted Writing

Table 3.4 summarizes the kinds of restricted writing activities favored by the subjects studied. Across subjects, the short-answer exercise (requiring anywhere from a phrase to a two-sentence response) is the most frequent, though there are subject differences in overall patterns of usage. Simple copying exercises play an important role in business education textbooks, where they provide practice in typing and clerical activities; math and science textbooks, as one would expect, include many activities requiring mathematical calculations. Surprisingly, relatively few of the foreign language activities involve direct translation from one language to another; the emphasis instead is divided between manipulation of constructions within the language and responding to comprehension questions or conversational drill.

Types of Extended Writing

Table 3.5 examines the nature of the extended writing activities provided by textbooks in different subjects. Informational uses of writing dominate in all subjects, with significantly higher numbers of exercises being provided by literature, social science, and science textbooks. Few personal writing activities are suggested in any of the textbooks, though composition/grammar books place significantly more emphasis on personal writing than do textbooks in the other subjects examined. When they do occur, these assignments ask either for a letter to a close friend, or for a journal or diary writing activity.

Imaginative writing activities occur significantly more often in literature anthologies than in any of the other textbooks examined, though they are rare in all

Table 3.5   Types of extended writing activities

| | Mean Number of Exercises per Textbook | | | | | |
| | Informational | | Personal | | Imaginative | |
	Gr. 9	Gr. 11	Gr. 9	Gr. 11	Gr. 9	Gr. 11
Composition/Grammar	36.7	41.3	8.0	4.0	2.0	1.3
Literature	488.7	556.0	2.0	3.3	21.3	13.3
Foreign Language	6.0	24.0	0.7	0.0	0.7	0.0
Social Science	464.7	633.3	1.3	0.0	4.7	6.0
Science	80.0	36.7	0.0	0.0	0.0	0.0
Math	1.3	15.3	0.0	0.0	0.0	0.0
Business	132.7	34.7	0.0	0.0	1.3	0.0

$N = 42$ textbooks.
Significant Multivariate Effects. Subject: $F (18;74) = 7.44, p < .001$. Text Segment: $F (9;20) = 2.50, p < .05$.

subjects. In the context of the anthology, such assignments are either very abrupt, with little development, or very analytic, asking students to examine the workings of a selection very closely, and then to imitate either its content or form. The following examples illustrate these two versions:

> Write your own blues song.
>
> —9th-grade literature

> Study the techniques McCullers used to build suspense, especially in the early part of the story. Then try writing the first few paragraphs of a suspense story. It is important to set a mood of tension and to give hints that foreshadow the events to come. But do not disclose these developments directly.
>
> —9th-grade literature

> Students might try writing an update of this story, in which a person sells his soul to the devil for money or some other reward. In this update they should use modern settings, characters, situations, and symbols. But the theme of the story should remain the same.
>
> —11th-grade American literature

Again, grade level effects and interactions were not significant for the analyses in Table 3.5.

Table 3.6 provides a more detailed analysis of the kinds of informational writing required in different subjects at different grade levels. The simplest sorts of informational writing tasks—those requiring only notetaking, recording, or reporting on a particular experience—are not heavily represented in any of the subjects. Science textbooks include a few notetaking and recording activities, usually in the context of out-of-class observations. Although laboratory work and observations play a major role in science, most of the writing involved is highly structured, requiring only a few words or phrases rather than extended writing. The following activity is typical of many that lead to short responses:

> Obtain a potato, a piece of bread, a banana, a carrot, and some tincture of iodine. Place a small piece of food in a dish. Put a drop of iodine on each. Record your observations. Iodine is used to test for the presence of starch. Which of these foods contains starch? Try this test on other foods.
>
> —9th-grade physical science

Though this is a very simple activity, the format in which it is presented continues as the work grows more complicated. Rather than connected text, such activities tend to produce lists of activities or results in the chronological order in which they occurred.

Reports on particular events require somewhat more structure than notes or recordings of ongoing activities, but again these are rarely suggested in the

Table 3.6 Types of informational writing

	Grade	Notes	Record	Report	Summary	Analysis	Theory
				Mean Number of Exercises per Textbook			
Composition/Grammar	9	1.3	0.0	15.3	7.3	10.7	0.0
	11	2.0	0.0	9.3	9.3	14.0	0.0
Literature	9	0.7	1.3	14.7	39.3	432.0	0.0
	11	0.7	0.0	6.0	78.7	462.7	8.0
Foreign Language	9	0.0	0.7	2.7	2.0	0.0	0.0
	11	0.0	2.0	0.7	14.7	6.7	0.0
Social Science	9	1.3	0.0	4.7	276.7	178.7	0.7
	11	0.7	0.0	16.7	240.7	372.7	2.7
Science	9	8.0	10.7	2.0	56.0	3.3	0.0
	11	0.0	0.0	1.3	27.3	8.0	0.0
Math	9	0.0	0.0	0.0	0.0	0.0	1.3
	11	0.7	0.0	0.0	0.0	0.7	14.0
Business	9	0.0	0.7	11.3	61.3	59.3	0.0
	11	0.0	0.0	4.0	22.0	8.7	0.0

$N = 42$ textbooks.
Significant Multivariate Effects (combined variables). Subject: $F_{(18;74)} = 9.31$, $p. < .001$.

textbooks we analyzed. They are somewhat more likely to occur in English textbooks, usually in the context of writing about personal experiences or, sometimes, a newspaper report. The examples below illustrate both types of activity:

> Activity 12. In activity 5 you collected facts for a news story and in Activity 9 you wrote the lead. Complete the story. Be sure you arrange the details in order of decreasing importance. Check your story for accuracy and editorializing. Apply the cut-off test. Perhaps your teacher will submit the best stories to the school paper.
>
> —9th-grade composition

> Have you ever been in a situation (in a poor neighborhood, a foreign country, a hospital ward) in which you felt guilty or embarrassed by your own comparative wealth or health? Describe the situation and your feelings in a brief composition.
>
> —11th-grade American literature

Summary writing tasks are the first type of informational tasks to be heavily represented in the textbooks. The social science textbooks suggested an average of 259 such exercises in the course of a year's work, while literature and business education textbooks averaged 59 and 42 per year, respectively. In social science textbooks, such questions focussed on students' knowledge of particular figures or events, as in the following selections from a variety of ninth grade world history textbooks:

> Describe a specific international problem with which each of these Presidents was involved: Harry S. Truman, John F. Kennedy, Richard M. Nixon.

> How did Stalin suppress opposition to his regime?

> Summarize the chief results of the Russo-Japanese War.

> How did medieval universities originate?

Such questions are typically stated quite briefly, and relatively brief responses are expected from the students. As writing tasks, they are really asking for summaries of summaries: The information has been presented directly earlier in the chapter, and it is there that the students are expected to look for the answers.

In literature textbooks, summary writing usually recapitulates one or another important incident, theme, or character, as in the following assignment:

> Write a brief sketch of Dr. Mortimer's character.
>
> —9th-grade literature

In business education textbooks, summary writing assignments usually focus on business practices or procedures, as in the following question from a unit on saving money:

> Explain what happens to your money when you deposit it in a savings account with a bank.
> —9th-grade general business

The other type of informational writing that is heavily represented in the textbook assignments is the analytic essay, in its various forms. Literature exercises at both grade levels are dominated by analytic tasks; some of these reflect the familiar exercise in textual analysis, but others focus on such topics as the motivations and development of the characters. The example which follows is drawn from a "unit review":

> The passage from innocence to experience that is associated with maturing is treated in several of the stories in this unit. Suppose you are the main character in one of these stories. Write to another character in that story and analyze how the experience you went through has matured you. What were you like before the experience? After? How do you define maturity?
> —9th-grade literature

In many of the anthologies, detailed textual analysis is relegated to short-answer discussion questions immediately following each selection, while longer writing tasks are used to address broader issues. The two questions below come from the beginning and end of a sequence following Stephen Crane's short story, "An Episode of War":

> What devices does Crane use to bring his scenes to life?

> Reread the discussion of realism and naturalism in the Unit Background. What elements of each school of writing are displayed in the subject matter, theme, and techniques of this story? In what way is its view of life naturalistic? Explain your opinion in a brief composition, quoting examples from the story.
> —11th-grade American literature

Social science textbooks also require a considerable amount of analytic writing, increasingly so in grade 11. Like the summary writing assignments we have already seen, however, these tend to be directly based on material that has just been presented, as in the following examples:

> In what ways did Summerian civilization compare with that of Egypt? In what ways did it differ?
> —9th-grade world history

What are the chief weaknesses of the United Nations? Can they be eliminated? Explain.
—11th-grade American history

Compare what Jesus taught about war with what Mohammed taught about it. How is it that, although Jesus and Mohammed differed in their views, their followers in the Christian Crusades and in the Islamic wars of expansion engaged in essentially the same methods to spread their faith?
—9th-grade world history

Occasionally a more ambitious analysis is proposed. The following question followed a 15-page unit on the history of the English speaking world between 1770 and 1911:

Prepare a class report on the revolutions of 1848 in Europe. Investigate the causes, events, and results of the various revolutions that occurred throughout Europe. Consult the following readings: [a list of 5 sources followed].
—9th-grade world history

A few further points are worth noting about the results in Table 3.6. Science and business education textbooks are dominated by summary writing activities, though as we have already seen the overall levels of extended writing activities are low in both subjects. Mathematics textbooks, though suggesting few extended writing activities, are the only set where the emphasis is on theoretical writing, with a sharp increase between grades 9 and 11. Composition/grammar textbooks require singularly few writing activities for a course that emphasizes written language skills; those activities that are suggested are spread relatively evenly among reporting, summarizing, and analyzing tasks.

Because frequencies are so low for some of the categories in Table 3.6, tests of significance were based on three combined variables: exercises requiring at least report-level writing, exercises requiring summary writing, and exercises requiring analytic or theoretical writing. Overall, only subject effects were significant.

AUDIENCE

The textbook exercises were also analyzed in terms of the relationship assumed between writer and reader. Table 3.7 displays the results by subject and grade level. Although there are minor variations, the predominant audience for student work is the teacher in the role of examiner. Only the literature textbooks consistently present even 10% of their exercises as part of an instructional dialogue; no more than 1% of the exercises in any of the textbooks provide for a wider audience for student work. The emphasis on teacher-as-examiner is so consistent across textbooks that none of the overall differences between subjects, grade levels, or textbook segments were statistically significant. At the level of

Table 3.7   Audiences for textbook exercises

	Grade	Self	Dialogue	Examiner	Wider
			Mean Percent of Exercises		
Composition/Grammar	9	2.0	2.1	94.9	1.0
	11	1.0	1.3	96.0	1.7
Literature	9	0.1	12.4	87.3	0.1
	11	0.4	11.0	88.4	0.2
Foreign Language	9	. . .	. . .	99.5	0.5
	11	10.8	0.6	88.6	0.0
Social Science	9	0.3	2.3	96.4	1.0
	11	3.1	0.1	95.2	1.6
Science	9	4.3	8.1	87.4	0.2
	11	1.3	0.5	97.1	1.1
Math	9	5.0	1.6	93.4	0.0
	11	4.8	5.2	90.0	0.0
Business	9	2.2	9.9	86.8	1.1
	11	3.4	5.0	91.6	0.0

N = 42 textbooks.
Significant Multivariate Effects: None.

individual variables, however, the proportion of teacher/learner dialogue was significantly higher in the literature textbooks than in the other subject areas ($p < .05$).

These exercises often occurred in contexts asking for students' personal response to literary selections, as in the following assignment, drawn from the teacher's manual for a ninth grade textbook:

> You will probably want to conclude with an impression of the joyful assurance in Psalm 96. Ask students why peace of mind would be gained by one who truly believes in lines 28–29:
> He shall judge the world with righteousness,
> And the people with His truth.
> Ask students to choose another Psalm and write an analysis-reaction, first telling what the Psalm says and then briefly describing their personal response.

Such an assignment at least invites a dialogue, even if it does not insure that the focus will not fall on the accuracy of "telling what the Psalm says."

The data in Table 3.7 are based on all exercises in the textbooks studied; it is possible that significant variations in the audiences for extended writing activities are being obscured by patterns in the more restricted writing activities. To examine this further, Table 3.8 summarizes the percent of activities directed to the teacher-as-examiner for the four major use-of-writing categories.

Comparing categories, restricted writing is slightly more likely to be directed

Table 3.8   Teacher-as-examiner in textbook exercises

	Mean Percent of Exercises			
	Without Composing	Informational	Personal	Imaginative
Composition/Grammar	97.2	94.8	. . .	. . .
Literature	92.9	84.2	. . .	88.0
Foreign Language	99.6	98.5	. . .	. . .
Social Science	96.5	76.2	. . .	. . .
Science	93.3	83.1	. . .	. . .
Math	89.2	. . .	. . .	. . .
Business	93.7	77.4	. . .	. . .

N = 42 textbooks.
Significant Multivariate Effects. Restricted vs. Extended: F (1;24) = 4.89, p < .04.

to the teacher-as-examiner than is extended writing, though the difference is relatively small (9.8% overall). Within the categories of extended writing, activities are slightly more likely to move out of the examiner role in literature, social science, science, and business classes. (Percents based on fewer than five items are omitted from the table.) Overall, however, the pattern remains one of using writing assignments, of whatever type, to test what students have learned.

CURRICULUM OPTIONS INFLUENCING WRITING ACTIVITIES

Textbook activities often provide options in the way the activities will be used. These options in turn may affect the balance of activities that students undertake in a particular textbook. Two such options were examined in the present analyses: whether the exercises were recommended for all students (versus intended for a particular ability level or for supplementary work), and whether writing was explicitly required to complete the task (versus exercises that could be assigned either for study or for discussion at the teacher's option).

Table 3.9 contrasts the extent to which extended writing activities as opposed to those involving more limited writing are likely to be recommended for all students. In general, the restricted writing activities are likely to be recommended for everyone, while the emphasis on longer writing activities varies with subject. Literature and social science textbooks (which include the largest number of extended writing exercises) also usually expect these activities to be undertaken by all students. Composition/grammar textbooks, though containing fewer extended writing exercises than either social science or literature textbooks, similarly expect all students to complete those they suggest. Math textbooks, which include few extended extended writing activities to begin with, are more likely to designate such activities as supplementary or for further study.

Table 3.9   Percent of exercises recommended for all students

	Mean Percent	
	Restricted	Extended
Composition/Grammar	92.5	97.3
Literature	100.0	99.8
Foreign Language	98.1	95.3
Social Science	99.7	97.9
Science	97.6	86.8
Math	81.8	32.1
Business	96.7	92.5
Overall	95.2	88.4

N = 42 textbooks.
Significant Multivariate Effects. Subject:
$F(12;46)$ = 3.72, $p < .001$.

Table 3.10 presents a similar breakdown of data for the percent of exercises that explicitly require a written response. Here there are very large differences between subjects. In general, history and literature textbooks are more likely to provide study or discuss options, while composition/grammar, mathematics, and business education textbooks are more likely to explicitly require a written response to both restricted and extended writing exercises. The slight overall

Table 3.10   Percent of exercises explicitly requiring writing

	Mean Percent	
	Restricted	Extended
Composition/Grammar	64.8	59.8
Literature	20.1	9.8
Foreign Language	24.7	35.8
Social Science	3.9	7.4
Science	33.5	18.7
Math	67.0	50.0
Business	50.6	64.2
Overall	37.8	33.5

N = 42 textbooks.
Significant Multivariate Effects. Subect:
$F(12;46)$ = 2.60, $p < .01$.

difference between restricted and extended exercises in the proportion requiring a written response is not statistically significant.

ACCOMPANYING MATERIALS

Teacher's manuals and supplementary materials accompanying each of the textbooks were also analyzed, in order to detect any major deviations from the patterns of emphasis emerging from the main analyses. With the exceptions noted below, few deviations were found; for the most part the analyses of teacher's manuals and supplementary materials simply confirmed the patterns we have already discussed.

Uses of Writing

We had anticipated that teacher's manuals might contain a higher proportion of extended writing activities, since such activities might require class discussion or other teacher-led introduction. In general, however, the percentage of activities requiring extended writing in the teacher's manual paralleled the percentage in the textbooks (Table 3.11). The one exception was science. Although few additional activities were suggested by the average teacher's manual in science (an average of 18 per manual for our sample), across science textbooks a mean of 48% of the activities that were suggested involved extended writing.

Supplementary student materials were if anything more limited than the main textbooks. Even in literature and social science supplementary materials, the percentage of activities requiring extended writing was relatively low. Rather than extended writing, such materials emphasized short-answer responses to comprehension exercises.

Table 3.11   Extended writing in accompanying
materials

	Mean Percent of Exercises	
	---	---
	Teacher's Manual	Supplementary
Composition/Grammar	9.2	18.4
Literature	41.7	34.0
Foreign Language	. . .	0.0
Social Science	65.5	13.1
Science	48.4	2.1
Math	1.1	. . .
Business	9.5	4.4
n of textbooks	25	20

Table 3.12   Teacher-as-examiner in accompanying materials

| | Mean Percent of Exercises | | | |
| | Teacher's Manual | | Supplementary | |
	Restricted	Extended	Restricted	Extended
Composition/Grammar	91.7	86.2	100.0	95.9
Literature	93.9	79.5	100.0	100.0
Foreign Language	. . .	. . .	93.8	. . .
Social Science	72.8	67.3	98.3	97.7
Science	33.3	66.7	71.7	68.8
Math	97.0	100.0	. . .	. . .
Business	85.4	. . .	88.0	72.7
n of textbooks	25		20	

Audience

As was true for the textbooks they accompanied, the teacher's manuals in our sample emphasized exercises intended to test students' learning of new skills or concepts (Table 3.12). The one exception was again for science, which included more experience-based activities including note-taking or observational records (where students are the only audience for the writing) or writing as part of a teacher–learner dialogue.

Supplementary student materials remained overwhelmingly examination-oriented, in most cases taking a drill-and-practice format.

CONCLUSIONS

The writing experiences provided in high school textbooks are narrow and limiting, whether one examines the role of the activity within the learning process or the kind of writing task the student is being asked to undertake. To an overwhelming extent, in all of the subjects and at all of the grade levels studied, the primary audience for student writing was the teacher in the role of examiner. Although our earlier studies of classroom instruction had led us to question such a one-sided emphasis, in retrospect it seems clear that teachers were abandoning or revising textbook activities in order to provide even a minimal level of other contexts for writing.

The types of activities suggested were also limited. Textbooks in all subjects seemed to be constructed around a base of exercises that required only minimal writing: fill-in-the-blank exercises, short answer responses, and the like. Some subjects—literature and the social sciences in particular—supplemented this base of restricted activity with more extensive writing tasks. Others, including the grammar and composition series, offered few if any suggestions for more extended tasks.

When writing activities were suggested, the various subjects examined showed characteristic preferences. Overall, analytic writing tasks were most prevalent, but summary tasks were important in the social sciences, and report writing had a place in science classes. Personal and imaginative writing, however, had almost no place in any of the textbook assignments.

The limited range of audience and function in textbook writing assignments is disappointing but not surprising. It may be almost inevitable, given the role of the standard textbook as a synthesis and presentation of what is known about a particular field of study. In Barnes's (1976) terminology, the underlying philosophy is one of transmission rather than interpretation of knowledge; and in such a context, writing serves appropriately within a rather narrow band of functions.

Although school tasks may seem to place students in a relatively passive role, the students find their own ways to extend their skills and knowledge within the contexts provided for them. These ways are rarely passive, nor are the lines of growth as orderly and linear as a transmission model of teaching might imply. In the remaining chapters of this book, we will explore in more detail how students function within the contexts provided to them for learning to write.

Chapter 4
The Students and Their Writing

Arthur N. Applebee

INTRODUCTION

Results from the case study analyses, examined with respect to a variety of special issues in Chapters 5 through 8, are based on our work with some 20 students (15 by the end of the 16 months of study). This chapter will focus on the kinds of writing experiences which these students had at school and at home, comparing them both with each other and with the results obtained in earlier phases of the study. The final half of the chapter will portray 3 of the students in more detail, to give a sense of the individuality that underlies the results in other chapters.

THE WRITING STUDENTS DO

One concern that has run throughout our studies has been to explore the nature and frequency of the writing experiences of high school students. In our earlier studies of classrooms, as well as in the textbook analyses reported in Chapter 3, we were able to describe general emphases across grades and subjects. In contrast, the data from our longitudinal studies allowed us to explore how these general emphases worked themselves out in the cumulative experience of individual students.

The best estimate of the amount of writing completed by each student comes from the interview data. From this, we were able to follow each piece through from initial assignment to completion, whether or not the paper was returned by the teacher, lost, or hidden in embarrassment. Table 4.1 summarizes the average amount of writing completed by each student, over a full academic year. (To provide the most accurate estimates, Table 4.1 is based on the second year of work with the 15 students who remained in the study throughout year 2; any

Table 4.1   Writing completed during one academic year: case-study students

	Mean Number of Papers per Student			
	All	Better	Poorer	ESL
School-sponsored				
English	13.8	13.2	14.3	16.0
Foreign Language	0.8	0.2	1.3	0.8
Social Science	8.8	6.0	11.7	0.8
Science	6.7	5.4	5.3	10.2
Mathematics	0.6	0.2	0.5	1.3
Other School	0.7	0.0	0.2	0.3
Total School	31.4	25.2	33.3	36.5
Self-sponsored	2.2	1.8	2.0	2.8
n of students	15	5	6	4

distortions due to unevenness in the pattern of assignments (e.g., term papers due at the end of a grading period) thus even out.)

On the average, the 15 students completed 31.4 pieces of writing for their various classes during 1 academic year, and another 2.2 pieces of writing on their own at home. English classes were clearly the focus of writing activity, with English papers representing some 44% of the sample of school writing. At the same time, it is important to note that on the average less than half of a student's writing assignments were completed for English; the majority of writing experiences were in other subjects. In turn, we must expect that these experiences in other subjects had much to do with both the skills our students developed and the attitudes they took away. Social science (with 9 papers per year) and science (with 7) placed particular emphasis on student writing.

Variations in the amount of writing completed are also interesting. The data in Table 4.1 indicate that the poorer writers completed slightly more papers than the better writers, and that the English-as-a-second-language students completed the most assignments. If we separate the students by grade level, a similar pattern emerges: The 10th graders completed an average of 42.3 papers; the seniors an average of 24.2. (Both patterns result from an inverse relationship between frequency and length of assignment, with the older students and the better writers writing less frequently, but at greater length.) The averages obscure some sizeable variations within each group, however. Among the 10th graders, for example, Li (with 58 papers) completed 1.8 times as many assignments as Sherri (with 32). Among the 12th graders the range was even greater. Emily and Tai (with 48 papers each) completed 2.8 times as many assignments as Sandy (with 17). From our work with these students, the vast range in amount of writing completed seemed more a function of their varying strategies for avoiding the work they were given than of the patterns of their teachers' assignments.

TYPES OF WRITING ACTIVITY

The significance of simple reports of the number of writing tasks completed in a particular time span is impossible to evaluate. We need to know more about the tasks before we can determine whether students are being asked to write too much, too little, or in appropriate ways. To begin to examine these questions, we can look at the variety of tasks represented in the writing collected from our students. As we saw in Chapter 2, the samples collected represent about 85% of the writing that they reported completing, with the highest collection rates for those subjects in which they wrote most often.

Audience

Table 4.2 summarizes the audiences addressed in the work of the case-study students. Overall, the teacher-as-examiner was by far the most frequent audience for school writing. Percentages of such writing ranged from a low of 64% for social science papers to a high of 98% for science writing. Opportunities to write for oneself (as in journals or exploratory writing) were relatively limited (about 4% overall for school-sponsored writing), as were papers which addressed a wider audience (6% for school-sponsored writing). On the other hand, student writing within a teacher–learner dialogue, in which teachers take on a more supportive role, was more substantially represented. Such papers represented an

Table 4.2   Audience for case-study writing samples

| | | Mean Percent of Papers | | | |
| | | | Teacher | | |
	Total Papers	Self	Dialogue	Examiner	Wider
School-sponsored					
English	263	4.0	20.8	66.9	8.3
Social Science	146	5.8	24.4	63.7	6.2
Science	89	0.9	0.9	98.2	0.0
Other	52	5.7	17.0	72.2	5.0
Self-sponsored	53	4.1	20.1	7.9	68.0
Overall	603	4.2	18.9	65.7	11.2

N = 15 students.

average of 21% of the writing collected from English classes, and 24% of the writing from social studies.

Students' out-of-school writing, however, showed a dramatically different pattern. An average of 68% of those papers managed to address a wider audience; only 8% read as though the student were still writing to the teacher-as-examiner.

Table 4.3 looks separately at the audiences addressed by the two age groups in our sample, dividing them by their initial achievement in writing. In general, better writers rarely had opportunities to write for themselves or as part of a teacher–learner dialogue. Rather, most of their work was directed to the teacher-as-examiner. Poorer writers and English-as-a-second-language (ESL) students, on the other hand, had greater access to a teacher–learner dialogue, though their work was still dominated by examiner audiences.

The 11th- and 12th-grade writers in the sample showed some movement away from examiner audiences in comparison with the comparable group of 9th and 10th graders, though this represented a different sort of shift for each of the achievement groups. For the better writers, the decrease in papers addressed to teacher-as-examiner resulted from an increase in the proportion of their papers that assumed a wider audience of interested readers (21% in the older sample), which in turn reflected their developing competence in tackling informative writing tasks. For the poorer writers, a somewhat smaller decrease in teacher-as-examiner in the older sample reflected an increase in the proportion of journal ac-

Table 4.3   Audiences for school writing: interaction of grade level and achievement

		Mean Percent of Papers		
			Teacher	
	Self	Dialogue	Examiner	Wider
Better Writers				
Grades 9–10	0.9	6.4	86.1	6.7
Grades 11–12	1.7	9.6	68.0	20.7
Poorer Writers				
Grades 9–10	2.2	24.9	63.4	9.5
Grades 11–12	10.4	23.0	55.9	10.7
ESL Students				
Grades 9–10	1.8	16.1	82.1	0.0
Grades 11–12	3.4	26.0	59.8	10.9

$N = 15$ students (548 papers).

tivities, with self as audience. Finally, for the ESL students a decrease in teacher-as-examiner reflected in part an increase in papers that were part of a teacher–learner dialogue, and in part an increase in papers addressed to a wider audience.

Function

If the audiences for school writing were dominated by the teacher in the role of examiner, its functions were dominated by informational tasks (Table 4.4). Overall, informational writing represented 89% of the school tasks collected from our case-study students; it ranged from 84% of the writing in English to 100% of that from science classes.

Papers from two subject areas, English and social science, showed somewhat more diversity. In social science, for example, 10% of the writing was coded as personal, while in English some 10% represented imaginative writing (primarily stories and poems).

Table 4.5 provides a further breakdown of the kinds of informational writing tasks completed for various subject areas. As the table makes clear, the bulk of student writing fell within a rather narrow range of functions. Approximately 88% of the school writing reflected either generalized summary or analytic writing. The balance between these two shifts from subject to subject; samples from English were 12% summary, 78% analysis, compared with science with 46% summary, 37% analysis. Still it is clear that the functions which help motivate and shape student writing were characterized more by their similarities than their differences.

Self-sponsored writing again showed a different pattern. Some 39% of the writing students undertook on their own was imaginative in function (Table 4.4), and another 5% was personal (primarily journals but including some letters to

Table 4.4 Function for case-study writing samples

	Total Papers	Mean Percent of Papers		
		Informational	Personal	Imaginative
School-sponsored				
English	263	84.4	5.2	10.4
Social Science	146	88.4	9.8	1.8
Science	89	100.0	0.0	0.0
Other	52	96.2	3.8	0.0
Self-sponsored	53	56.4	4.8	38.9
Overall	603	85.9	5.6	8.5

N = 15 students.

Table 4.5   Types of informational writing

		Mean Percent of Papers				
		School-sponsored				
	English	Social Science	Science	Other	Self-sponsored	All
Notes	1.0	3.5	4.6	4.0	0.0	2.1
Record	0.9	2.0	2.1	0.0	0.0	1.3
Report	3.9	0.7	10.6	15.9	10.2	5.6
Summary	12.2	28.6	46.6	28.8	14.8	22.3
Analysis	78.3	63.1	37.1	51.3	57.9	65.4
Theory	3.3	0.5	0.0	0.0	5.2	2.0
Persuasive	0.5	1.7	0.0	0.0	11.9	1.2
Total papers	217	123	89	51	27	507

N = 15 students.

close friends). Though self-sponsored informational writing continued to be dominated by summary and analysis, the papers collected also reflected some reporting, theorizing, and persuasive tasks (Table 4.5).

If we look separately at the kinds of school-sponsored writing tasks undertaken by our three samples of students, some differences in their experiences emerge (Table 4.6). The poorer writers in our sample wrote more extensively in the personal and imaginative modes than did the better writers or the ESL students. Overall, these modes accounted for some 22% of their writing, compared with only 4% for the better writers and 2% for the ESL students.

Table 4.6   Function of school writing by grade level and achievement

	Total Papers	Mean Percent of Papers		
		Informational	Personal	Imaginative
Grades 9–10	292	91.2	2.4	6.4
Grades 11–12	256	86.5	7.8	5.7
Achievement				
Better Writers	157	95.9	1.9	2.3
Poorer Writers	230	78.1	10.8	11.1
ESL Students	163	98.0	1.0	1.0
All	550	88.4	5.7	5.9

N = 15 students.

Table 4.7   Functions of school writing: interaction of grade level and achievement

| | Mean Percent of Papers | | | | |
	Record/Report	Summary	Analysis	Theory	Other Writing
Better Writers					
Grades 9–10	7.5	25.4	61.9	0.9	4.3
Grades 11–12	1.5	10.5	80.2	3.8	4.0
Poorer Writers					
Grades 9–10	14.3	33.0	35.4	0.6	16.7
Grades 11–12	3.3	20.6	44.0	2.1	29.9
ESL Students					
Grades 9–10	10.7	32.1	55.4	0.0	1.8
Grades 11–12	8.8	5.9	80.6	0.9	3.7

N = 15 students.

Table 4.7 takes the analysis further, showing the types of writing tasks completed by the two different age groups within each achievement group. For both the better writers and the ESL students, school writing narrowed even more sharply around analytic writing tasks in the 11th and 12th grades. For the poorer writers, on the other hand, the pattern was quite different; the proportion of analytic writing which they were expected to attempt was only about half that of the other two groups, while assignments devoted to other kinds of tasks (in particular, imaginative and personal writing) increased to some 30%.

Information Needed for the Writing Task

If student writing is meant to convey information, the source of that information is of interest. Table 4.8 presents a simple analysis of source, contrasting tasks answered from information drawn from a teacher or text with those in which students could draw upon their own experience or their own reactions to the material. (Since some assignments integrate new material with students' experience or reactions while others point them toward other sources, totals can be greater or less than 100%.)

The majority of the writing tasks completed by our sample were based on information drawn from teacher or text. English assignments were slightly less likely to draw on such syntheses of information, but even for those papers the percentage was high (67%). In most of the school writing tasks we discussed with our case-study students, opportunities to use personal experience as the basis for writing were limited. (When they did occur, they were usually part of

Table 4.8   Knowledge drawn upon in writing

	Papers Discussed	Mean Percent of Papers	
		Personal Experience	Teacher or Text
School-sponsored			
English	118	32.6	67.4
Social Science	39	12.5	81.1
Other School	39	26.0	77.1
Total School	196	27.3	71.5
Self-sponsored	14	86.2	18.5
Achievement			
Better Writers	66	22.1	79.0
Poorer Writers	74	40.4	54.5
ESL Students	56	29.3	71.9

N = 15 students.

personal or imaginative writing tasks, rather than of informational ones.) Not surprisingly, writing produced outside of school drew much more heavily on personal experience, and only occasionally on information from other sources.

Table 4.8 also summarizes differences in the sources of information drawn upon by our three groups of students. These again reflect differences in the amount of personal and imaginative writing completed by these groups: for the better writers and ESL students, a higher proportion of the tasks were based on information from teacher or textbook (79 and 72% for the two groups, respectively). Poorer writers, meanwhile, drew primarily on personal experience for some 40% of their school writing.

The Case Studies in Context

In Chapter 2, we pointed out that the case-study students were selected to allow us to study the development of writing skills within as favorable a context as possible—a good school with a well developed program in writing, and an overall academic orientation. Even with these advantages, however, it is clear that the writing experiences of the case-study students shared many of the same emphases we have found in our earlier studies of schools and programs in general.

The most important features which the work of our case-study students shared with the national samples were (a) the emphasis on teacher-as-examiner in their writing for all subjects, and (b) the concentration on informational writing tasks, particularly those requiring summary or analysis. In the national sample, 55% of the papers had been directed to the teacher-as-examiner, and 12% had been addressed to a wider audience. As with the case-study students, papers addressed to a teacher as part of an instructional dialogue were most common in English and social science, and less common in science and other subjects (Applebee, 1981, p. 49). Results for function in the national sample were similarly close to those from the case studies, with some 39% of the samples representing analytic writing and another 23% representing summary tasks. Again, English and social science classes showed somewhat more variety than the other subjects (Applebee, 1981, p. 37).

Where the case-study students may differ most from the results from the national samples is in the frequency of their writing experiences, and in the amount of systematic instruction that accompanied their writing, particularly in their English classes. (We will examine the nature of that instruction in Chapters 7 and 11.)

PROFILES OF THREE STUDENTS

We will turn now to a more detailed introduction to three of our case-study students. Rather than being "typical" of the students in our sample, the profiles are intended to provide a sense of the uniqueness and individuality of the students with whom we worked closely. Donna, the subject of the first profile, was a highly successful 11th grader at the time our study began; Mark, the second student profiled, was also an 11th grader, but his academic work was at best a bothersome intrusion on the rest of his life; Jan, introduced in the third profile, began the study as a 9th grader struggling to accommodate herself to a new school and new tasks.

All three profiles are based on analyses prepared by the team members who worked most closely with each student. Donna was studied by Russel Durst and Kay Butler-Nalin; Mark by Russel Durst and Bracha Rubinek; and Jan by James Marshall and Anne Katz.

Donna

Donna joined the study during her 11th-grade year and continued until she graduated. Friendly and self confident, she was almost a textbook example of a successful high school student. During her senior year, for example, her activities included taking three advanced-placement courses, composing music, painting, drawing, writing poetry and short stories, learning foreign languages for fun, working part-time for an architect, running on the track team, serving as an advisor for a church youth group, and participating in our longitudinal study of her experiences as a writer. Donna's self-confidence and articulateness made her in some ways an ideal subject for a writing study. She freely provided explanations of what she thought about her writing, and of how she went about doing it.

Writing Processes. Donna's writing divided into three major types, each of which she approached differently. For her English classes, most of her writing was expository, usually involving critical essays on literary works. For social science classes, her writing was usually based directly on information presented in her texts or reference books; this typically required summarization of previously presented material, with little integration or exploration on her part. Donna also wrote stories and poems, either at home in her spare time or during a boring class to fill the time.

Donna wrote her school papers directly at a typewriter, after gathering whatever information she felt she might need. Her English papers, with their emphasis on analytic writing, were usually revised substantially, though she focussed her efforts on the first paragraphs. Her choice of a thesis statement and its amplification in the opening paragraph established the basis for the entire paper:

> The beginning is most important to me. If it's not right, it is almost impossible to get anything else. The thesis is in the first paragraph and then [when the first paragraph is written] I have the paper outlined. I need a paragraph to prove each point made in the thesis.

Because this paragraph played such an important role, it was sometimes rewritten as many as 10 times before she felt comfortable with it. Her concerns as she revised were to get the thesis "right" and to "be concise" in her language.

The rest of the paper would expand on and illustrate the points she had made in her opening. To get material for the body of the paper, Donna would spend considerable time "looking through the book for good quotes that fit the topic." She was very skillful at weaving these illustrations into her discussion.

Most of her writing for other subjects involved summary rather than analysis. She described this type of writing as,

> Where I don't have to think. I just read the book and it's already there. I just kind of paraphrase it and write it down. . . . I read it all and then I write it out. It's so much easier [than writing for English class]. There isn't a main idea in paragraphs. It just kind of . . . I figure, well, it's long enough, I'll make another paragraph.

Elaborating on this distinction, she added:

> In English class, you can't just take the information right out of a book, so it takes a lot more to organize it. And also when you're writing for English class, each paragraph has to have its own little meaning, and a conclusion, thesis. But in [a social science essay], you never have thesis's or anything like that.

Donna considered this kind of writing easier, since she didn't have to worry so much about it. She also made fewer revisions in her social science drafts.

When she did revise, she again focussed on the beginning of the paper, "putting in nice sentences" to "make it sound better."

In her writing at home, Donna was more likely to throw off the constraints of exposition and to experiment with poetry and short stories. This writing was "for fun," and sometimes directly parodied work she had been doing in her English classes. Most such pieces were written quickly and few were revised. During her junior year, her English teacher encouraged students to turn in unassigned writing, but Donna did this with only one of her poems. The teacher suggested some revisions, which Donna incorporated along with a few more of her own. But revision was the exception rather than the rule in her imaginative writing. Donna shared this writing with her family and friends, occasionally publishing a piece in the school literary magazine.

Writing Instruction. The instruction that shaped Donna's writing took place so long ago that she could not remember it. Yet the effects of earlier instruction were completely ingrained. She knew exactly what should go into a thesis paragraph. She knew that simple sentences were boring, complex ones "nice." She knew that word choice should not be haphazard and spent a good deal of time choosing the "best sounding" words. She knew that writing more than one draft was important.

During both years that we worked with her, Donna's teachers took such knowledge for granted. Their assignments consisted simply of a topic, due date, and length of paper. Donna felt that this was enough: "Everyone knows how to do it so they don't have to tell you anything." She did remember being taught about topic sentences and paragraph structure while in junior high school, and about the "funnel paragraph" at the beginning of high school. (The first sentence is a broad statement, the second one narrower, the third states your thesis, the last is a mini-conclusion.) Her teachers' comments on her work usually emphasized logical argument and development of the thesis. Rarely, an alternative wording might be suggested. Donna knew that to get good grades you must use "concise, descriptive words but not run on and on. Your points must relate to the thesis."

Donna was extremely grade conscious, and would sacrifice her time and personal interests to get a better grade on an assignment. She preferred to play it safe rather than to experiment with either form or content: "Even though a lot of it I might not believe myself, as long as the teacher does, that's what counts."

Audiences. Donna nearly always wrote by herself, sharing it later with her mother and a group of friends she met for lunch. Her mother's help was most likely to be enlisted when she was having a problem with a school assignment; they would discuss ideas for the paper and her mother would usually suggest she "let it rest" for a while. The lunch group often shared unassigned writing, which Donna felt was "more interesting" than their school work. In general, the circle of friends served to sanction completed work rather than to critique it; "that's good" was the typical, and expected, reaction.

Conclusion. For Donna, writing was important as a means to an end. The end might be a good grade or an amusing poem, but writing was not important to her as an activity in itself. She wrote fluently and without any major problems. She also knew what her teachers were looking for, and wrote to those concerns to insure she would receive a good grade. At the same time, her writing developed little during these last two years of her high school career. She rested comfortably within the structures she knew well, avoiding new formats or new approaches. The one area of her writing where she was willing to experiment—her poetry—she treated casually and playfully, never using it to do more than entertain herself and her friends for a passing moment.

Mark

Mark, like Donna, was an articulate and self-confident student who participated in the study during both his junior and senior years. Although a reasonably hard-working student, Mark was not particularly interested in his school subjects, concentrating most of his time and energy on tennis. He played for the school team, spent much of his out-of-school time training or coaching, and spent the summer after his senior year touring Asia as part of a travelling tennis clinic. Though he was conscientious about completing his writing assignments, Mark invested far less time and energy in them than he put into his tennis playing.

As a writer, Mark was struggling to overcome what he viewed as a weak background in writing skills. Raised on a farm in the east before moving to California for his last two years of high school, he was not accustomed to the high academic standards at his new school. Contrasting the two experiences, he noted that "Before, you could just write a short paragraph, a couple of sentences, and you didn't have to give examples or anything. You could get away with a lot less writing." Compared with his classmates, Mark felt he had much to learn about writing. In addition to matters of grammar and punctuation, Mark was working during these two years to master the intricacies of exposition, including topic sentences, paragraph structures, and appropriate conclusions. His approaches to writing tasks reflected his growing awareness of these conventions, as well as his concerns with grammar and punctuation.

Instruction. Mark was placed in remedial English, and his teachers provided quite a bit of instruction about how to structure an essay. During his senior year, for example, the teacher began by providing students with a topic, thesis statement, and outline replete with supporting details for each essay. As the year progressed, she gradually removed these supports, so that by the end of the course students were providing their own details and organization. The writing component of the class was organized as a workshop, so that the teacher was available to provide help when it was needed.

Mark wrote very little for his other courses, and when he did so relied upon the opening/body/conclusion structure that he had learned in English class. His experiences outside of English were similar to those that we have seen Donna reporting: The class would be given a topic and a due date, and little other guidance. The topics were more likely to draw on his personal experiences, however, as in a report on family expenses for his Family Life class during his senior year. One of his best papers was an interview about communism, for his eleventh grade Government class. Here he was able to interview a friend who, as a professional tennis player, had travelled in China.

Writing Processes. Typically, Mark began his writing assignments by sitting down, looking through his book, and thinking about what to write. When a thesis and an outline had been provided, he focussed on those parts of his textbook that dealt with the points in the outline. As he put it, "[The teacher] has us exemplifying every little thing, so it gets really hard." Even when he had been told what to write about, Mark had trouble keeping to the outline. In an essay on *Brave New World,* for example, he was to support the thesis that the novel uses three types of comic effect: wit, satire, and irony. Although the teacher's outline included examples of each type of effect, Mark never got beyond his discussion of wit; nor did he manage to provide a conclusion.

Mark's approach to more open-ended writing changed during his senior year, in response to his experience with writing for English class. As a junior, he followed a loose opening/body/conclusion structure emphasized by his English teacher. Rather than planning in advance, he moved through his writing point by point—thinking of one idea and writing it down, thinking of another, and so on. This approach worked reasonably well when he could organize his writing as a narrative, but for more analytic tasks he often found himself in trouble.

As a senior, his first priority became to create a thesis statement and accompanying outline. As he explained:

> I've always had problems in writing, 'cause I'd jump back and forth to and from different points. So what I do now is make a little order of how [the essay] is going to go and I work from that. It makes it more organized, flows it together more.

He was not so enthusiastic about working from his teacher's outlines, however: "It cramped my writing style. . . . Instead of trying to think what you're thinking, you had to try to think what she was thinking."

Mark spent relatively little time on his assigned writing, usually between 1 and 2 hours per essay. Once he had his thesis and outline, he would try to keep to them. The goal, as he explained it toward the end of his senior year, was "to be factual, to get the message across properly."

When he had finished his first draft, Mark invariably wrote out a second version in which he polished his language but rarely examined larger issues of organization or development: "My rough draft to the good draft, it's basically just a proofread, grammatical errors and stuff like that." Nonetheless, Mark felt that this was an important part of writing, because of the problems he had: "Like I'll start out with 'is', then I'll say 'was', and I won't notice it when I read it over. Things like that." He often asked his tennis coach, or a friend of his father's who works as an editor, to read over his drafts for problems with grammar and punctuation.

Although Mark completed his assignments relatively quickly, he disliked writing in class because it gave him little time to reread and correct his work.

Conclusion. Mark's writing developed considerably during his last 2 years of high school, though writing (like the rest of his academic life) was at best a secondary interest. He accepted writing as one of the things you have to do for school, though he did not enjoy it. In general, he preferred narrative tasks (at which he was relatively successful), and was particularly uncomfortable with analytic writing in which points must be defended logically and systematically. As he neared the end of his senior year, however, he was beginning to master at least some of the forms of the analytic essay, though he was not yet comfortable enough to adapt them for his own purposes.

Jan

Writing Processes. Jan participated in the study during her 9th- and 10th-grade years. As a 9th grader, Jan had very positive feelings toward her writing, particularly when it was personal or creative. She had been keeping a journal for several years, and wrote in it almost every night, "about things I do during the day . . . . teachers being awful, crabby, students being bad . . . if I had trouble with anything." This was a very personal form of writing; she claimed it helped her as a "way of understanding" herself, of sorting out her thoughts.

Both her family and prior schooling had encouraged Jan to be creative and expressive. Before high school, she attended an "open" school where she was allowed to develop at her own pace. She and her mother had saved her writing throughout her school years, and many of the samples from elementary school were poems and short stories. As a 9th grader, she still enjoyed writing such pieces, centered on things that had happened to her, and felt a genuine sense of satisfaction when they were completed. She had some trouble with school writing, mostly because of the constraints of time and teacher-set topic, but she received a great deal of support from her mother during the writing process, and her attitude toward writing remained almost buoyantly positive.

For a variety of reasons, Jan's attitudes toward writing shifted dramatically over the course of her second year in the study. The journal was abandoned early on in the year, as were the poetry and short stories. All of the writing Jan brought to the interviews was school sponsored, and when asked about her personal writing, she answered, somewhat reluctantly, that there didn't seem to be enough time. Instead, "learning how to do" school writing became important. Jan became very concerned about grades—they figured in every interview—and with the rules she was to employ in writing for her teachers. At the end of the year, she registered for an elective course in composition because she

> wanted to get a better understanding of how to write an essay—to get the thoughts together quickly—so I could do it. . . . I would like to learn to write more rapidly. I know people who can write a really good paper in just a few minutes. . . . It causes a lot of tension in me because I know I'm not getting done as fast as I should be.

By the end of the year, Jan had virtually stopped attending to the personal uses of writing, and had become interested, almost exclusively, in alleviating the "tension" that writing for school brought on. This shift seemed to derive, at least partly, from the writing instruction Jan was receiving.

Writing Instruction. As a freshman, Jan was enrolled in an accelerated English class; the following year, on the recommendation of her teacher, she had dropped to a less competitive track:

> I'm in a lower-lane class. It's for people, um, who aren't as smart. . . . I was recommended for the class. Last year, the class was really hard. It was a good class, but I don't feel like working that hard.

In spite of the last disclaimer, however, Jan was displeased with her sophomore English class because it wasn't demanding enough:

> I think the teacher is a lot more lenient in grading. I don't like it as well. . . . You need the insistence on perfection or you don't learn anything. I have to be constantly pushed.

Jan never resolved the tension between "wanting to be pushed" and "not wanting to work that hard." On the one hand, she felt that grading was a necessary part of the process of writing for school. She wanted to be evaluated honestly for her work, and she wanted her teacher to respect her enough to maintain high standards. On the other hand, she was somewhat resentful of the kinds of assignments she was given, and especially resentful of the time constraints of writing for school:

> I can never write in class. I have trouble doing all kinds of things in class. I really need breathing space between the time I get a topic and the time I have to write. I also think it would be good to know the topic before you read the book. I forget a lot of stuff in the book when it's time to write the essay.

The frustration Jan felt with some of her school assignments led her to fall back on a series of rules—culled from the instruction she had received—for solving the problems those assignments present. She knew, for example, that English essays are "supposed to have five paragraphs, a thesis statement, and all that other garbage." A typical English essay on *All Quiet on the Western Front* began with a quotation and a list of 3 examples supporting Jan's thesis. When asked why she chose 3 examples, Jan replied:

> Because that's the minimum you can have. I've never written [an essay] that had more than that. You have to have three. You have to have 5 paragraphs in an essay.

The ready-made structure defined the minimum requirements, but it did not help her with time and, perhaps more importantly, it did not solve the problems she encountered in other subject areas:

> I have trouble applying it [the five-paragraph frame] to some things, like my social studies reports. It's supposed to work for any essay you have to write, but in social studies, it's hard to explain in a short phrase what the paragraph is going to be about. Like on certain characteristics about a person if you're writing a biography or autobiography.

Jan wanted to do well when writing for school, but the instruction she received provided insufficient support for the writing tasks she had to face. Not only did it limit her thinking ("I've never written one that had more than that"), but, at times, it seemed inappropriate to the assignment.

If the rules she was given for writing sometimes frustrated Jan, her assignments were also a matter of concern. Near the beginning of her sophomore year, she was told to keep a journal for social studies. At first, she kept this separate from her personal journal, writing for herself, then "removing the personal stuff" that she didn't want the teacher to see; she turned in the edited version for a grade. Eventually, however, Jan dropped the personal journal altogether, partly because there was no time to keep two, and partly because she felt that it was interfering with her performance on school assignments:

> If I write in my journal, I lose my creativity in other writing. It's like water in a hot-water heater—it runs out. If I just write straight facts in my journal, like "I had a math test today," then it's OK. But if I'm creative, I don't have anything left for my other writing.

In the personal journal, Jan was able to write "very abstractly, jumping around from one thing to another"—but when writing for a teacher, she was more careful about organization, because she knew she would "be graded down if they don't understand it."

During her sophomore year, Jan's personal purposes for writing—the purposes that led her to keep a journal and compose poems—were "taken over" by

the purposes of schooling. The pattern seemed especially clear on an assignment
Jan was offered in English class:

> We were supposed to write two essays on <u>Hamlet,</u> but if we could only write
> one, we had a list of alternative assignments about a thing or a place or a person.

From that list, Jan selected this one: "Choose an object and write a 150-word
descriptive paragraph about it, beginning with a general statement and supporting that statement with specific details." The assignment seems straightforward
enough: a paragraph-length version of the thesis/support essay. Yet it caused Jan
considerable concern. First, she was unwilling to believe that the teacher really
wanted something of paragraph length only. Her sense of the rules for essays led
her to argue, somewhat vehemently, that the teacher must have made a mistake
on the assignment:

> You can't have a 1-paragraph essay. I'm sure that's not what the teacher wants.
> We're supposed to write an <u>essay.</u> I suppose you could do it [write one para-
> graph], but you would probably be graded down for it.

Clearly, Jan has taken her previous instruction seriously—so much so that she
seems inflexible in the face of even a slightly different task. In spite of the
clearly-stated directions, Jan wrote a 5-paragraph essay.

   Conclusion. Jan came to high school with positive attitudes toward writing
and with a confident view of herself as a writer. It would be too much to claim
that schooling completely undermined that confidence and that attitude, but it
seems clear that both were displaced, at least temporarily, with a rather grim
concern for getting her written products in the correct form. Such a shift—if it is
temporary—may be a necessary step in Jan's growth as a writer. Yet it seems
unfortunate that the instruction Jan received took so little account of her original
purposes for writing. Rather than building on those purposes or making constructive use of them, this instruction provided Jan only with a rather arbitrary set of
rules which she had trouble applying in an intelligent fashion. Further instruction
may solve the problem—or it may exacerbate it by further removing Jan from the
center of her writing and causing her to rely even more heavily on external
evaluation as a sign of success. In any case, the kind of writing Jan did and the
attitudes she brought to it altered significantly between her freshman and sophomore years, and it is not clear that Jan was the better for it.

CONCLUSION

This brief look at the writing experiences of three of the case-study students
suggests a number of issues that we will explore further in the chapters that
follow. One theme that runs throughout these chapters concerns the prevalence

of tasks designed to evaluate previous learning, and the consequences for the writing that results. Another theme involves the challenges posed by the analytic writing that is such an important part of the high school curriculum, and the ways in which students learn to work within these initially unfamiliar analytic frames of reference. A third concerns the tensions that exist between the goals which a teacher may hold for a particular assignment, and the purposes that the students may develop in the process of making that assignment their own. None of these issues has simple answers, but together they shape the process of learning to write in the secondary school.

Chapter 5
The Demands of School Writing

Arthur N. Applebee
Russel K. Durst
George E. Newell

INTRODUCTION

This chapter will explore in more detail the writing skills and strategies required by school writing tasks, drawing comparisons between the approaches of the students we have been studying and those of the adult authors of the textbooks they use.

Following Britton et al. (1975), most of our analyses of writing have been holistic, relying on native speakers' intuitive understanding of the conventions of language for judgments about the intended audience and purpose of completed writing samples. Our data are drawn from observations of ongoing instruction, rather than from interventions or assignments structured by the research team; as one result, we have found (as we would expect) that virtually all of the writing we have examined has been addressed to the teacher. Because the functions or uses of school writing show more variability, we will focus upon them in exploring students' developing skills.

The function categories have been described in Chapter 2, and in more detail in Britton et al. (1975) and Applebee (1981). One of the assumptions underlying our analysis of function was that the various uses of writing involve different "logics" or rules of evidence and organization; these, in turn, pose different cognitive and linguistic demands for the writer, requiring the exercise or orchestration of different combinations of skills in the process of writing. As a consequence, we would expect that growth in writing abilities would involve a gradual differentiation of more sophisticated uses of writing, and that effective writing programs would provide students with a range of different kinds of writing tasks to foster this differentiation.

We have also assumed that the various secondary school subjects would differ in the types of writing required. To some extent, this variation results from an emphasis on different writing functions: English teachers are more likely than other teachers to ask students to write stories or poems; business education classes are more likely than others to emphasize letters and reports. Even within specific types of writing, however, academic disciplines may differ in their rules of evidence and organization. History and science teachers both require reports on specific events, for example, but the focus of the students' attention (and the formats to be followed) are likely to differ. Again, these assumptions have led us to expect that effective writing programs will involve writing across the disciplines, not just in English classes.

The analyses presented in this chapter represent an initial examination of our assumptions about the different demands posed by specific rhetorical contexts. Two aspects of context were examined: subject area and function (or use). Within specific contexts, two sources of writing were examined: novice writers, represented by ninth graders in the various strands of our study, and adult writers, represented by authors of our textbook selections.

We chose to examine textbook selections because they are one of the major sources of adult writing that students encounter in school contexts. Though textbook selections probably differ in significant ways from other forms of published academic writing, the forms of writing embodied in the textbooks are the forms that students are expected to emulate. For our purposes, these passages seemed an appropriate contrast to the writing produced by our ninth grade students.

Three aspects of text structure were chosen for initial examination: overall coherence, as reflected in Hasan's (1980) measure of interaction among cohesive chains; local operations, as reflected in Odell's (1977) measures of intellectual strategies; and global structure of text content, as reflected in Meyer's (1975, 1981) hierarchical rendering of content structure. (All three systems will be explained in more detail later in this chapter.)

SAMPLE SELECTION

For these analyses, passages were selected to represent important contrasts in the study as a whole. Science and social science were chosen as the subjects in which students are most frequently asked to write, and in which textbook passages and writing assignments reflect similar functions or uses of writing. (Although students also write frequently in English, their reading and writing tend to reflect differing language functions.) Summary and analysis were chosen as the most frequent types of writing required in these subjects. These two types of writing are of further interest because the category system implies some clear differences in the writing strategies required for the two tasks. Summary (or "generalized narrative" in Britton et al.'s [1975] original formulation) is assumed to be a generically simpler task, relying to a large extent on narrative frameworks.

Analysis, in contrast, requires a shift to logical modes of argumentation and organization, relying more heavily on classification and categorization.

For student writing, we chose samples for which there had been complete agreement about function category when they were scored independently by two raters. These samples were further reviewed by members of the research team to insure that all selections clearly represented the intended function category and subject, and that the samples represented complete texts rather than excerpts from student work. Textbook passages were similarly selected on the basis of a clearly represented writing function and on the ability of the passage (though drawn from a larger chapter) to stand on its own as a complete text.

Passages were selected from among the ninth grade samples available in the study as a whole, in a 2 × 2 × 2 factorial design contrasting function (summary, analysis), subject (social science, science), and source (student writing, textbook writing). Forty passages were selected in all, five per cell. Length was not controlled for either textbook passages or student writing; mean length of all selections was 270 words ($SD = 13.0$), with no significant differences between functions, or between students and textbooks. Science passages were significantly shorter than social science samples (F [1;32] = 4.3, $p < .05$).

TEXT ANALYSES

Each passage was separately analyzed for quality, coherence, local operations, and global structure using the systems outlined in the following sections.

Ratings of Quality

Two raters rated each passage holistically for overall quality, using a 5-point scale. Holistic scorings were carried out separately for textbook passages and student writing. Ratings were summed to obtain a total quality score ranging from 2 to 10 for each passage. Interrater reliabilities for the total scores were .86 for the textbook selections and .82 for the student writing samples.

Overall Coherence

Hasan's (1980) measure of text coherence is based on an examination of the ways in which chains of related lexical items interact with one another through formal syntactic relationships. The analysis involves (a) identifying lexical chains, (b) specifying all instances of interaction among chains, and (c) quantifying the degree of interaction as the ratio of the number of lexical items directly involved in chain interaction to the number of lexical items in chains.

Chains of lexical items can result from a variety of cohesive devices (Halliday & Hasan, 1976). In an *identity chain,* each item in the chain refers to the same person, item, or event. For example: "*Mary* once lived in Utah. Now *she* lives in

New York,'' where *Mary* and *she* refer to the same person. In a *similarity chain*, members belong to the same class of items, such as musical instruments (piano, violin) or travel verbs (go, walk). Members of this type of chain can also be related through synonymy, antonomy, part–whole relationships (e.g., chassis, car), and subordinate–superordinate class structures (e.g., father, parent).

Chain interaction occurs when two or more items from one chain stand in the same case grammar relationships with two or more members of another chain. In the example above, *Mary* and *live* are members of cohesive chains, and since they stand in the same case grammar relationship (doer, doing) in the two sentences, there is a chain interaction as well as a set of cohesive ties between the two sentences. (In this particular example, *Utah* and *New York* also from a cohesive chain, and are similarly involved in chain interaction between the two sentences.)

To quantify the degree of chain interaction, the system distinguishes three kinds of lexical tokens. *Relevant tokens* are those lexical items included within cohesive chains; *peripheral tokens* are those items not included in a cohesive chain; and *central tokens* are the subset of relevant tokens that figure directly in chain interaction. Hasan (1980) states that central tokens contribute the most to the coherence of a text. Thus she proposes using the ratio of central tokens to relevant tokens as a primary measure of text coherence.

Figures 5.2 and 5.3, in the results section below, illustrate this analysis when applied to particular passages. Appendix 3 presents our specific scoring procedures in more detail.

Local Operations

Odell's (1977) analysis of intellectual operations is based on a variety of linguistic signals of processes that may be used to consciously examine information, attitudes, or concepts. In applying the system to a particular passage, each instance of a process is noted and totals per process calculated for each passage. The processes are "local" in the sense that they can be identified through a sentence-by-sentence analysis, without attention to overall text structure. Whether the sentence-level features identified serve to organize inter-sentence relationships is irrelevant to the analysis.

Five operations were examined:

1. *Contrast*—After focussing on an item of information, an attitude, or a concept, we set it in a field to see how it differs from other items. Indicated in surface structure by comparatives, superlatives, negatives, and contrasting connectors, e.g., "He's 40, *but* looks 25."
2. *Classification*—Labelling, classifying items. Indicated by phrases such as "for example," words like "similar" and "resemble," and by linking verbs.
3. *Physical Context*—Reference to geographical location. Indicated in sur-

Figure 5.1   An Example of the Analysis of Local Operations

Passage (ninth-grade social science; analytic writing):
First of all people were buying more things on credit and people today are buying a lot on credit too. People also in the 20's were carefree and spent more money on a good time and we're getting a little like that today. However, lately we have slacked off. (51 words)

Operation	Surface Features	Total	Frequency/ 100 words
Contrast	more, good, a little, a lot, more, however	6	11.8
Classification	people were carefree	1	2.0
Physical Context		0	0.0
Time Sequence	first of all, today, today, in the 20's, lately	5	9.8
Logic		0	0.0
Total Operations		12	23.5

---

face structure by prepositional phrases of location, such as "the warm sun *in Bermuda.*"

4. *Time*—Reference to chronological sequence. Indicated by time or frequency adverbials, such as "*Yesterday,* he began working."

5. *Logic*—Reference to causality. Indicated by linguistic cues to logical sequence, such as "consequently" or "therefore."

Two further operations suggested by Odell, *focus* and *change,* were not examined in the present study. Focus is more appropriately examined qualitatively (in terms of the specific focus adopted or of the patterns of varying focus through a passage) rather than quantitatively, since focus in the sense of a grammatical subject is present in every clause. Change was not examined because of problems in obtaining consistent ratings.

The five local operations were identified on the basis of surface linguistic features, and prorated to yield frequency/100 words for each passage. Interrater agreement was 87% on a subsample of 222 individual operations rated independently by two raters.

Figure 5.1 illustrates the application of this analysis to a brief passage comparing the depression and contemporary society.

Global Structure

Each of the passages was analyzed for hierarchical structuring of information using the text-analytical procedures outlined by Meyer (1975, 1981). Meyer's system yields hierarchical tree structures which represent the organization of the information presented by the author.

Meyer's analysis is based on two sets of relationships among items of content. At the level of individual propositions, structure is imposed by case grammar relationships governed by *lexical predicates*. Inter-propositional relationships are governed by *rhetorical predicates* which specify superordinate and subordinate relationships among propositions. Top levels of the content structure are typically governed by rhetorical predicates, except in the case of a passage organized as thesis and elaboration; in that case, the top-level structure is typically a lexical predicate (the thesis), with various types of elaboration at lower levels in the content hierarchy.

We identified four general types of top-level structures, in addition to the thesis and elaboration structure already mentioned:

1. *Causal*—antecedent and consequent are specified, at equal levels in the hierarchy.
2. *Response*—problem/solution, question/answer, remark/reply are specified, again at equal levels.
3. *Alternative*—two or more equally weighted views or options are compared or contrasted.
4. *Sequence*—steps, episodes, or events ordered by time at equal levels in the hierarchy.

A variety of other rhetorical predicates occur at lower levels in the content hierarchy:

1. *Explanation*—causal antecedents, subordinate in staging to the idea or event being explained.
2. *Adversative*—comparison between alternatives, where one alternative is less favored (and subordinate).
3. *Description*—a variety of types of subordinate elaborations, including manner, attribution, specific, evidence, equivalent, setting, and identification (Meyer, 1975).

Collection, which Meyer treats as a separate rhetorical predicate, was treated here as an optional replication of any node in a content hierarchy; thus a problem could have a collection of solutions, a consequent could have a variety of antecedents, or an item could have a variety of specific descriptions. Sequences, which in Meyer's system are represented as collections plus time ordering, were analyzed as a separate category.

Procedures for analysis followed those outlined by Meyer (1975, 1981). Because we were interested in overall organization rather than in the microstructure of the text, lexical predicates were indicated but not elaborated when they occurred. Analysis included the top three levels in the superordinate structure, where a level consisted of all rhetorical predicates and embedded content from the text occurring at the same level in the hierarchy. (See Figures 5.5 through 5.7 for examples of tree structures and labelling of levels.)

These analyses were completed by one analyst and the top-level structures checked by a second analyst. Differences were resolved through discussion.

DIFFERENCES IN OVERALL WRITING QUALITY

Analysis of quality ratings showed no significant differences between subjects or between function categories; the main effect for source (student vs. textbooks) was artificially set to zero by the scoring procedure. Quality ratings were significantly correlated with length in the student writing sample ($r = .45$, $df = 18$, $p < .05$) but not in the textbook sample ($r = .10$). The significant correlation between quality and length for the student sample reflects the tendency of the better writers to write more easily, and at greater length, in responding to typical school assignments. Because of the strong relationship with length in the student samples, partial correlations controlling for number of words were used to investigate associations between quality ratings and other features.

DIFFERENCES IN COHERENCE

In presenting the rationale for her interpretation of chain interaction as a fundamental aspect of coherence, Hasan (1980) points out that a coherent text:

> says similar kinds of things about similar kinds of phenomena. Thus the "girl" not only "goes" somewhere, "she" also "gets" somewhere; "she" does not only "go to sleep," "she" also "wakes up" and so on.

If a text has a low ratio of central to relevant tokens, it "does not stay with any of the things [being talked about] long enough to establish a sense of continuity." The passages which follow illustrate these tendencies. The first passage is an excerpt from a discussion of the Indian Nationalist Movement:

> At the end of World War I, Indian nationalists had changed their goal from self-government to complete independence for India. I am going to discuss three factors that influenced this independence movement.
>
> The first factor that influenced the movement was the Round Table Conference. Between 1930 and 1932, Parliament held the round table discussions, but they were failures. The Indian National Congress boycotted the meetings. Mohandas K. Gandhi, who was fighting for the rights of the Indian nationals, demanded that congress should dominate a new system of government. The princes objected to any plan that might limit their powers or threaten their privileged position in the subcontinent. If Great Britain learned anything from

Figure 5.2 Analysis of Chain Interaction, High-Coherence Passage

Passage: The Indian Nationalist Movement (ninth-grade social science; analytic writing)

Cohesive chains
1. Indian (5), India, the Subcontinent
2. independence (3), self-government, nationalist, national, nationals
3. factor, factors
4. influenced (2)
5. Round Table Conference (2), discussions, meeting
6. Great Britain (2), Parliament
7. Princes (3)
8. Gandhi (2)
9. plan (3)
10. held (discussions), boycotted
11. Movement (2)
12. dominate, limit power, threaten privileged position, fight for rights, demanded

Chain interactions

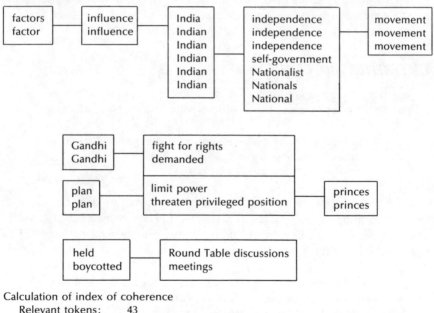

Calculation of index of coherence
Relevant tokens: 43
Central tokens: 34
Coherence: (34/43) = .79

the Round Table Conference, it was that they never satisfy all parties. (126 words)

The analysis of chain interaction in this passage is presented in Figure 5.2. There are 12 separate cohesive chains, containing 43 lexical items. Of these 43 items (*relevant tokens,* in Hasan's terminology), 34 are directly involved in chain interaction (these are the *central tokens*). The index of overall coherence is thus 34/43, or .79. This is a relatively high proportion, reflecting the fact that the student established a single topic (the Round Table Conference), and elaborated on it at some length before moving on to the next point in the argument (which is not included in the excerpt analyzed).

In contrast, consider the following excerpt, from a paper titled "Chemistry vs. Photosynthesis":

> Chemistry and Photosynthesis are alike in there is chemistry involved in making photosynthesis. When the sunlight make the plant make food. And chemistry is going on all the time in photosynthesis. And a chemical change is taking place, light–energy.
>
> They are different in they are spelled differently. Photosynthesis has a p and an o in it and chemistry doesn't. They both don't rhyme either.
>
> My opinion of photosynthesis is without it all the plants would die. And with no plants, we would die. Then their would be no life on the planet earth.

Compared with the previous writer, this student seems to know very little about the topic. Rather than developing any point at some length, the writer keeps grasping at new ones. This tendency is captured by the analysis of chain interaction, presented in Figure 5.3. Although the passage is shorter than the previous example, there are nearly as many words included in cohesive chains (37 versus 43 relevant tokens). The number of central tokens (those involved in chain interaction) is much lower, however, leading to a lower ratio of central to relevant tokens (.46 compared with .79).

To the extent that these passages are representative of the way this index varies, we would expect that adult writers (reflected here in our textbook passages) should maintain a higher level of coherence than novices, who may have difficulty managing organizational patterns or simply having enough to say about a new topic.

Table 5.1 displays the results from an analysis of variance for the measure of overall coherence (the number of central tokens as a percent of relevant tokens). Means for the textbook passages are remarkably consistent across functions and subjects; means for student writing are significantly lower ($p < .01$). The mean for students' analytic writing in science is particularly low, producing a nearly significant three-way interaction ($p < .06$).

Partial correlations (controlling for length) between Hasan's measure of co-

Figure 5.3   Analysis of Chain Interaction, Low-Coherence Passage

---

Passage: Chemistry vs. Photosynthesis (ninth-grade social science, analytic writing)

Cohesive chains
1. Chemistry (8), Chemical change
2. photosynthesis (9)
3. plants (2), plant, life, we
4. sunlight, light
5. die (2)
6. alike, different, differently
7. make (2), making
8. has, have
9. going on, taking place

Chain interactions

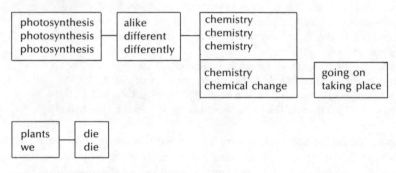

Calculation of index of coherence
Relevant tokens: 37
Central tokens: 17
Coherence: (17/37) = .46

---

herence and the holistic ratings of overall quality were not significant ($r = -.25$, $df = 17$, for the textbook passages and $r = +.27$, $df = 17$ for student writing).

DIFFERENCES IN LOCAL OPERATIONS

The five categories of local operations represent surface linguistic features hypothesized to reflect more fundamental manipulations of content. In the present analysis, we would predict that summary writing would be marked by operations involving time sequence and placing content within a situational context, while analysis should be characterized by greater use of contrast, classification, and logical sequence.

Mean frequencies/100 words for each of the five types of local operations are

Table 5.1 Overall coherence: central tokens as percent of relevant tokens

	Means			
Source:	Textbooks		Students	
Function:	Summary	Analysis	Summary	Analysis
Subject				
Social Science	72.9	72.9	60.0	61.0
Science	67.2	69.3	69.4	37.9

Analysis of Variance				
Main Effects	df	Mean Square	F	Significance
Function	1	505.7	2.48	.13
Subject	1	331.9	1.63	.21
Source	1	1823.1	8.94	.01
Interactions				
Function × Subject	1	575.1	2.82	.10
Function × Source	1	667.8	3.28	.08
Subject × Source	1	12.1	0.06	.81
Function × Subject × Source	1	753.9	3.70	.06
Residual	32	203.9		

displayed in Figure 5.4. In general, summary and analysis differ as predicted, particularly for the textbook passages. Indications of time sequence and of physical context are significantly more frequent in summary writing than in analysis; indications of contrast and classification are significantly more frequent in analytic writing. Surface indicators of logical sequence are also slightly more frequent in analytic writing, but the overall frequency is very low and the differences between functions are not significant.

Subjects also show differences in the patterns of local operations. Indicators of contrast and classification are more frequent in science writing, while physical context and markers of time sequence are more frequent in social science passages.

In comparing student writing with the textbook passages, the overall impression is that the students are moving toward the same general pattern of local operations, but with less consistency than the adult writers. In this sample, the differences are particularly sharp for the use of physical context (which the

Figure 5.4 Mean Frequencies of Local Operations

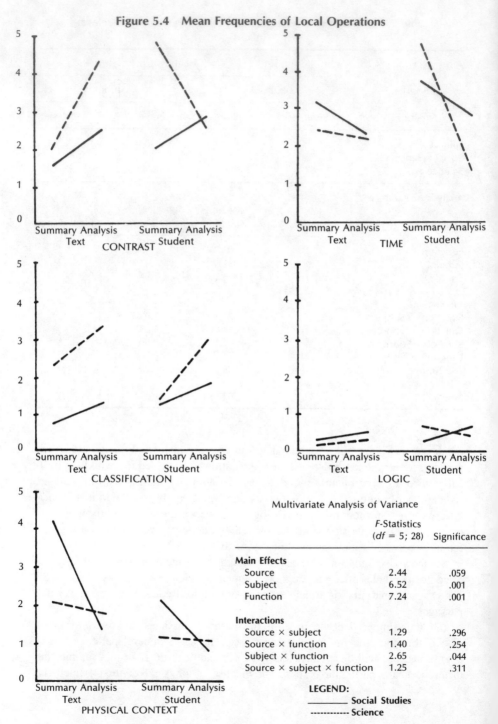

Multivariate Analysis of Variance

	F-Statistics (df = 5; 28)	Significance
Main Effects		
Source	2.44	.059
Subject	6.52	.001
Function	7.24	.001
Interactions		
Source × subject	1.29	.296
Source × function	1.40	.254
Subject × function	2.65	.044
Source × subject × function	1.25	.311

LEGEND:
——————— Social Studies
------------- Science

students tend to specify less frequently in all categories of writing) and with contrast (which students seem to use disproportionately in science summary writing).

Although Odell (1977) hypothesizes that the total frequency of use of the various operations may be an important indicator of writing quality (with higher frequency reflecting fuller development of content), these analyses suggest that the pattern of use of individual operations is at least equally important. Total operations/100 words showed a complex pattern, being particularly high for science analytic writing in the textbook selections, and science summary writing in the student samples (three way interaction, F [1;32] = 4.53, $p <$ .04). Mean totals/100 words for textbooks and students were virtually identical (9.7 and 9.9, respectively).

Associations between writing quality and total operations were also not significant ($r =$ .21, $df =$ 17, for the textbooks; $r =$ .01, $df =$ 17, for the students). In general, writing in various contexts seems to produce special demands that make quality relative to the context rather than to measures of overall frequency of use.

GLOBAL ORGANIZATION OF CONTENT

Meyer's (1975, 1981) system of analysis describes the relationships between the propositions or *idea units* included in a particular passage; the superordinate structures analyzed for the present study reflect the overall logic or structure in the material being discussed. Table 5.2 presents the results of our analyses of the top level of the content hierarchy in each of the passages in our sample. In the textbooks, summary writing is organized primarily through time-ordering, in both science and social science passages. Analytic writing tends to be structured

Table 5.2 Organization of top level of content hierarchy

	Percent of Passages							
	Summary				Analysis			
	Social Science		Science		Social Science		Science	
	Text	Student	Text	Student	Text	Student	Text	Student
Causal	0	20	0	0	80	20	0	0
Response	0	0	0	60	0	0	0	0
Alternative	0	0	20	20	0	20	80	20
Sequence	80	40	60	20	0	0	0	0
Lexical predicate	20	0	20	0	20	60	20	40
Mixed	0	40	0	0	0	0	0	40
n	5	5	5	5	5	5	5	5

around causality (antecedent/consequent) in social science writing, and around comparison of alternatives in the science passages.

The student writing samples are less consistent in their dominant structures. In summary writing, they make more use of response (question/answer) formats, while in analysis the content structure is more likely to be dominated by a lexical predicate (producing a thesis and elaboration structure). The ninth graders are also more likely to produce an essay with two parallel and unintegrated content structures (indicated in Table 5.2 as "mixed").

The full range of rhetorical predicates used in the top three levels of the content hierarchy are displayed in Table 5.3. In summary writing, the primary means of elaborating upon the initial rhetorical predicate is through various types of descriptive structures, including manner, attribution, specifics, evidence, equivalent, setting, and identification (Meyer, 1975).

Table 5.3 Rhetorical predicates in top three levels of content hierarchy

	Passage Means							
	Summary				Analysis			
	Social Science		Science		Social Science		Science	
	Text	Student	Text	Student	Text	Student	Text	Student
Causal	0.2	0.2	0.0	0.0	1.0	0.6	0.2	0.2
Response	0.0	0.4	0.0	0.6	0.0	0.6	0.0	0.0
Alternative	0.0	0.0	0.6	0.4	0.0	0.2	1.0	1.0
Sequence	1.2	1.2	0.8	0.2	0.0	0.0	0.0	0.0
Description	5.8	5.8	5.8	1.0	2.4	5.8	4.8	5.4
Explanation	0.2	1.8	0.4	0.2	0.4	0.6	0.6	0.0
Adversative	0.8	3.4	0.4	0.2	0.6	1.8	0.6	0.4

Multivariate Analysis of Variance

Main Effects	F-Statistics ($df = 7;26$)	Significance
Source	2.64	.034
Subject	5.30	.001
Function	3.65	.007
Interactions		
Source × Subject	1.13	.377
Source × Function	1.61	.177
Subject × Function	1.46	.225
Source × Subject × Function	1.07	.405

$N = 40$ passages.

Students' summaries make more use of response (question/answer) structures, and, in science, markedly less use of descriptive elaborations. For analytic writing, descriptive elaborations continue to be important, but are augmented in the social science textbooks by causal structures. In judging overall quality of the textbook writing, raters tended to prefer passages whose elaborations represented *explanations* ($r = .46, df = 17, p < .06$) rather than *descriptions* ($r = -.18$). In the student samples, both associations tended toward zero. In general, student writing samples relying on narrative structures were preferred ($r = .31$), while causal structures were rated less highly ($r = -.52, df = 17, p < .03$).

Other aspects of the content structure in these passages are best illustrated by examining individual passages and their corresponding tree diagrams. The passage below is taken from a science textbook. It introduces a contrast between hardwoods and softwoods, and elaborates the distinctions between them. Numbers in brackets key specific parts of the passage to their place in the content structure, diagrammed in Figure 5.5a.

[1] Two groups of trees can be cut into lumber: [2] softwoods and [3] hardwoods. [4] Most softwoods are <u>conifers</u> (cone-bearing), such as [5] pine, [6] fir, and [7] hemlock. [8] Conifers normally keep their leaves or needles all year [9] and are called evergreen trees. [10] The second group, the hardwoods, are mostly <u>deciduous</u> trees. [11] Deciduous trees are those that shed their leaves in the fall of the year. [12] Examples of hardwoods are oak, [13] gum, [14] ash, [15] birch, [16] walnut, and [17] maple.

The tree diagram in Figure 5.5a has been elaborated to reflect the parallel development of content in describing the two types of trees, though the surface representation is somewhat different. (The examples of softwoods, for example, are embedded in the sentence introducing the term *conifers,* while the examples of hardwoods are presented in a separate sentence.)

The next passage, written by a ninth grader, similarly seeks to introduce a contrast between two concepts (diesel and gasoline engines), and to elaborate upon their differences:

[1] The two types of engines are [2] diesel and [3] gasoline. [4] The diesel engine depends upon the hot expanding gases for operation. [5] The differences from a diesel engine and a gas engine are: [6] During the intake stroke, only air enters the culinder. [7] There are no spark plugs to ignite the fuel. [8] There is no carburetor to mix the fuel and the air. [9] The compression ratio is about 16 to 1.

[10] When the piston is pushed up the air is so highly compressed it gets hot enough to ignite the fuel when it is injected into the cylinder. [11] When the piston reaches the bottom of the cylinder the exhaust valve opens. [12] When the piston moves up it forces the burned gases out. [13] The cylinder is ready again to take in more air. [14] In the winter the engine is hard to start [15] so they spray ether or [16] they might have glow plugs.

Figure 5.5 Examples of an Alternative Rhetorical Predicate

a. Science textbook: Analysis (types of trees)

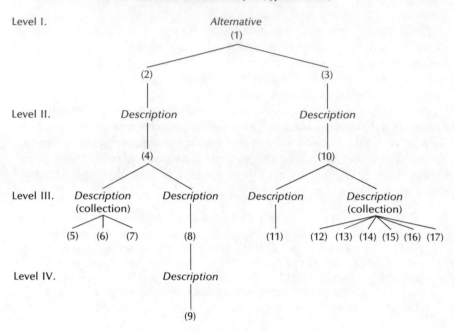

b. Science student: Analysis (types of engines)

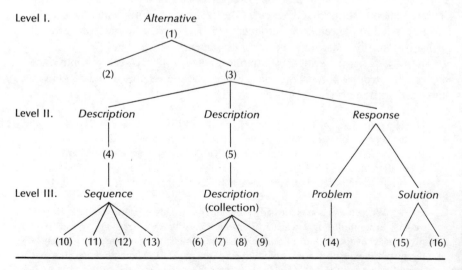

Figure 5.5b outlines the structure of this passage. (Numbers in parentheses indicate specific content from the text, in the order in which it occurred.) Although the student begins with the overall organizational pattern preferred in the textbook passage, her use of the structure is very primitive, with one branch of the alternative highly elaborated and the other (equally weighted) alternative left undeveloped. Rather than a comparison among alternatives, the piece is really a discussion of only one of them.

What seems to be happening, in fact, is that the student has taken a relatively familiar structure of thesis and elaboration and embedded it under one alternative, ignoring the other. (The thesis/elaboration is reflected in the tree structure by the various elaborations on node 3 in the diagram.)

This pattern of relying on familiar structures in the transition to more complicated forms is common as students extend their writing skills.

The next two passages illustrate another common contrast between the more expert writing represented by the textbooks and the novice writing of the students. Again the passages are of similar length and discuss similar topics, in this case summarizing the history of a particular military campaign. First, the textbook passage:

[1] The Soviet Union took advantage of the time it had gained by signing the Nazi–Soviet pact. [2] With German troops busy in Poland and French and British troops concentrated on the Maginot Line, Russia forced Latvia, Lithuania, and Estonia to sign treaties granting the Soviets naval and air bases. [3] The Soviet Union then ordered Finland to surrender some of its territory near Leningrad. [4] When the Finns refused, the Russians launched a brutal attack against Finland in November 1939. [5] Finland met the attack with stiff resistance, [6] but the Russians, far outnumbering the Finns, broke through their defenses in March 1940. [7] The Finns were forced to surrender land and to lease important military bases in Russia.

[8] Stalin, who was becoming increasingly distrustful of his German ally, began to build a buffer zone between Russia and the German frontier. [9] In June 1940 Russian troops moved into Rumania to occupy almost 20 thousand square miles of that country. [10] In August, the Soviet Union annexed the countries of Latvia, Lithuania, and Estonia.

As diagramed in Figure 5.6a, this passage is organized around a sequence rhetorical predicate. Within the general sequence of events, however, the narrative is "chunked" into two episodes which organize specific events into larger units. (A more elaborate structure could be generated for the content represented by Items 2 through 7, by analyzing the content within as well as between independent clauses. The level of detail in analyses such as these is ultimately arbitrary; for our purposes, remaining at the level of independent clauses was sufficient for our quantitative comparisons. We analyzed to a lower level only for purposes of illustration, as in Figure 5.5a.)

Figure 5.6   Examples of a Sequence Rhetorical Predicate

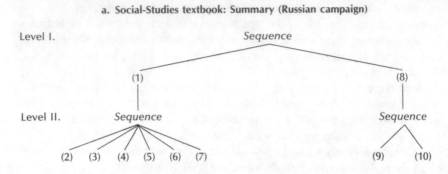

a. Social-Studies textbook: Summary (Russian campaign)

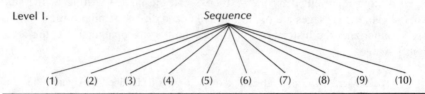

b. Social-Studies student: Summary (Napoleon's campaigns)

In contrast, consider the following sample of student writing:

[1] When Napoleon invaded Russia he lost most of his men. [2] The Battle of Leipzig then crushed Napoleon's empire and forced him to surrender and abdicate as emperor. [3] The victorious allies restored the Bourbon nomarchy and banished him to the little island of Elba. [4] He escaped from Elba and landed in France. [5] He reigned again as ruler for 100 days and [6] his return united the allies who determined to crush the common enemy and disturbed the world's peace. [7] In 1815, the end came at the village of Waterloo. [8] The Duke of Wellington and a Prussian army destroyed the unprepared French army. [9] Then he was taken to the lonely Island of St. Helena in the south Atlantic. [10] He died of cancer in 1821.

As the diagram in Figure 5.6b illustrates, this passage similarly begins with a sequence at the top of the content hierarchy. Unlike the textbook passage, however, the student sample relies almost exclusively on the superordinate narrative structure, without clear intermediary episodes to provide further organization to the events being recounted. (Though it is possible to infer some further structure among the events in this passage, the structure is not clearly marked; as a general rule in these analyses, when alternative representations were possible, we chose the most conservative, least structured representation, for student and textbook samples alike.)

The lack of intermediary structure evident in Figure 5.6b has some effects

Table 5.4   Embedded content

	Mean Number of Items of Content			
	Textbook	Student	$F(1;32)$	Significance
Level I	1.8	4.8	5.46	.026
Level II	6.0	7.3	0.85	.365
Level III	5.6	5.2	0.11	.744
Total	13.4	17.2	1.79	.190

$N = 40$ passages.

which can be examined quantitatively in the sample as a whole. One effect is to embed more individual items of content at upper levels in the content structure; another is to include more individual items within each sequence or collection, without further structure.

Analyses of these aspects of the content structure are summarized in Tables 5.4 and 5.5. Student writers embedded significantly more content at the top level of the content structure, and showed a similar pattern at Level 2. Overall, students embedded 2.3 content items per rhetorical predicate, compared with 1.9 for the textbooks ($p < .04$). They also included more individual items per collection or sequence, particularly in summary writing (the function × source interaction is significant, $p < .04$).

In the next example of student work, a lab report that began as a piece of

Table 5.5   Items per collection or sequence

	Means	
	Textbooks	Student
Summary		
Social Science	3.3	13.3
Science	3.9	5.3
Analysis		
Social Science	4.3	3.3
Science	4.0	4.6

$N = 36$ passages that used collections or sequences.
Significant Effects. Mode: $F(1;28) = 3.70$, $p < .07$.
Source: $F(1;28) = 3.59$, $p < .07$. Function × Source:
$F(1;28) = 4.68$, $p < .04$. Function × Subject × Source:
$F(1;28) = 3.45$, $p < .07$.

analytic writing reverted through a series of critical ellipses into a summary of steps in a procedure. The task facing this student was one of determining the number of substances in a particular mixture. The writing was to be organized around three subproblems, each of which would contribute part of the answer. By pooling the results of the three subproblems, the overall problem could be solved. In drafting the report, however, the student included only the steps that were taken, and the final conclusion:

[1] In order to separate the liquids from the solids, we poured the liquid through a filter, and boiled some of the liquid away to supersaturate the solutions and then filtered the solids out. [2] In order to separate the solids, we put the mixture of solids in water, dissolved one, and poured it out and evaporated the water. [3] In order to separate the liquids, we fractionally distilled the mixed liquid.

[4] I conclude, because of our results, that our mixture contained 8 different substances.

Figure 5.7 depicts the analytic structure that might have governed this report if it had been carried through as the teacher had intended. The effect of the deletions (indicated by bracketed structures in the tree diagram) was to produce a summary of steps: "To separate liquids," "to separate solids," and so on. This is a characteristic form of summary writing, and the piece was so categorized by our raters.

Figure 5.7   Structure of a Science Lab Report

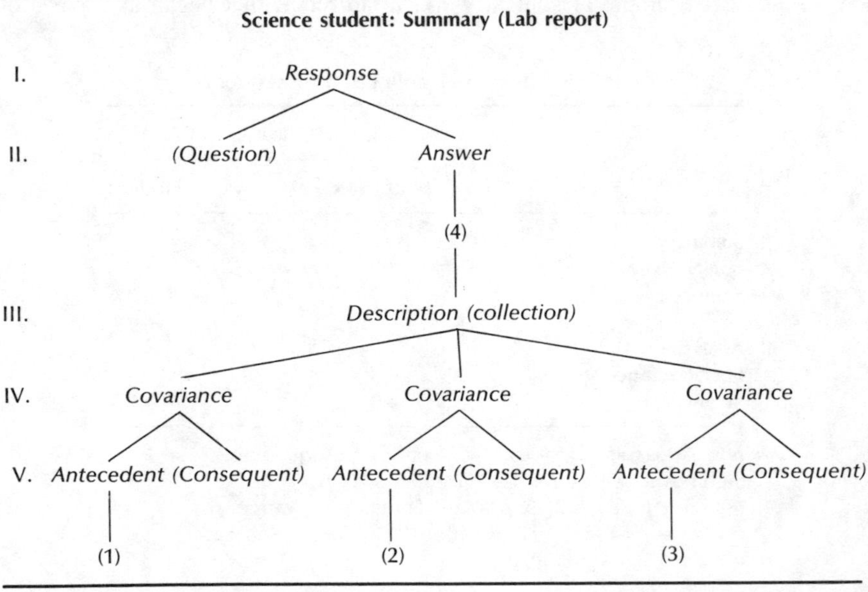

Science student: Summary (Lab report)

Figure 5.8 Structure of a Biographical Report

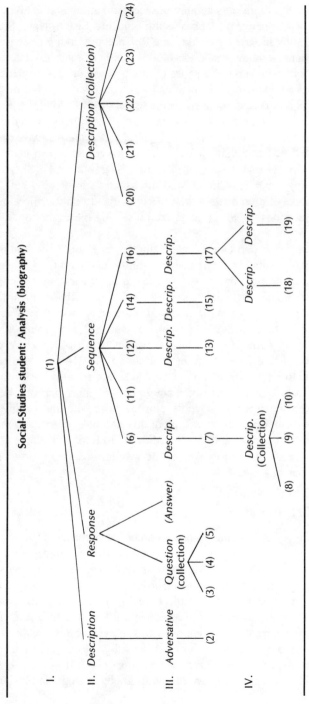

Social-Studies student: Analysis (biography)

Figure 5.8 represents another unsuccessful attempt at analytic writing, in this case drawn from one of our case-study students, Sherri. Here, Sherri was preparing a lengthy biography of Madame Roland, attempting to analyze the extent of her influence on the French Revolution. Early in the essay (Items 3, 4, and 5 in Figure 5.8), Sherri poses a series of questions about this influence, but she lacks strategies for using biographical material to answer the questions. What emerges instead is an essay dominated by the initial thesis, "Madame Roland was influential during the French Revolution" (Item 1), with a simple life history embedded beneath it (Items 6 through 19), unrelated to the *response* (question/answer) rhetorical predicate that Sherri seems to have intended to use as an organizing device. At the end of the essay (Items 20 through 24), Sherri turns to a few concluding statements about Madame Roland's influence, but again as another isolated elaboration of the initial thesis, without relationship either to the earlier set of questions, or to the narrative presenting the events of Madame Roland's life.

Figure 5.8 is particularly interesting because some 14 months after the essay on Madame Roland, Sherri began a similar essay on the influence of Susan B. Anthony. Without conscious reference to the earlier attempt, she developed an initial organization for her essay that was essentially identical to that in Figure 5.8; she gathered the information for a life story, formulated specific questions about the influence Susan B. Anthony had had, and found that the evidence available in a life story is of little direct help in answering questions about influence. The difference in the process was that 14 months after writing about Madame Roland, Sherri recognized and struggled with this problem, eventually seeking a different set of organizing questions more appropriate to the material available. She seems to have developed, during the intervening year, a sharper sense of the constraints on writing of this sort, and of the ways in which the parts of a long essay must fit together if they are to form a coherent whole. Even with this new sense of form, however, she was not successful in shaping her material around her new questions.

CONCLUSION

The analyses in this chapter had a number of purposes. One was to begin to test our assumptions about the relationships between our description of rhetorical contexts (in terms of such features as audience, function, and subject) and the underlying demands of the writing task. The data suggest that, at least for the two uses of writing and the two subject areas examined here, there are characteristic differences in the structure of argument, at both the local and global levels.

Another purpose of the analyses was to explore the sensitivity of various text analytic frameworks to patterns of growth and development. Hasan's (1980) measure of overall coherence showed consistent differences between the novice and adult, as represented by the ninth grade writing samples and the textbook passages. In general, the students tended to move on more quickly to new topics, rather than staying with a topic long enough to develop a strong sense of continuity and elaboration. Coherence in this sense, however, was not a major factor in readers' judgments of overall quality.

The analysis of content structures, using Meyer's (1975, 1981) system, was more revealing about strategies adopted by individual writers. In general, the students had a tendency to multiply detail and minimize superordinate structure, while the textbook passages imposed a clearer and more fully developed superordinate structure. Analytic writing seemed to pose more problems than summary; frequently, students approached analytic tasks by grafting newly developed analytic frameworks alongside earlier organizational structures that they could manage more successfully.

The ratings of overall quality of the student samples seem best interpreted as ratings of fluency within particular contexts, rather than as direct reflections of writing ''ability'' or level of development. Associations between particular structures and overall quality were low, because of the complexity inherent in the development of writing skills. A student attempting a new task that may represent real growth in writing ability may manage that task poorly; another, adhering to familiar patterns, may produce a fluent and highly rated text that represents little progress at all. Others develop a compromise, embedding familiar structures that help them maintain overall fluency in new and more difficult contexts for writing. Sherri's paper, illustrated in Figure 5.8, is in fact a good example of such a compromise. Though unable to manage the overall analytic framework, the fluency of the life story she embedded within her paper earned her the highest overall quality rating in the sample studied.

There are other aspects of these passages which seem important to examine in further analyses. One has to do with the genre conventions that also shape a text at both a local and global level, and which students must learn in the process of becoming more expert writers. At a local level, these conventions govern such features as tense, types of evidence, and such markers as ''Once upon a time. . .'' in a fairy tale or ''In summary. . .'' in an analytic essay. At a global level, they define the parts of a lab report in science, the structure of a five-paragraph theme, and the setting, episode, outcome structure of a story. None of these structural elements are captured by a system such as Meyer's, where the focus is on relationships among the various sets of information being presented, rather than the discourse frames which are in turn superimposed upon that information. We will examine some of these issues further in Chapter 6, drawing on a different sample of student work.

Chapter 6
The Development of Analytic Writing

Russel K. Durst

INTRODUCTION

In Chapter 5, we have seen that the move from summary to analytic writing can be difficult. Many students lean heavily on summary formats even when more analytic modes of written organization are called for, as in a critical essay. To investigate this further, in this chapter we will trace the evolution of three students' writing from third through twelfth grade, focussing on the development of such forms of analytic writing as the thesis/support essay in English and the lab report in science.

By analytic writing, we are referring here to writing which is organized around a set of critical issues rather than as a chronology. As we shall see, however, analytic comments may also be embedded within a wider chronological framework, as in a summary in which the writer occasionally explains the causes of particular events. This too is a form of analytic writing. The development of both types of analytic writing will be examined in this chapter.

THE SAMPLE

Three of our case-study students had saved much of their extended writing from previous years. Two, Margery and Donna, were usually successful in their school writing, while the third, Jan, was somewhat less successful.

Because we had few examples of extended writing from the earliest years of elementary school, the analysis focussed on writing from third grade onwards. We have looked in particular at writing in three subjects: English, social science, and science.

The number of papers available for analysis varies from year to year and subject to subject. This is because students saved varying amounts of their

Table 6.1   Student writing samples

	English	Social Science	Science	Total
		Number of Papers		
Grades 3 and 4				
Margery	10	0	1	11
Jan	33	2	5	40
Donna	6	1	0	7
Grades 5 and 6				
Margery	18	8	9	35
Jan	51	4	1	56
Donna	1	3	0	4
Grades 7 and 8				
Margery	20	5	1	26
Jan	38	10	7	55
Donna	13	0	0	13
Grades 9 and 10				
Margery	15	4	0	19
Jan	21	6	10	37
Donna	12	0	0	12
Grades 11 and 12				
Margery	17	9	9	35
Donna	20	5	0	25

writing, and wrote more for English than for science or social science. The sample for our analyses is summarized in Table 6.1.

TEXT ANALYSES

The overall structure of each writing sample was analyzed using a method of analysis adapted from Rumelhart's (1975) research on story grammars and Applebee's (1978) study of children's narratives. A set of typical patterns of passage organization was isolated for each content area, with each pattern represented by a tree diagram.

Previous studies, such as Applebee's (1978) analysis of children's discussions of stories, have shown that, as children get older, the complexity of their discourse increases. In the school writing we are analyzing here, the students similarly address more complex and abstract material as they grow older. They are also increasingly likely to analyze and interpret what they write about for school, rather than simply to describe it within a narrative framework. These shifts in the nature of student writing for school are reflected directly in the structures they adopt to organize their texts; it is these structures that we will be studying here.

The development of students' text structures will be discussed for English, social science, and science writing, highlighting the evolution of analytic writing across the three subjects.

WRITING FOR ENGLISH CLASS

Our case-study students' writing for English fell into several broad categories: journal and story writing, book reports, idiosyncratic analyses, and thesis/ support essays. Each of these broad types will be discussed in turn.

Journal and Story Writing

Our students' earliest writing for English consisted of stories, poems, and class journals; these pieces were primarily concerned with relating events, whether fictional, as in students' imaginative writing, or real, as in journal entries. Some of the early stories and journal entries were organized as narratives, with setting information followed by an event structure in chronological order. Other early writing samples consisted of descriptions of particular objects or places.

The following example, from Donna's third grade year, suggests the flavor of our students' earliest efforts at story writing:

Zip and Zap

One day the were to cats named Zip and Zap. They were a brother and a siter. They went down to the stream. They wented fish in the stream. They went to fish zeabra fish because they liked them.
—Donna, grade 3

In the original, this story is accompanied by a drawing of two cats fishing at a stream. Such illustrations appeared with over half of the stories from the elementary school years.

Despite a relative lack of elaboration, these early stories do suggest command over an array of story conventions. The third and fourth grade stories from our three students regularly began with a title, used conventional introductions such as "one day" or "once upon a time," and concluded with "the end" or "and they lived happily ever after." The stories also used dialogue (complete with quotation marks), provided background information about characters and setting, and attempted to indicate the motives underlying characters' actions.

The next example, from Jan's fourth grade year, reveals a slightly more elaborated narrative pattern than was evident in Donna's story. More is happening both formally (with the use of such conventions as quotation marks for dialogue, and of parentheses to mark an aside), and in terms of content. Note the way in which Jan stepped out of her story with a parenthetical remark about practicing the recorder. This aside illustrates the conversational tone which characterized much of the early writing in our sample.

Harold's Adventure

One day Harold was practcing his recorder he did not like to practice, (I do not like practcing eather) so he decided to runaway. He ran to Alice's house. Alice was his girl freind only she liked Al now so she started yelling "Hairless Harold! Hairless Harold!" and he ran even farther away. He ran all the way to Spooky woods where he hid in a cave. He did not know that the cave was really a monster. He finaly found out that he was in monster when the cave shut its mouth. "Chomp! Chomp! Chomp! and that was the end of Harold!

—Jan, grade 4

The students continued to write stories and poems in class contexts until junior high. As might be expected, these literary efforts gradually increased in complexity, with greater detail of setting and plot, and more extensive character development.

The nonfiction counterpart of the story in our students' early writing was the journal. Two of the three students, Jan and Margery, kept in-class journals in which they recorded their daily activities and discussed their feelings and attitudes toward school. These entries were shared with teachers, who responded with brief written comments. These tended to be informal and chatty rather than evaluative.

Like their stories, our students' journal entries usually had a narrative structure, listing events and reactions to them. The entry below, from Jan's fourth grade year, reflects the summarizing nature of much of the journal writing, as well as its informal, conversational tone.

May 20, 76

Thanks for puting a birdie on my jounol. I had a good day (but it was hot!).
My faveroit foods are stroganof and hash. Stroganof is made from hambuger, mushrooms and cream.
Hash is made from hambuger, mushroom, potatos and sometimes carrots. Mostly just leftovers.

—Jan, grade 4

Journal writing continued in our sample through ninth grade. The journal entries written during the later grades reflect the students' growing propensity to analyze and comment upon events, though the basic "what I did today, and how I felt about it" structure remains. Feelings and attitudes were also discussed in

greater detail and with more sophistication in later journals. The following excerpt from a ninth grade travel journal illustrates these tendencies:

> The dinner was at an old fashioned Japanese restaurant. When we went in we
> took our shoes off and walked up some steep steps to a small room where there
> was a long table. We had to sit on the floor except in the middle of the table
> there were four seats where people could put their feet in a hole in the floor. The
> dinner was served in about twenty courses, including raw fish, squid, and
> strange vegetables, little of which I could bear to eat. The ladies who served us
> noticed that I wasn't eating anything and they worried about me and fussed over
> me the whole dinner. They brought me extra of the dishes I liked so I wouldn't
> starve. They were really nice and kept looking at me and smiling. Hiromi was
> also at the dinner and she was very nervous because it wasn't normal for her to
> be at a dinner with a group of men. She wanted to pour drinks for everyone and
> she started to but I told her not to and she agreed with me, but she kept reaching
> out to pour and then remembering and stopping.
>
> —Margery, grade 9

Book Reports

Book reports first appeared in our sample in the fifth grade and lasted until the
eighth grade, when they were replaced by more critical, analytic writing. The
structure Margery, Donna, and Jan used in writing book reports is perhaps most
remarkable for its rigidity. Starting with title and number of pages, each went on
to describe the main characters, setting, and plot (or, if reporting on a nonfiction
book, the main events). The conclusion consisted of an opinion statement in
which they typically stated, first, whether or not they liked the book, perhaps
added a sentence stating why or why not, and then told what type of audience
would enjoy reading the book. This structure seems to have served as a scaffold
for these students, operating as an instructional support which allowed them to
accomplish a new and at first difficult task within explicit guidelines. Donna's
report on *Jade* reflects this formula:

Jade

1. Jade is by Sally Watson and is 270 pages.
2. Jade is a girl in her teens. She is very adventuresome and refuses to be
bullied. Jade is very loyal and stands by her friends even when she could leave
them easily.
3. This book takes place on a pirate ship, a big planatation in India, and a
hanging platform during the early 1800's.
4. The main plot is about how Jade rebels from her guardians and runs away
to become a pirate with the famous Anne Bonney. Eventually their pirate ship is
caught and they are sentenced to be hanged after a term in prison. In the prison
Anne, Jade, and Mary suffer a great deal and spend time thinking up retorts for

the head of the prison when he comes to make fun of them. When they are about
to be hanged Jade makes a statement which saves her life and the others.

5. I liked this book very much and would recommend it to any one who
likes adventuresome fictional stories, especially young teenage girls.

—Donna, grade 7

In spite of the book report's formulaic structure, there was considerable
variation in the ways in which students accommodated themselves to writing
within that structure. Jan, the least successful of the three writers, often found it
difficult to keep the various parts of a book report separate. In describing the
main characters of *The Wolves of Willoughby Chase*, for example, she also
brings in minor characters, and ultimately summarizes the plot (rendering her
later plot section superfluous):

The Wolves of Willoughby Chase by Joan Aiken pp. 168

The main characters are: Bonnie, a bright girl with a slender figure, beautiful
black hair, and dancing blue eyes (sometimes scornful and fierce), Sylvia,
Bonnie's cousin, a frail girl whose parents died, and lived with her poor, old
aunt (but was recomended to go to Sir Willoughby's.) And Miss Slighcarp, (a
distant cousin of Sir Willoughby.), who is hired to care and teach the girls while
he and his wife were away. But, unknown to him, she is really a wicked and
fiendish woman, wanting to take the Chase and money.

And some important minor characters are: Simon, a carefree, trustworthy,
parentless boy who lived in a cave near the boundarys of Willoughby Chase and
raised geese to sell. (And who helps the girls escape the clutches of Miss
Slighcarp.)

And James and Pattern, the faithful servants who also assist the girls, even
when it endangers them.

The story takes place sometime in the 1800's in the country out side of
London. It opens in midwinter with harsh weather and half-starved wolves
everywhere. (And closes in the beautiful greenery of spring.)

And the main conflict was: Miss Slighcarp's want of the mansion and money
as opposed to Bonnie and Sylvia's want of a home.

I greatly enjoyed The Wolves of Willoughby Chase, and I believe that
almost anybody would enjoy reading it.

—Jan, grade 7

In this report Jan has piled so much content into her character section that the
piece as a whole seems rather top heavy.

The three students also differed in the extent to which they took up the
demands of the opinion statement. Jan rarely recommended a book to any particular audience, keeping her evaluative comments brief and general, as in the
example above. Donna was somewhat more incisive, usually suggesting a group,
such as "young teenage girls" who like "adventuresome, fictional stories."

Margery consistently gave the most elaborate opinion statement, discussing in some detail her appraisal of a book, and intrepidly putting forward her opinions. In this sense, the book report was a precursor of the critical writing these students would eventually undertake; in their book reports, they began to develop strategies for analysis and evaluation, in addition to summary.

Idiosyncratic Analysis

Jan and Donna developed another structure in their seventh and eighth grade English writing, which we have labelled *idiosyncratic analysis*. Margery, perhaps the best of the three writers, moved directly into more mature forms of critical writing.

Idiosyncratic analyses are further along the continuum toward critical analytic writing than book reports. Rather than the formalized and limited opinion statement of the book report, idiosyncratic analyses contain a summary of characters, setting, and plot, followed by an analysis of comparable length. This analysis section focusses on selected aspects of the literary work under scrutiny, and tends to be evaluative rather than explanatory. In other words, Jan and Donna passed judgment on what they perceived to be the merits or debits of the work, rather than providing an interpretation of its meaning. Their analyses centered around their personal, subjective reactions, and lacked the critical detachment and systematicity of later efforts at literary analysis. Donna's reaction to the film version of *The Pearl,* excerpted from a longer piece which includes a summary of the film, illustrates this approach:

> The dress in the film was authentic looking, and the setting was, too. The complaints I have are, for one, when Keno was diving for the pearl, he stayed under the water about five minutes it seemed, and I don't think he could have really held his breath that long. Another complaint is that the people in the movie whispered almost, even when the projector was turned up, and Keno when he hit the door of the Dr.'s house in anger because the Dr. wouldn't heal his baby's infection, the blood from supposedly hitting the door seemed fake. All in all though, the movie was done well, considering the film was made a long time age.
>
> —Donna, grade 7

Donna's comments here are a laundry list; they are not systematically presented or supported, just mentioned. Moreover, her complaints deal with side issues rather than central features of the flim. Though presumably important to her, the questions she raises reveal a student in the earliest stages of learning to write critically.

In the book-report format, students had a powerful scaffold within which to frame their evaluative remarks. There was safety in that structure: an opinion, thumbs up or thumbs down, and a recommendation, were all that was required.

The idiosyncratic analysis appears to have arisen when this scaffold, the rigid but familiar book-report structure, was removed. Hence, Donna seems to have been struggling at this point to find her footing in a new structure. The strategy she adopted here was to focus on aspects of the film which were poorly done, and to list them. She is moving toward more analytic writing but without an effective organizing principle. During the seventh and eighth grades such a principle, and the critical focus that comes with it, was being introduced to our students, in the form of the thesis/support essay.

Thesis/Support Essay

The thesis/support essay differs from earlier writing in that a chronology or summary will not suffice. Students must move back from the text they are discussing and lay an interpretive framework onto it. Whether they analyze a literary work's thematic structure or give a book review, they must do so systematically, providing arguments and specific evidence to support their points. Moreover, the thesis/support essay poses its own formal demands; points must be framed in a well-marked hierarchical structure, and linked to the thesis statement. Consequently, all three students experienced some difficulty in learning this new format. However, once they had mastered it, they tended to rely on the thesis/support structure almost exclusively in their English critical writing. Overall, 90% of the critical essays in our sample were organized using this structure.

Essentially, the thesis/support essay requires students to state a main idea, or thesis, and to elaborate and exemplify that idea in the body of the essay. This model for writing has its roots in classical rhetoric and the British essayist tradition, but owes its current popularity to texts such as Baker's (1977) *The Practical Stylist* and McCrimmon's (1980) *Writing With a Purpose*. For the most part, the students in our sample used this structure to analyze a work of literature. They also occasionally applied it to autobiographical, informative, and argumentative essays, and even to writing outside of English class.

The opening paragraph of a thesis/support essay contains the thesis statement, usually found in the final sentence of the paragraph. The thesis itself is often preceded by a lead-in, in which the writer introduces the subject and sets up the thesis. This pattern is illustrated below in the thesis paragraph from Donna's twelfth grade essay on *Hamlet*. Notice that this paragraph contains the seeds of the entire essay, which will elaborate the point that Hamlet's struggle is a plot device used by Shakespeare to heighten readers' interest in the play:

> The thought of a tragedy generally brings to mind images of evil and confusion, a fairly straight forward plot with a few good, innocent people caught in the midst, and a significant number of deaths by the end of the play. Though usually true, Shakespeare's Hamlet is an important exception. In accordance with the accepted definition of a tragedy, there is an underlying seriousness and a disastrous ending, yet the pathe to the end is anything but straight forward or

easily anticipated by the reader. Hamlet, confronted with his father's wish for revenge and the corruption of Denmark due to the king's murder, is involved in a very difficult situation. With this background, Shakespeare creates a kind of schizophrenia in Hamlet, a struggle between passion and reason which captures the reader's interest and gives the play an element of suspense which would otherwise be lacking.

—Donna, grade 12

Interior paragraphs elaborate the thesis, providing examples which support it. In Donna's *Hamlet* essay, she referred to particular portions of the play to depict Shakespeare's dramatic technique. Typically, the concluding paragraph is a "mirror image" of the thesis statement, and Donna followed this pattern in her essay.

Occasionally, the conclusion of a thesis/support essay contains a generalization following from the interpretation presented. For example, in a ninth grade essay on the nature of justice in the novel *The Ox-Bow Incident,* Donna moved from the concept of justice as depicted in the novel to make a statement about justice in our own times. Similarly, in a ninth grade essay on the novel *What Makes Sammy Run?,* Margery concluded with a statement about her own view of ambition.

With its hierarchical, analytic structure, and its requirement that critical arguments be systematically supported, the thesis/support format represents a new and more complex set of constraints. The three writers in our sample used varying strategies in learning this new format. The least successful of the three writers, Jan, appears to have followed a different pattern of development in learning to use this new format than the successful writers, Donna and Margery, who progressed in similar ways.

Jan's first strategy, employed in her eighth and ninth grade writing, can be called a *pseudo-analysis.* Here she began with a thesis statement but switched immediately to narrative, summarizing the literary work rather than elaborating the thesis. For example, Jan opened with the following thesis in an essay on the novel *The Yearling:*

Ma Baxter, a very different and interesting character, in The Yearling by Marjorie Kinnan Rawlings, is portrayed as a harsh but likeable mother and wife. It is understandable why she behaved as she did if you consider the circumstances of her life.

—Jan, grade 8

Instead of providing explicit links between aspects of Ma Baxter's life and the formation of her personality, Jan gave a detailed life story of the character. She appears to have been reluctant, at this point, to depart from the chronological summary format she had already learned.

In ninth and tenth grades, Jan adopted an organizing principle that allowed her to shift somewhat from summary or pseudo-analysis, though she still leaned rather heavily on a chronological presentation in her critical writing. The main difference was that she became more discriminating in choosing points to discuss, and in adapting these points to a thesis/support framework. In structuring a paper, she would form a thesis and support it with specific examples, but her thesis and her examples were rooted in concrete, narrative aspects of the plot. She found a way, in effect, to satisfy the minimal demands of the thesis/support structure without giving up her allegiance to narrative summaries. Her essay on the novel *Summer of My German Soldier* reflects this new strategy. Her thesis paragraph reads:

> Everyone encounters obstacles in their lives which they must deal with. In the book Summer of My German Soldier, Patty, the main character, encountered many. Some of them were racial prejudice, talking too much and asking too many questions, and being of above average intelligence . . .
> —Jan, grade 9

In the body of the essay, she develops her thesis by giving examples of each obstacle Patty faced, but she does not discuss the wider significance of these obstacles in the novel, or the ways in which Patty did or did not overcome them. Similarly, in an early tenth grade essay on the novel *1984*, Jan's thesis again seems broad and likely to lead toward plot summary:

> In the book 1984, by George Orwell, there were two important figures that affected life in Oceania.
> —Jan, grade 10

In this case, however, she attempted to go beyond a mere summary of plot details, saying what she thought the characters represented in the novel, and contrasting their respective roles.

At this point, Jan has learned the basic structure of the thesis/support essay. Her further development throughout tenth grade represents an attempt to achieve the critical perspective needed to go beyond the relatively superficial forms of analysis with which she has begun.

In contrast, Donna and Margery adapted more smoothly to the thesis/support format. Their most common strategy in making the transition to critical writing had its roots in their earlier book-report writing. This can be called the *thesis book review*. For these pieces, Donna and Margery chose a thesis which expressed an evaluation of the literary work being discussed. They then developed the thesis by pointing to aspects of the work which supported their evaluation, much as a professional reviewer would. For example, Donna opened a ninth grade essay in the following way:

A Connecticut Yankee in King Arthur's Court is a fast moving tale by Mark Twain which starts with a 19th century man awakening under a giant oak in a strange country, only to find the gleaming tip of a lance coming at him with a large knight on the other end. From here it proceeds quickly, rapidly capturing your interest, as it is told in the friendly conversational tones of the "Boss" as they later call the Connecticut Yankee. It is basically a light-hearted book with appeal for all ages, but it also raises some serious questions which add depth for the adult reader.

—Donna, grade 9

In the body of the essay, Donna provided examples of the novel's lightheartedness, and its seriousness, using quotes and anecdotes to demonstrate the book's appeal.

Interestingly, almost all instances of the thesis book review strategy conveyed favorable impressions of the book under scrutiny, whereas earlier book reports were often negative. This tendency to emphasize the positive may be one way in which students limited the dimensions of the task. Teenagers, with little background in literature or criticism, were being asked to pass judgment on respected works of literature, and to support their evaluations with "evidence." Lacking the skills and knowledge to systematically evaluate the merits of such works, a positive review was much safer.

Margery and Donna left the thesis book-review strategy behind after ninth grade. From this time on, their critical writing focussed mainly on analysis of literary devices, rather than on evaluation of a work's literary merits.

Margery and Donna also quickly became adept at linking their thesis explicitly with supporting points. This was done at regular intervals throughout an essay (typically at the beginning and end of interior paragraphs) through the use of topic sentences and end-of-paragraph summaries. This structuring strategy gave a sense of tightness and hierarchical ordering to the essays, helping to cement the bonds which hold the essays together. Figure 6.1 illustrates how tight this structure can be. It contains the first and last sentences of each of the interior paragraphs of Donna's *Hamlet* essay, as well as her concluding paragraph—all of which refer to or restate her initial thesis. (For the first paragraph of this essay, see page 86, above.)

Despite different degrees of mastery of the form, the three students were almost totally faithful to the thesis/support essay in their high school English writing, using it in virtually all of their essays from ninth grade on.

Summary of Growth in Writing for English

The organizational structures which have been described in this section are depicted graphically in Figure 6.2. Narrative structure, with setting information typically followed by relating of events, is depicted in Figure 6.2a. (Arrows at

Figure 6.1   Reinforcement of Thesis Statement in Donna's *Hamlet* Essay

---

Paragraph 2
First: Though <u>Hamlet</u> is most famous for the soliliquies, it is Hamlet's bursts of passion which frame the play in the reader's mind.
Last: The first two choices are common among tragedies and allow little room for the unusual, but the third and chosen one gives Shakespeare much more latitude in selecting a path to the end.

Paragraph 3
First: Hamlet's waverings between passion and reason begin from the moment he sees the Ghost.
Last: This uncertainty, once begun, stays with the reader throughout the play despite Hamlet's anguished and seemingly firm "The time is out of joint: O cursed spite that I was born to set it right!"

Paragraph 4
First: Shakespeare, catering to Hamlet's oscillations by regulating the action and inaction in the play, carefully spaces the soliliquies and their counterpart intense physical or mental confrontations.
Last: By this time, the reader has probably noticed the action-inaction pattern, though it is still not yet clear what Hamlet plans to do.

Paragraph 5
First: The conflicting nature of Hamlet's heart and mind are most easily noted in the change in his attitude towards his mother and the killing of Claudius.
Last: Finally, though, by the time of the death scene and Hamlet's last outburst, his passion, by sheer fate, culminates his waverings with the murder of Claudius.

Concluding Paragraph
   Thus, Shakespeare by simply creating a character not quite sure of himself or his motives, injects some mystery in a play, the ending of which by its very definition is more or less known. And the reader, caught up by the reality of Hamlet's uncertainties has much more enjoyment of the plot and its intricacies.

---

the bottom of the triangle reflect narrative movement.) The invariant book-report structure, with its five-part format, is shown in Figure 6.2b. The lack of a superordinate analytic framework for the idiosyncratic analysis is apparent in Figure 6.2c, where analytic comments can be seen to focus on particular aspects of plot, without a unifying analytic principle. Finally, the thesis/support format, illustrated in Figure 6.2d, consists of a hierarchical structure in which students set forth and systematically support an argument.

   We have already looked in some detail at the gradually shifting patterns of emphasis which the three students placed on these structures. These patterns are summarized quantitatively in Table 6.2, which illustrates the gradual move from narrative to analytic modes of writing for all three students.

Figure 6.2 Major Organizational Patterns in English Informational Writing

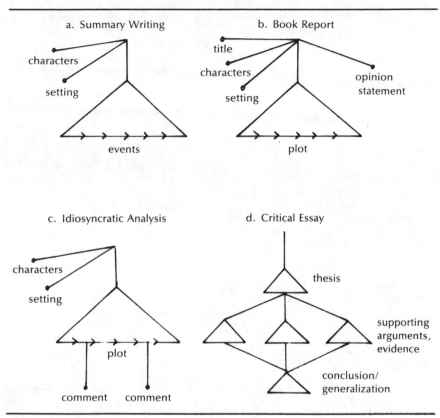

WRITING FOR SOCIAL SCIENCE

As with English class writing, early social science writing usually dealt with a subject chronologically, as in a life story of George Washington, or provided a *National Geographic*-type description of a place. In their descriptions of either events or places, the writers stayed close to the concrete, with little interpretation or analysis. Frequently, these pieces were quite elaborate; a fourth-grade report that Donna prepared about the Puritans, for example, had separate sections on religion, agriculture, education, architecture, politics, and history.

Though analytic writing was rare in the elementary school writing samples, Margery prepared a comparison of two deserts as part of a geography lesson during her fifth-grade year. The idiosyncratic and attenuated nature of her comparison illustrates her unfamiliarity with the demands of analytic writing at this point:

Table 6.2   English class writing

	Number of Papers				
	Stories and Poems	Summary	Book Report	Idiosyncratic Analysis	Critical Essay
Grades 3 and 4					
Margery	0	10	0	0	0
Jan	14	19	0	0	0
Donna	5	1	0	0	0
Grades 5 and 6					
Margery	3	5	10	0	0
Jan	17	34	0	0	0
Donna	0	1	0	0	0
Grades 7 and 8					
Margery	1	19	0	0	0
Jan	0	22	3	3	10
Donna	0	2	5	2	4
Grades 9 and 10					
Margery	0	11	0	0	4
Jan	0	7	0	0	14
Donna	0	0	0	1	11
Grades 11 and 12					
Margery	0	3	0	0	14
Donna	0	4	0	0	16

Two Deserts

Two deserts, the Sonora and the Sahara, both entirely different.

The Sahara desert is a sandy, barren place. It is very hot and sometimes a mirage will appear because of the angle of the sun.

In the day, the sand in the Sahara desert will be about 180 degrees but at night it will be freezing.

The Sonora desert is very different from the Sahara desert one thing different is that they have water. They built a canal all the way from Colorado to California therefore they are more civilized.

You may think that the people in the Sonora desert have a better living. Now they do but people are now finding oil in the Sahara desert so they could make a good living on that.

—Margery, grade 5

At this age, Margery is much more adept at narrative and descriptive writing. This is evident in the opening of a report on Yugoslavia:

Yugoslavia
The Land

If you like many different kinds of people, enjoy good food, and are a very loyal person, you would probably like to live in Yugoslavia.

Yugoslavia is a very mountainous country bordered by Italy, Austria, Hungary, Rumania, Bulgaria, Greece, and the Adriatic sea . . .

—Margery, grade 5

The writing flows smoothly in this piece and others like it, where students were relating information obtained from a book or similar source. And, despite the factual, concrete nature of most of the students' elementary school social science writing, these pieces were often surprisingly elaborate. All three students wrote reports over 10 pages long, on subjects as diverse as Aztec foods, the life of Ben Franklin, De Soto's expeditions, and Greek Myths. These reports contained a variety of sophisticated conventions, and were typically broken into semi-autonomous sections. For example, Margery's report on Yugoslavia contained sections on land, climate, sports, food, points of interest, chief products, cities, and people. In addition, there was a title page, a table of contents, maps and other illustrations, section headings, and a bibliography. Obviously, a serious amount of work went into pieces of this nature. This work focussed on the form, however; the contents of these reports rarely went beyond listing information obtained directly from encyclopedias or similar sources.

The formal nature of such pieces led students to emphasize "cleanness" of presentation. These reports generally contained few errors in spelling, punctuation, or grammar. In terms of content, the pieces stayed at a descriptive level. Writing of this nature was common until tenth grade, when the genre disappeared from the writing of all three students, being replaced by somewhat more analytic forms of writing.

Interpretive Summary

We have labelled the first type of analytic writing to appear in our students' work for social science *interpretive summary*. This is essentially a more mature form of earlier summary writing. Students relied, for the most part, on narrative structure, but interspersed their text with occasional explanatory comments (much as in their idiosyncratic analyses in English). The overall structure of the text remained chronological, however, with comments being offered in the context of particular events.

The interpretive summary was often used in students' biographical writing. Donna, who used this format for all of her high school social science writing, wrote interpretive summaries of figures such as Marx and Keynes. These essays combined ideas and events in a chronologically organized intellectual history, ending with a brief statement about the person's place in history. There was little attempt, however, to deal directly with the relevance or meaning of the ideas or theories of the people discussed.

Donna also used this format to organize broader pieces, including a history of early France and a description of Eskimo culture. These essays did not go beyond a recapitulation of information that could be found in a textbook, describing and commenting on events in a panoramic fashion. Margery and Jan also used this approach in their later social science writing, providing interpretive summaries of social and political personalities and events. The focus in all such writing remained on the gathering and presenting of information, rather than on the defense of a thesis.

The Critical Essay

The critical essay accounted for about half of the analytic writing in our social science sample. These essays moved further from chronology and description by applying either a compare/contrast or, to a lesser extent, a thesis/support framework to the events being discussed.

Compare/contrast pieces seemed to follow their own developmental path. Early attempts, such as Margery's comparison of two deserts, stayed at a fairly concrete level. For example, in a seventh grade piece, Jan compared life in America with life among the Bushmen of southwest Africa. She focussed on tangible aspects of life in the two cultures, such as food, clothing, and shopping, without speaking to more global concerns, or reaching any conclusions. The following excerpt is typical:

> The bushmen think that having scars and being 5 feet tall are desirable, while we think that being tall and slim, with non chapped lips and no pimples is desirable. Also bushmen go out and hunt down meat, bring it back and divide it according to law, and we have a butcher do the killing; then we go and buy it at the store. The bushmen also just pick up a piece of meat and stick it in their mouths and cut it off just past their mouths; they also have no tables or dishes, and we cut it into small pieces and then pick it up with a fork and put it in our mouths . . .
>
> —Jan, grade 7

Her strategy here seems to be to generate as many comparisons as possible, listing them in the order they come to mind.

Similarly, in a later paper comparing the democratic decision-making process with other forms of government, after a classroom simulation of various political systems, Jan's discussion centered almost wholly around what actually happened in class. She made only a token attempt to deal with the wider issues, and concluded in a manner reminiscent of her pseudo-analyses in her writing for English class, with only the pretense of having systematically worked through an argument and arrived at a position:

> . . . In conclusion, I feel that, in thinking about it, the democratic decision making system is probably the best we have developed yet.
> —Jan, grade 8

Later efforts at the compare/contrast format showed a greater ability both to lay an interpretive frame onto a narrative structure, and to organize the result into a coherent essay. In eleventh grade, for example, Margery compared two books about Supreme Court justices. To organize her writing, she picked one aspect of the books on which to base her essay, rather than focussing too widely and diffusely. She contrasted the two authors' approaches—one was a legal historian and the other a professional biographer—to show how the authors' differing perspectives led them to emphasize different aspects of the justices' lives.

In their attempts to use a thesis/support structure in social science writing, the students gradually learned to lay an analytic frame onto earlier summaries of events, and to pick from the summary selectively in making a specific point. Again, as in English, Jan began by writing pseudo-analyses, where she mainly related events, with a thesis statement tacked on.

In later essays, Jan moved further from summary, but even at the end of tenth grade was still relying heavily on chronological presentation in her writing. Consequently, she tended to choose thesis statements allowing her to fall back on her summarizing skills. In a tenth-grade essay on the Amish, for example, her thesis statement refers to the group's tendency to cut themselves off from the rest of society, a tendency which she claimed led them into a legal conflict with the government. She supported this thesis be telling the story of the Amish, rather than by systematically giving examples of the group's behavior.

Margery, on the other hand, had greater mastery over the thesis/support format. In an essay about a book on the depression, for example, she chose a strategy reminiscent of the thesis-book review format used in some of her writing for English. Her thesis was that the book's strength lay in its analysis of both the economic and the psychological aspects of the depression. This provided an organization for her essay; rather than simply summarize the book, she could critique it in elaborating her thesis.

Summary of Growth in Writing for Social Science

The major organizational structures the students used in social science writing are depicted graphically in Figure 6.3, not including the less frequently used thesis/support structure, which is depicted in Figure 6.2. The uses which the three students made of these structures are summarized in Table 6.3.

Figure 6.3   Major Organizational Patterns in Social Science Writing

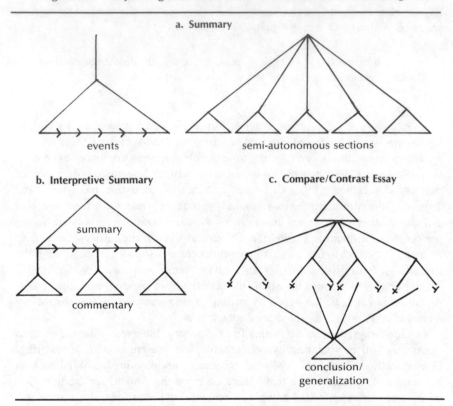

As we have seen, the development of students' social science writing seems to take two forms. All three students grew within the summary format, bringing more analysis and interpretation to this type of writing as they grew older. Jan and Margery, unlike Donna, also used more of an analytic framework in some of their work, extending their use of compare/contrast formats to social science writing. However, even here, Jan tended to rely heavily on her expertise at the summary form, while Margery learned to use a global organizing principle, or thesis, which allowed her to go beyond summary.

WRITING FOR SCIENCE

In their science writing, Jan and Margery show a gradual shift from summary to interpretive summary, and a rise of analytic writing in the context of highly structured lab reports. Donna did not save her early work in science, so could not be included in this analysis.

The earliest efforts at science writing were very concrete: biographical pieces on scientists or rough descriptions of scientific processes, such as friction, and of

Table 6.3 Social science writing

		Number of Papers	
	Summary	Interpretive Summary	Critical Essay
Grades 3 and 4			
Margery	. . .	. . .	. . .
Jan	2	0	0
Donna	1	0	0
Grades 5 and 6			
Margery	7	0	1
Jan	4	0	0
Donna	3	0	0
Grades 7 and 8			
Margery	5	0	0
Jan	3	0	7
Donna	. . .	. . .	. . .
Grades 9 and 10			
Margery	4	0	0
Jan	0	4	2
Donna	. . .	. . .	. . .
Grades 11 and 12			
Margery	0	5	4
Donna	0	5	0

natural objects, such as rocks. As in social science, these sometimes took the form of elaborately structured reports.

The narrative quality of early science writing is illustrated in Margery's report on a trip to a science museum. As with early writing in English and history, the focus is on specific events. Organization is chronological rather than hierarchical. This piece ends with a brief meta-comment describing Margery's reaction to the museum experience:

> This weekend we went to the exploratoryom. We went with Marcia, Sandra and Mark. And of course Robie too. It was neat. There was this box and it looked like there was a spring in it, and you try to grab it but your hand goes through it and you can't see were it really is. And there was barrle that you put money in and there was a pole that made sparks stick out, and it was really neat.
> —Margery, grade 3

This example is unusual in its emphasis on personal experience. Even in elementary school, the majority of science pieces seemed to strive for a more technical, detached quality. Margery's description of three types of rocks is more typical in its emphasis on presenting the facts, with little of the writer's personality slipping through:

Rocks

Sedimentary rocks are rocks that are formed mostly in the water but you can also find them in the dessert were there is one layer then a different kind of sand and on and on. Then it gets alot of pressure on it and turns hard.

The Igneous rocks are formed by heat. Deep down in the earth the ground is very hot the heat make the rocks and minerals melt to molten rock, magma. When the magma comes to the surface of the earth it cools and becomes hard then it is called Igneous rock.

Metamorphic rocks are rocks that have changed. When limestone is changed it turnes to marble. When shale changes it turns to slate.

—Margery, grade 5

At times, though, a sense of the writer's excitement and interest in the topic did emerge. Jan's engagement in her reports on endangered birds, for example, came through occasionally in her prose:

Another bird of those years ago was Hesperornis. It was a very big bird about 4ft. long. It lived about 70 million years ago. Unlike Archopteryx, Hesperornis had wings too small for flying use.

Hesperornis, like most sea creatures, eats fish and just like modern birds all of a sudden . . . disappears under water to catch a fish.

If you like modern birds better, the Ichthyornis is your bird. It lived about 100 million years ago and looked like a fern or gull.

It lived off the coast of North America. It could fly very well, but it had weak legs.

—Jan, grade 4

Such reports for science were usually embellished with tables of contents, bibliographies, and detailed illustrations, corresponding in style and structure to the social science reports we discussed earlier. Continuing through ninth grade, such multisection pieces were used for biographies of scientists and detailed descriptions of animals or of other phenomena. These pieces were essentially Jan's and Margery's versions of encyclopedia entries, with the primary task being to summarize the information presented in the source text.

For eleventh-grade biology, Margery wrote a number of papers which added an interpretive dimension to the basic descriptive format. These papers began to classify and analyze, to a degree, the organisms and processes they described, though they did not depart entirely from a chronological or descriptive mode of organization. In this regard, they paralleled interpretive summaries in social science writing.

The following example of Margery's biology writing fits this pattern. Throughout the first paragraph, which is principally summary, she occasionally stepped back and made an analytic comment about some aspect of the cell cycle. Her second and third paragraphs, which are not shown, were similar in format.

> The cell cycle is the combination of interphase and cell division. During interphase the chromosomes and their proteins are replicated so that nuclear division can proceed. Interphase has three sub-phases: S-synthesis, G1 and G2 gaps. G1 preceeds synthesis and the cycle always stops in this phase. Something must be produced in G1 that inhibits or stimulates S. This is a control mechanism of cell division. Some cells (R.B.C.'s) reproduce continually but others (nerve cells) stop reproducing once they are mature, and others (liver cells) reproduce when a part of the tissue is removed and stop once the tissue reaches its original size. More knowledge of these control mechanisms (and the cell cycle) would help with the control of cancer.
> —Margery, grade 11

In another report, Margery moved beyond summary to a compare/contrast format, almost identical to the one she occasionally employed in social science writing. In examining the differences and similarities between mitosis and meiosis, she opened with a general point about how the two processes were both similar and different in three dimensions: structure, function, and development. Then, in separate paragraphs, she discussed those three aspects of the two processes. In a sense, she had combined the compare/contrast and the thesis/support format, by making her thesis a compare/contrast statement, and developing it systematically in the body of her piece. This was the same pattern she used for her compare/contrast essays in social science.

Lab Reports

The other form of science writing in our sample was the lab report. Jan, the only one of the three students for whom we have lab reports, exhibited a pattern of development similar to that which she experienced in English and social science analytic writing.

For an eighth-grade lab report, Jan was to frame her discussion in terms of observations and conclusions, with an analysis of results leading toward a formal conclusion. But she came up instead with a description of what happened rather than an explanation of why it happened. Her token conclusion was stated as if a systematic argument had been presented, but it appeared incongruously against her summary of what had happened, much as her theses dangled in early pseudo-analyses in English and social science.

By tenth grade, in chemistry lab reports, Jan's writing conformed more to the analytic framework. All her reports consisted of the following sections: purpose, hypothesis, materials, procedures, results, and conclusion. The arrangement was intended to be inductive, with observation, analysis, and conclusion building upon one another.

However, the structure provided by the teacher took most of the analysis out of the writing itself. Jan's conclusions consisted of a series of short answers to questions posed by the teacher. Consequently, as an extended writing task, these lab reports ended up as summaries (of materials and procedures) rather than as arguments proving or explaining some scientific outcome. An excerpt from the conclusion of one of her lab reports illustrates this pattern. (Interestingly, she received an A− for this particular report.)

> 7. Several students measuring the same potato core got the following data for length: 30 mm, 31 mm, 29 mm, 28 mm. How do you account for the variations in data? The measurements were taken carelessly.
> 8. Has this investigation answered the question stated in the title? Explain.
> Yes, the investigation has answered the question.
> Summary:
> In conclusion, we did this investigation to prove osmosis.
> —Jan, grade 10

Figure 6.4   Major Organizational Patterns in Science Writing

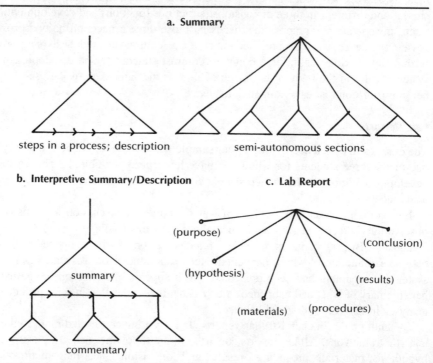

a. Summary

steps in a process; description

semi-autonomous sections

b. Interpretive Summary/Description

summary

commentary

c. Lab Report

(purpose)

(hypothesis)

(materials)   (procedures)

(conclusion)

(results)

Table 6.4   Science writing

	Number of Papers			
	Summary	Interpretive Summary	Compare/ Contrast	Lab Report
Grades 3 and 4				
Margery	1	0	0	0
Jan	5	0	0	0
Grades 5 and 6				
Margery	7	2	0	0
Jan	1	0	0	0
Grades 7 and 8				
Margery	1	0	0	0
Jan	4	1	0	2
Grades 9 and 10				
Margery	0	0	0	0
Jan	1	0	0	9
Grades 11 and 12				
Margery	0	8	1	0

Though Jan learned to use the analytic lab report format, she did so little writing of her own in these reports that their status as extended writing activities can be questioned. This is not to say, of course, that no serious thinking was involved in her completion of lab reports, simply that, for Jan at least, not much of the thinking went into organizing the writing itself.

Summary of Growth in Writing for Science

The main structures that Jan and Margery used to organize their science writing are depicted graphically in Figure 6.4, except for the compare/contrast format, used only once, which is depicted in Figure 6.3. Use of each of the structures is summarized in Table 6.4.

On the whole, Jan and Margery's science writing, like their writing for English and social science, moved from more concrete to more abstract forms. For Jan in particular, a tight, formulaic structure helped her frame the increasingly complex content of the writing. This structure operated as an organizing scaffold, much as the thesis/support essay in English helped students organize the complexity of their critical analyses.

CONCLUSION

These analyses have charted the development of three students' analytic writing strategies over time and across content areas. Overall, we have seen movement away from a pure summary format, organized chronologically or descriptively, toward more interpretive or analytic forms of writing. We have seen that, even in elementary school, the students' writing was often elaborately structured, making use of a considerable repertoire of formal conventions, at both a local and a global level.

At a local level, students' early efforts showed, for the most part, appropriate use of grammar and punctuation. At a global level, writing was often organized into multiple sections, and included such readers' aids as introductions, a table of contents, glossary, and conclusions. It should be noted that even Jan, the weaker of the three writers, wrote elaborate reports in elementary school, and used a number of formal devices correctly, at both a local and a global level.

In high school, new patterns of organization were introduced, as students went from summary to more logical modes of analysis. The thesis/support essay in English and social science, and the lab report in science, both required students to frame a formal argument. However, both formats were so rigid and formulaic that students were often able to simply "slot in" points, which took their shape and plan from the overall structure. Helpful at first, these structures may eventually have limited their further development.

The overall developmental pattern that emerged was one of students gradually learning the requirements of different patterns of organization, and, once having learned and found safety in a particular format, adhering to it as closely as possible. What the three students seemed to need most was a loosening of some of the formal constraints, the scaffolds they had come to rely on at the global level, to lead them towards other, more heuristic forms of writing.

Chapter 7
Schooling and the Composing Process

James D. Marshall

INTRODUCTION

In the decade since Emig (1971) characterized composing research as "disheveled," the field has grown in both size and coherence. On the one hand, the focus of such research has been expanded from high school writers (Emig, 1971; Matsuhashi, 1979; Mischel, 1974; Stallard, 1974) to include elementary students (Graves, 1975; Sawkins, 1975), college students (Pianko, 1979), remedial students (Perl, 1979), and adults (Flower and Hayes, 1980). On the other hand, the tools available to researchers have grown in number and sophistication, increasing the precision with which writers at work may be described. Yet in spite of the widening body of research, the picture of writers has remained remarkably consistent. Whatever their age or ability, writers usually must struggle with the conflicting constraints of generating ideas, translating those ideas into text, and editing that text into a coherent whole. Even Graves's (1975) elementary students "learned to make writing difficult" when the creation of a final product became important to them.

At the same time that writers' processes have drawn increasing research interest, a number of works on the teaching and learning of writing skills have suggested means of easing the process, arguing that all the constraints facing a writer need not be met at once. Elbow (1973), for example, dismisses the notion that "to form a good style, the primary rule and condition is not to express ourselves in language before we thoroughly know our meaning" and asserts instead that one should "think of writing . . . not as a way to transmit a message, but as a way to grow and cook a message." Murray (1978) defines writing as a "process of using language to discover meaning in experience and to communicate it" and goes on to state that the "process can be described, understood, and therefore learned." Both of these authors perceive writing as a process that proceeds in stages—stages which should be kept separate if the cognitive systems employed in writing are not to become overloaded. Meaning must be discovered before it can be communicated, and writing can be used to accomplish both ends.

In the present chapter, we will examine in some detail the ways in which our case-study students approached their writing tasks. Much of the data we will be drawing on comes from analyses of discussions of individual papers, in the biweekly meetings which we had with each student. Some comes too from our analyses of the papers themselves, as reported in earlier chapters.

STUDENTS' REPORTS ON THEIR WRITING INSTRUCTION

As we saw in Chapter 4, some 88% of the writing our case-study students produced for school was informational in function, and most of that was limited to summarizing or analyzing material drawn from textbooks or teachers' presentations. Given the widespread use of such highly specific writing tasks, one might expect that students would be well schooled in their use. Yet student reports on the writing instruction they received indicated the contrary: in many cases, instruction on how to produce a piece of assigned writing was limited—if it took place at all—to a description of the final form the piece was to take.

Student interviews were coded for descriptions of class discussion that took place as writing assignments were made. Table 7.1 presents the average results for 15 students in the 96 interviews in which such discussions were mentioned. Some 22% of the time students reported that discussions focussed on content that should be included; another 27% of the time discussions focussed on appropriate form. Audience and evaluation criteria were mentioned less often. Only 27% of the time did students report a teacher-sponsored prewriting activity as part of their preparation for writing. (Approximately 10% of the time, students reported classroom discussions prior to writing without indicating the specific nature of the discussion.)

Individual students' responses to the lack of more specific instruction took a variety of forms. Bill, for example, an 11th grader classified as a better writer, reported that the instruction took place a long time ago; further efforts were unnecessary: "Everyone knows how to do it, so they don't have to tell you anything." On the other hand, Jan, whose struggles we have examined in Chapters 4 and 6, was pleased to have received a mimeographed sheet from her English teacher entitled "The Instant Essay Success Formula." Basically, the formula outlined the dimensions of the five-paragraph essay: write a clearly stated thesis in the first paragraph (usually in the last sentence), prove that thesis in the body of the paper (usually three paragraphs long), and then provide a conclusion.

Other students discussed what they already knew about school writing, stressing always the form that writing was to take. Margery, for example, told us

Table 7.1   Student reports of classroom discussion

Topics Discussed	Mean Percent of Papers
Content	22.0
Form	27.2
Evaluation Criteria	10.4
Audience	0.9
References	3.7
Prewriting Exercises	27.2

N = 15 students discussing 96 papers.

during her 11th grade year that: "Paragraphs should be at least three sentences long and there should be at least three paragraphs in an essay. Be sure to have a beginning, a middle, and an end." Emily, another 11th grader, was one of several students to mention the "funnel" when writing for English:

> The top of the funnel . . . you have to open it with a very broad statement. Then you have to narrow it down a little bit, generally mentioning at this point the author and the book. And then the third (sentence) is the thesis statement. Then you . . . there are the three paragraphs. Three paragraphs to back up what you said in the first paragraph. That's the straight part of the funnel. Then you start out with a fairly narrow thing and recap what you said. They never say exactly what they want in the summary. All of my English teachers have told me this. Five-paragraph essays. . . .

Each of these reports is striking in the specificity with which students can describe the form their writing is to take. The shape of the product—even to the precise number of sentences per paragraph and paragraphs per essay—has been made clear to them. What remains unclear, however, is the motivation for the form. Emily, for example, went on to describe her frustration with the conclusion of essays:

> Every teacher seems to want a recap of what I've just written . . . which I think is stupid . . . I don't think you need a summary. Unless I'm arguing for 50 pages, then I could see the need, but not for a little five-paragraph essay. It's dumb, it's redundant, and it's really ridiculous. And a waste of time.

Emily knows what to produce, but she does not know why she is producing it. Moreover, she—like other students in the sample—did not report receiving instruction on *how* to produce it. Instead, she has been given an organizational model into which she must slot whatever information is required for the task. The unexplained constraints of the form are clearly causing her some frustration.

There was more evidence of instruction after students' writing had been completed—in the form of grades and comments—than there was before. Yet student reports as well as the collected papers indicate that such instruction was specific to the paper in question and rather unspecific about how students could incorporate improvements into their next effort. Students' comments on teachers' responses are presented in Table 7.2.

In general, students were rarely impressed by the helpfulness of their teachers' comments. They were, however, more likely to make such reports about their English papers than about papers from social science or ESL classes. Poorer writers, on the other hand, were more likely than better or ESL writers to make such reports. Not surprisingly, better writers more often reported being pleased with a teacher's evaluation, but not by a very large margin.

The relatively small number of students mentioning helpful teacher comments can perhaps be explained by examining a small sample of those comments. Larry, for example, classified as a poorer ninth-grade writer, received a grade and the following on one of his English essays: "You have some good ideas, but you need to be more careful about your word choice and your sentence structure. Make your sentences grammatically correct and as precise in vocabulary as possible."

It is difficult to see how Larry, or any other student, could make use of such advice. First, he has not been told which of his ideas are good—or why they are good. The remark may simply be a buffer protecting Larry from the negative remarks which follow. Second, he has been told to make his sentences grammatically correct, yet unless Larry was trying to make his sentences incorrect, it is probably the case that he has not mastered some of the sentence forms attempted. Should he avoid them in the future? Third, he has been told to be "precise" in his choice of vocabulary, but the suggestion is itself imprecise in indicating which words need clarification. The production of proper and varied sentences containing an intelligent choice of words is a task at which even the best writers sometimes fail. Telling Larry to do something without showing him how to do it seems unhelpful at best.

Table 7.2   Student reports on teacher comments

| | Mean Percent of Papers | | | | | |
	Better Writers	Poorer Writers	ESL Students	English	Social Studies	ESL
Grading Helpful	14.4	23.7	15.6	21.8	9.1	12.7
Student Pleased with Evaluation	31.3	26.5	12.4	21.2	32.0	13.5
Papers discussed	38	25	33	56	22	11
n of students	5	6	4	15	15	4

When teachers' comments were more specific, they were sometimes insensitive to the writing in question. Emily, for example, received a grade and the following pieces of advice in response to a story she had written for an 11th grade English class:

1) "Avoid 'so' as a conjunction." (Emily's sentence read, "The rain pelted down hard against the window that night so my companion Sherlock Holmes and I were surprised to hear a knocking at the door.")

2) "Avoid beginning a sentence with 'but'." (Here, Emily's prose ran, "Without a word, he took off his overcoat and galoshes. But when he took off his hat, his beard went with it, revealing light blond hair and a young slim face.")

3) "Use a more exact word (for 'ass')." (Emily had written, as part of a dialogue, "And he's such a complete ass, always telling lies about people. He said that he had our father's blessing for the marriage, the bloody liar.")

In each of these cases, the teacher had applied a rule where the rule could be more properly finessed—especially in a short story where a wider latitude of expression can be assumed. Emily responded with "why not?" to each of the comments. She did not understand the reason for the rule cited, and more importantly, her own reading had given her a sense of what was right in the situation. In this case, her judgment was arguably more appropriate than her teacher's.

Finally, teachers' comments often moved beyond advice to an actual reshaping of the students' sentences. Lynn, an ESL student, received the response illustrated in Figure 7.1 to a paper for her English class. The strategy employed here—modelling corrections for Lynn to follow—might have been helpful if Lynn had been given more guidance on how to follow the model. But that guidance was absent. The researcher working with Lynn reported that "The teacher turned back this paper with the first paragraph only corrected for grammar mistakes. She told Lynn that she didn't understand what Lynn was talking about and told her to fix the grammar throughout the paper." Again, instruction in how Lynn is to "fix" the grammar remains vague at best. She is clearly having trouble expressing herself in English, but it is difficult to see how the teacher has helped matters. In this case, Lynn visited an ESL tutor who helped her correct the mistakes, basically by rewriting the paper with her. Unless the principles behind the rewriting are made clear, however, Lynn's future work is likely to be just as problem-ridden as this was.

The comments that students received on their writing, then, sometimes seemed less than helpful. As the examples show, teachers' comments tended to focus on form—especially at the word and sentence level—without providing guidance as to how or why a more appropriate form was to be achieved.

Taken together with the analyses of work completed (reported in Chapter 4), these responses suggest that our students had very few options available to them when they wrote for school. They shaped their messages within a narrow range

Figure 7.1 Teacher's Corrections of an ESL Student's Work

The Bicycle Thief is the movie really get people on and put sympathy into it. The whole structure of the story in film which the editing and characterization (actors) are more important than other skills. and then combine the different establishing shots, sequence and black and white color, music and sound made the performance perfect and believable.

of purposes and within rather severe formal constraints. When they moved outside of these constraints, they were corrected, but they rarely reported receiving instruction about the processes they were to employ in writing. They were given a rather austere picture of what writing was to look like in finished form, but little direction as to what steps they might take to achieve it. The effect such instructional patterns can have on students' attitudes and writing processes will be discussed in the following sections.

ATTITUDES TOWARDS THE WRITING TASK

What were students' attitudes toward the writing tasks they were assigned in school? Were these attitudes consistent across students or did some report a higher level of engagement than others? What factors affected students' attitudes most clearly?

Students' discussions of particular papers were rated for the extent of their involvement in the writing task. Results are presented in Table 7.3. Better writers were evenly divided in their attitude toward school writing, while ESL students were most likely to express a perfunctory attitude. Poorer writers, on the other hand, reported a higher level of involvement for some 82% of the papers they discussed. These results may be partially explained by reference to the wider variety of purposes for which poorer students wrote and their more extensive reliance on personal knowledge. (See Chapter 4, Tables 4.7 and 4.8.)

One of the factors strongly affecting our students' attitudes toward school writing may have been the audience for whom they were writing. As we saw in Chapter 4, that audience was most often the teacher as examiner (Table 4.2). While there was some variation across subjects and achievement levels, students' sense they they were to be judged for the quality of their written products informed many of their reports.

One can hypothesize that the effect of a judgmental audience for student writing would be to displace student interest in the task itself with an interest in the teacher's response to the finished product. Individual reports from students appear to bear this out. Bill, a 9th grader classified as a better writer, explained that, for him, writing is a ''mundane'' activity whose major purpose is to teach

Table 7.3   Student reports of attitudes toward specific writing tasks

	Mean Percent of Papers		n of Papers	n of Students
	Perfunctory	Involved		
Better Writers	52.1	47.8	35	5
Poorer Writers	17.7	82.3	25	6
ESL Students	76.1	23.8	10	4

"discipline." He asserted that to get a good grade on an assignment, one must use "nice sounding words" and "nice sentences" and that one should use "concise, descriptive words, but not run on and on. You must relate to the thesis." Donna, an 11th grader also classified as a better writer, described her pleasure in getting a good grade on an assignment because "It was longer than one page, which was the minimum. And I put effort into it . . . nothing major, but a little bit. And it had a lot of information, which is what [the teacher] wanted."

In both of these examples, students appear to be distancing themselves from the writing task, focusing on surface details ("nice sounding words" and "nice sentences") and almost exclusively on teacher expectations (". . . it had a lot of information, which is what [the teacher] wanted"). They reveal both the perfunctory attitude expressed by better writers in the sample—and its cause. When students had to shape their message constantly to fit the expectations of an examining audience, then whatever interest they had in the message eventually gave way to the details of its presentation.

The somewhat cynical attitudes expressed by better writers when writing for the teacher as examiner had their counterpart among the poorer writers when they were asked to undertake similar tasks. Terri, a 9th grader, pointed out that "The things I read are more like journal writing . . . you know, honest. [When you write for school] you want to make it sound good to get a good grade, but you don't really mean it."

Some of the poorer writers' attitudes were shaped by failure. An 11th grader, Emily, said:

> I don't think much of my essays. I don't like them . . . I don't like essays really. I just think they're kind of a waste of time. . . . Not really that. I'm really not good at them is what it really is. I don't think that logically or something. My logic is not that logic.

Whereas Donna can meet her teacher's specifications—delivering "more than one page" with "a lot of information"—Emily cannot. It is difficult to see how her sense of failure will enhance her skills as a writer.

The students' sense of audience, then, had a profound effect on the attitudes they brought to the writing task. Still another factor influencing those attitudes was the pressure they felt to complete the task on time. As we saw in Chapter 2, students reported that the majority of their writing assignments had to be completed within one day—frequently within one class period. To examine the relationships between time constraints and student attitudes toward writing, students' reports of liking or disliking assignments were compared with the amount of time given to complete the assignments. Table 7.4 presents the results.

As Table 7.4 shows, students most often reported liking two kinds of assignments: those completed during a class period (and thus often less sophisticated),

Table 7.4 Relationship between writing time and attitude toward the writing

| | Mean Percent Liking the Task by Writing Time | | | |
	Class	One Day	More than Day	Week or More
	63.9	7.2	40.9	58.9
Number of papers discussed	12	24	9	25

N = 15 students.

and those for which they were given more than a day to work. Nearly 60% of the time, students reported liking assignments on which they had extended time to write. On the other hand, the least favored assignments were those that had to be completed within a day, usually for homework. Here, assignments may have required some thought, but students were not given adequate time for thinking.

When one considers the tight constraints of form, purpose, and audience that were already operating upon students as they wrote, it is not surprising that the added constraint of time affected their attitude toward the task. Consider the in-class essay illustrated in Figure 7.2, which Sherri wrote for her advanced-placement history class. In the time allotted (20 minutes) she was able to write only the two and one-half paragraphs reproduced in Figure 7.2. Her teacher's comment was that "You should have gotten more written given the preparation time and in-class time. It is imperative for you to speed up!"

Sherri, however, was clearly responding to training about the form her writing was to take. In the first, crossed-out effort, she attempted to open with a broad statement (the opening of the funnel discussed earlier), then realized that there would not be time to go anywhere with it, and thus, in the second draft of the first paragraph, collapsed the first two sentences into one. Even in the second effort, she stopped to correct lexical infelicities. Sherri was extremely disappointed in her performance, but given the constraints under which she was operating, it is surprising that she was able to produce even what she did.

The attitudes of our students toward their school writing, then, appeared to be shaped by particular features of that writing. The fact that almost all of their work was done for the teacher as examiner meant that they were less likely to engage themselves fully in the task—to commit themselves to a message and a form that was uniquely theirs. Rather, students kept their distance, designing the written product so as to meet the somewhat strict specifications of their audience. Further, they met those specifications within tightly constrained time limits, often having to submit a final version of their work at the sound of a bell. The effect of

Figure 7.2 A Better Writer's In-Class Essay

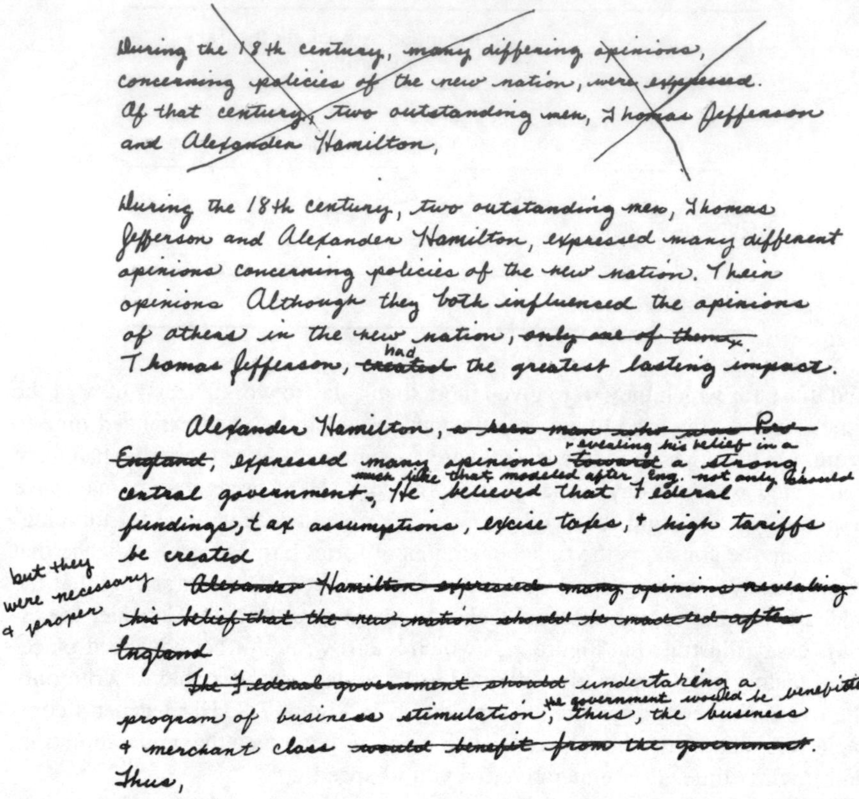

~~During the 18th century, many differing opinions, concerning policies of the new nation, were expressed. Of that century, two outstanding men, Thomas Jefferson and Alexander Hamilton,~~

During the 18th century, two outstanding men, Thomas Jefferson and Alexander Hamilton, expressed many different opinions concerning policies of the new nation. ~~Their opinions~~ Although they both influenced the opinions of others in the ~~new~~ nation, ~~only one of them,~~ Thomas Jefferson, ~~created~~ had the greatest lasting impact.

Alexander Hamilton, ~~a keen man who was Pro-England~~, expressed many opinions ~~toward~~ revealing his belief in a strong, central government much like that modeled after Eng. He believed that not only should federal fundings, tax assumptions, excise taxes, + high tariffs be created but they were necessary + proper ~~Alexander Hamilton expressed many opinions revealing his belief that the new nation should be modeled after England~~

~~The federal government should~~ undertaking a program of business stimulation; the government would be benefitted + thus, the business + merchant class ~~would benefit from the government~~.
Thus,

these constraints was to remove students even further from a sense of personal control over the task at hand. With the rules set so rigidly, there was little student ownership of the product they created—and thus little commitment to it. The cumulative impact of the constraints placed on these students is shown most clearly in the processes they employed while writing. Those processes will be discussed in the following section.

THE WRITING PROCESS

In producing a piece of writing for school, students go through several steps, both prior to and during the act of writing itself. These steps fall into three general categories: generating information, organizing, and drafting. In the first, generating information, students go through a period of incubation—however brief—in which they consider the dimensions of the task and the strategies they will use for completing it. They may read or reread texts containing the information they need, consider a thesis around which they can marshal their arguments, and search for specific facts or selected quotations that may help them prove that thesis. In the second, organizing, students begin to use writing as a tool for shaping their message, writing and rereading notes, drafting an exploratory piece in which they attempt to explain the task and its demands to themselves or constructing an outline, in whatever form, to stake out the order of their presentation. In the third, drafting, students may begin the act of producing text, writing one or more rough drafts until the piece takes the form students want it to have. Neither the three categories nor the steps within them represent orderly or sequential stages in the writing process. Rather, the categories represent a template which can be laid over the complex process of composing, allowing us to see more clearly what steps are most often taken as students write.

Interviews were coded for students' reports of these aspects of the writing process. From the results in Table 7.5, we can see the extent to which writing in different subjects encouraged the use of these steps. For example, an average of 64% of our students' reports on social science papers mentioned reading as part of the writing process, compared with about 36% of the reports on English papers. On the other hand, papers in English classes were more likely to involve thinking and organizing around a thesis than were those from social science classes. Like students in social science classes, students in ESL classes tended to report relatively often on reading and note-taking as part of their writing process, while they did not report as often on organizing around a thesis, and never reported on thinking through the task before writing.

Table 7.5   Writing processes reported on papers for selected subjects

Processes	Mean Percent of Papers			
	English	Social Studies	ESL	Out of School
Incubate	35.7	21.6	0.0	24.5
Read	35.6	63.6	46.8	19.8
Reread	9.0	18.1	14.2	21.7
Thesis	37.5	9.5	20.2	13.8
Quote	19.3	14.8	0.0	0.0
Notes	9.9	31.1	60.1	6.8
Outline	28.3	28.9	27.0	19.5
Exploratory Writing	25.1	33.1	0.0	42.9
Rough Draft	44.5	40.2	53.2	33.1
Multi-draft	17.2	9.9	13.8	50.5
Papers discussed	129	40	21	16

N = 15 students.

Table 7.6   **Relationships between writing process
and writing ability**

Processes	Mean Percent of Papers		
	Better Writers	Poorer Writers	ESL Students
Incubate	36.7	35.3	20.1
Read	49.8	38.5	41.7
Reread	16.9	13.3	2.7
Thesis	37.7	22.5	24.2
Quote	25.3	6.5	12.1
Notes	23.5	11.4	28.2
Outline	20.3	26.9	43.6
Exploratory Writing	38.1	30.2	11.0
Rough Draft	37.3	36.4	55.6
Multi-draft	29.2	12.8	7.3
Papers discussed	79	82	69

N = 15 students.

Reports on out-of-school writing, while few, showed a different pattern of results. Here, students seldom read or took notes as part of the writing process. Instead, they were more likely than in their school work to engage in exploratory writing, and were much more likely to go through several drafts of a piece.

In general, better writers took more steps while writing than did poorer writers (Table 7.6). Some 50% of the time, for example, better writers reported that they used reading as part of the writing process, while poorer writers made these reports only 38% of the time. Likewise, better writers reported taking notes, searching for quotations, and organizing around a thesis more often than did poorer writers. On only one step—outlining—did poorer writers report more frequently than better.

Results from the ESL students showed a somewhat surprising pattern. While reporting least frequently on incubation, exploratory writing, rereading notes, and multiple-drafting—a function, perhaps, of the the limited time in which they had to work—they reported more frequently than the native-speaking poorer writers on taking notes, outlining, and producing a rough draft. On certain specific steps, in other words, the pattern for ESL students more closely resembled the pattern for better writers than it did the pattern for poorer writers.

These trends may be explained in one of two ways. First, it may be that one of the characteristics of the better student writers was that they had learned to take specific steps in producing an assignment for school—to go through a recogniz-able series of stages, in whatever sequence, that supported the writing process and eased its constraints. The poorer writers, in contrast, may not have learned to take these steps—or may not often take them—and have become classified as "poorer" partly because the process is thus rendered so difficult. The ESL students, on the other hand, may have been receiving a substantial amount of teacher guidance and support during the writing process. It seems likely that assignments for such students would be structured more rigidly, perhaps proceeding in teacher-designated steps, than were assignments for native speakers.

The second explanation derives from the nature of assignments given to students in the three ability groups. We have seen, for example, that our better writers and ESL writers were somewhat more likely than poorer writers to write for informational purposes, to operate from text-based knowledge, and to write for the teacher as examiner. Since poorer writers more frequently relied on personal knowledge when writing—and more frequently worked within the teacher–learner dialogue—it seems likely that the writing they produced for school sometimes served a different, perhaps more personal, function than the writing done by other students. Their reports on process perhaps reflect that fact.

Yet, to draw the argument even tighter, poorer writers may have been assigned different tasks precisely because they had trouble with the assignments given better students. At the same time, they could not conveniently be given the instructional support provided to the relatively smaller number of ESL students in the school. Thus, for them, the rules of school writing were shifted slightly. As poorer writers, they were not as frequently assigned the types of tasks given to better writers (who could handle them on their own) or to ESL students (for whom some intensive help was available). Yet when poorer writers were given such tasks, which still represented the majority of their efforts in school, they appeared to lack the process supports other students in the sample possessed.

The problems students faced when they wrote reflected both the abilities they brought to the task and the constraints placed upon them as they composed. As can be seen in Table 7.7, ESL writers most often reported difficulty with grammatical forms, and to a lesser extent with generating ideas. Better students, on the other hand, reported little trouble with word and sentence level skills, instead indicating that their major problems were in generating ideas, organizing, and constructing a thesis—perhaps because they were also worried about having insufficient time. (Sherri's inability to write a satisfactory first paragraph in 20 minutes reveals how these problems can converge.) Finally, poorer writers also reported having trouble with time and with generating ideas, but additionally indicated difficulty understanding the assignments they were given. This may be related to the lack of prewriting and during-writing support described earlier.

The relatively high proportion of writers reporting difficulty with generating ideas may be due to several factors. First, the somewhat narrow range of purposes available to students when they wrote for school meant that many of the ideas they might have had could not be included in their school writing. Second, the organizational form much of their writing had to take—with a thesis state-

Table 7.7   **Student reports of problems while writing**

Problem	Mean Percent of Papers		
	Better Writers	Poorer Writers	ESL Students
Organization	18.6	10.9	20.7
Grammar	4.1	2.2	62.4
Words	6.3	15.1	31.9
Time	29.2	25.9	7.1
Thesis	25.7	15.7	3.9
Understanding	10.3	19.7	5.0
Generating Ideas	32.5	22.6	25.3
Papers discussed	40	41	39
n of students	5	6	4

ment, elaboration, and conclusion—may itself have abetted students' inability to generate ideas.

Under the thesis/support model, the overall argument of the essay is to be laid out at the very beginning, showing the reader exactly where the writer will go. Realizing this, students frequently reported that the opening paragraph gave them the most trouble. Wayne, for example, a better 11th-grader writer, stated:

> The beginning is the most important to me. If it's not right, it is almost impossible to get anything else. The thesis is in the first paragraph. . . . I need a paragraph to prove each point made in the thesis. It kind of outlines everything for me.

Wayne perceived the first paragraph as a microcosm of the paper as a whole, and therefore had to "worry" it until it was just right. Yet in focusing so intensely on the first paragraph, Wayne not only determined the direction his essay was to take, he eliminated every other direction. Because the first paragraph of the thesis/support essay requires exactitude, because it is a microcosm, the paper as a whole is contained within it. Donna, another better 11th-grade writer, suggested that she relaxed a little once the thesis and the first paragraph containing it had been constructed:

> The beginning paragraph ends with the thesis sentence. That's just what I want my examples to show. Examples are the next three paragraphs. Each one of those examples has two or three more examples to show that that's true. Then the last paragraph is just a conclusion, restating the thesis.

The two uses of "just" in the above may illustrate Donna's attitude toward the process. The first seems synonymous with "exactly," the second with "merely." Once the first paragraph is completed, the rest of the effort becomes the more-or-less mechanical one of filling out a pre-established design. Conclusions, rather than exploring the implications of the thesis, are simply restatements of it.

Because of the time constraints under which they operated, our students could not generate ideas through exploratory drafts—at least they did not frequently report doing so. Rather, they drafted in a top–down fashion, struggling over the first paragraph and moving with greater ease through the rest of the process. The problem with generating ideas might be alleviated were students given more time and much more guidance as to the purposes to which writing can be put. Unfortunately, neither of these were available in their school setting.

When students confronted problems—and had sufficient time—they sometimes sought help. Interviews were coded for student reports of writing conferences held with teachers, parents, and peers. Results by achievement level are presented in Table 7.8.

The patterns here are rather clear. The better and poorer writers who reported on conferences indicated that they conferred least often with their teachers and most often with their parents and peers. ESL students, on the other hand, reported conferring with their teachers far more often than did writers at the other achievement levels, indicating the higher level of instructional support they received while writing in school. They also reported conferring less frequently with parents and peers.

Why did better and poorer writers fail to confer with their teachers? Time may well have been a factor. When student reports of conferences were compared with their reports of time given for assignments, results showed that when

Table 7.8   Student reports of conferences about their writing

Discussed with:	Mean Percent of Papers		
	Better Writers	Poorer Writers	ESL Students
Teacher	6.6	19.3	60.7
Parent	65.6	47.4	0.0
Peer	63.3	50.7	26.2
n of papers	30	31	14
n of students	5	6	4

students were given one day or less to work, they reported consulting with teachers only 16% of the time; whereas when they were given more than a day, the likelihood of reporting such a conference increased to 31%.

Still another factor may have been the students' perception of the teacher-as-examiner. Since the teacher is the one who will judge their work, students may feel hesitant about sharing work in progress. Sherri explained that conferring with a teacher made her feel guilty:

> Then it becomes somehow not my own work and I feel guilty about it. The paper is how they would have written it. It would be their grade. You're using someone else's ideas.

While there may be a sense of compulsion to accept ideas from a teacher—and possibly alter one's own—suggestions from parents and peers can be accepted or rejected. Students can thus retain ownership of the grade they receive. Whatever the explanation, it appears that native-speaking writers in the sample did not often look to their teacher when confronting problems in writing.

CONCLUSION

The results from the analyses reported in this chapter make it clear that discussions of composing processes must include not only descriptions of writers and their writing, but also descriptions of the environments in which they first learn and practice their skills. Emig (1971) suggests as much when she argues that:

> The first teachers of composition—by giving certain descriptions of the composing process and by evaluating the products of student writing by highly selective criteria—set rigid parameters to students' writing behavior . . . that the students find difficult to make more supple.

Britton et al. (1975) go further when they state:

> It may well be that some of the assumptions about students' writing implicit in various teaching methods will be challenged when we know more about [the] psychological processes [in composing] . . . a start can be made by shifting the focus . . . away from the product and on to the process.

Whether the current state of composing research is strong enough to challenge traditional teaching methods may not be clear, but what must come clear is the relationship between these methods and the composing processes of students. While students may come to school with some attitudes and practices already in place, these attitudes and practices are influenced greatly by the school environment. The nature of the writing students are asked to produce, the instructions they are given, and the responses they receive must have dramatic impact, not only on the written product, but on the writing process as well. To speak of composing processes without reference to the schooling which shapes them may be to isolate an effect from its cause.

Chapter 8
Revising Patterns in Students' Writing

Kay Butler-Nalin

INTRODUCTION

A decade ago, before descriptive studies on the writing process emerged, composition textbooks suggested that writing occurred in a sequence of stages; first there was *prewriting* or planning; next there was *writing* where the text was produced; and last there was *post-writing* where editing changes were made to the text. Recent studies of composing processes, however, have documented that these stages occur throughout text production in a recursive rather than a sequential way. This finding emphasizes the importance of planning and revising throughout a writing experience, rather than relegating them to less important stages occurring before or after "real" writing.

The importance placed on the revising process by many researchers and educators occurs because, theoretically, revising should improve writing. Models of the composing process suggest that when the writer perceives a discrepancy between the intended message and the written text, the writer revises the text to make the message clearer. Thus, descriptive studies of revision can illuminate where writers have problems in text production. Further, this kind of research can show what parts of the text the writer is concentrating on and which aspects of language are being considered.

Revising has been investigated by a number of researchers. One line of research has looked at the patterns of revisions made by such differing groups as professional writers, college "basic" writers, or "good" writers (Bridwell, 1980; Faigley & Witte, 1981; Murray, 1978; NAEP, 1977; Perl, 1979; Sommers, 1978). These studies typically categorize and count kinds of revisions, and then compare them to writer characteristics. Collectively, these studies suggest that as writers mature (in age or ability), their pattern of revision shifts toward higher level rhetorical concerns, away from a focus on word and sentence level changes.

Though the results of these studies have shown how writers actually revise their own text, this research has been limited in several ways. Because documenting writing processes is time-consuming, much of the work has been based on a few writers. Often the writing task has been artificial in the sense that students write to a specially designed task for an unusual audience (the researcher) or produce their drafts under the scrutiny of the investigators. Sometimes first drafts have been returned with explicit directions to revise. Such factors led Faigley and Witte (1981), at the close of their own study on revision, to state: "Perhaps what we need now are more observational studies of writers revising in nonexperimental situations rather than more studies of student writers in contrived situations."

A study of the revising patterns in the school assignments of our case-study students allowed us to broaden the portrait of revising in the ways suggested by Faigley and Witte. Because we had a large number of papers written for ongoing school tasks, the limitations necessarily imposed on the many other studies of revising could be ameliorated.

PROCEDURES

Of the 15 case-study students who remained with the project until its conclusion, 13 began their participation in the project at the same time. This study of revision is based on their work.

The 13 students were distributed according to the selection criteria as follows (F is female; M is male):

	Grade 9	Grade 11
More successful writers	FM	FFF
Less successful writers	F	FFM
ESL students	M	FMM

During the 16-month case-study period, 465 pieces of writing were collected from these students. For these analyses, all papers were first coded as revised or not revised. Papers which contained any changes in the writing were designated as revised papers.

The revised papers were then coded for number and kind of revision using Bridwell's (1980) system. Bridwell defined seven categories of linguistic structures, reflecting a movement from smaller to larger linguistic units: surface, lexical, phrase, clause, sentence, multi-sentence (two or more consecutive sentences) and text. The system is workable and reliable; in the present study, coders reached 86% agreement in categorizing revisions.

One change was made to the system. In Bridwell's system, "text" seemed to refer to the entire paper. In her work, no revisions at this level were found. For this study, *text* was redefined as any unit represented as a separate paragraph, or as four or more consecutive sentences; this allowed us to examine revisions of paragraph length.

Following the categorizing of all the revisions, we combined Bridwell's seven categories into three levels of revision: surface (punctuation and parts of words); lower (words, phrases and clauses); and higher (one or several sentences).

PAPERS THAT WERE REVISED

The case-study students were encouraged to share all of their writing with project staff, including any rough drafts that had been developed along the way. As we saw in Chapter 2, the case-study procedures led to a collection rate of about 85% for completed work. It is likely, however, that the collection rate for early drafts was lower, since most students throw these away as soon as they are finished with them. Because of this, our estimates of the total amount of revision are probably underestimates. However, since the majority of the assignments completed by case-study students were first-and-final drafts, we believe that the underestimation introduced by missing first drafts is low.

Of the 465 papers collected, 40% contained revisions. Table 8.1 shows the percentages of revised papers in terms of audience, function, subject, and writer proficiency.

The likelihood of revision was directly related to the audience being addressed. Only 20% of the writing that was primarily for the writer's own use had any revisions, compared with nearly 40% of the papers addressed to the teacher. (Perhaps surprisingly, papers written as part of a teacher–learner dialogue were revised just as frequently as those written to the teacher-as-examiner, though we might expect the examiner audience to be perceived as more demanding.) The highest proportion of revised papers occurred when the students addressed a wider audience; nearly 60% of these papers showed revisions of one kind or another.

Just as revisions increased as audiences became more public, they also increased as the writing task became more abstract and theoretical. Just over one quarter of the papers that involved reporting or summarizing showed revisions of any sort, compared with 42% of the papers that required analysis, and fully 83% of those involving theorizing.

If we look at revisions by subject, the proportion of revised papers roughly parallels the frequency of extended writing in the particular subject involved. Thus English papers were most likely to be revised (52%), followed by social science papers (27%), and science papers (8%).

The writing proficiency of the case-study students had a diverse influence on revising. Poorer writers were most likely to revise their papers (51%), while students who spoke English as a second language (ESL), in spite of their language difficulties, were least likely to do so (20%). Papers from the better writers fell in between, with some 42% reflecting revisions.

Table 8.1 Proportion of papers that were revised

	n of Papers Analyzed	Percent with Any Revision
Audience		
Self	25	20.0
Dialogue	93	38.7
Examiner	291	37.8
Wider	56	58.9
Chi-square = 13.9, df = 3, p < .004.		
Function		
Report	25	28.0
Summary	76	28.9
Analysis	266	41.7
Theory	6	83.3
Chi-square = 9.48, df = 3, p < .024		
Subject		
English	208	51.9
Social Science	117	27.4
Science	60	8.3
Chi-square = 45.31, df = 2, p < .001.		
Writing Proficiency		
Better	165	42.4
Poorer	144	51.4
ESL	156	25.6
Chi-square = 21.63, df = 2, p < .001.		

In general, the pattern of whether or not a paper was revised depended on the writing task. As the writing task became more demanding (in terms of audience, function or emphasis placed on writing by the particular subject), students were more likely to revise their papers. And perhaps because any writing task is more demanding for less proficient writers, this group tended to revise more papers than the other writers.

The group which does not fit neatly into this pattern is the ESL writers, for whom writing must be somewhat different but at least equally difficult as it is for the less proficient writers. Their surprisingly low proportion of revised papers may result from a tendency to hand in reworked and recopied papers and to destroy earlier drafts without sharing them with us.

VARIATIONS IN REVISING PATTERNS

In addition to examining whether a paper is likely to be revised at all, we examined the variations in revising patterns in those papers that were revised.

Were revising patterns constant across tasks, or did the types of revision vary depending upon audience, subject, or writer proficiency?

To insure a substantial enough base for interpretation after deleting unrevised papers from the sample, our analyses of revising patterns concentrated on those categories of writing where our samples were largest. These were analytic papers written in English or social sciences classes and directed to a teacher audience. Because there were many more papers in the English/analysis/teacher-as-examiner classification, one third of each student's papers in this classification were randomly selected for study. For all other classification, all papers were used. The number of papers in each cell of the analysis is as follows:

	Audience	
	Teacher-as-Examiner	Teacher–Learner Dialogue
English	37	19
Social science	11	8

All revisions made on these papers were categorized using our adaptation of Bridwell's system. Revisions per 100 words as well as the overall percentage of each kind of revision were calculated for each paper. Repeated measure multivariate analyses of variance were used to evaluate the significance of main effects and interactions for audience (dialogue, examiner), subject (English, social science), and writer proficiency (better writers, poorer writers, ESL students).

Influence of Audience on Revising Patterns

We noted in Chapter 4 that most of the writing done in schools is directed to the teacher, either in the role of examiner or as part of a teacher–learner dialogue. Our assumptions about the nature of these two teacher roles would lead us to predict differences in the focus of the student-writer's attention, and thus in the revising patterns that would be evident in the papers that result.

Writing as part of a teacher–learner dialogue allows the writer to experiment with ideas that are in the process of development. Attention is focussed more on what is being said than on how to say it; the paper may ramble or jump from topic to topic as the writer discovers new facets of the subject being written about. Revisions in such papers are more likely to involve changes in words or phrases, as the writer looks for "the right words" to express evolving ideas.

In writing for the teacher-as-examiner, on the other hand, the focus is on displaying previous learning. The organization of information is important, particularly in analytic writing where each bit of evidence must be presented concisely and relevantly. Students sensed these demands, and often spoke about them in their interviews with project staff. The following samples are typical:

Well, they always say, "Give three proofs that back up your statements." And I hate doing that because I'm not too sure that the proof I give will back it up.
—Emily, grade 11

I work on a paragraph at a time. . . . It has to be organized. I have to do it by paragraph. Because my thoughts sometimes wander. Sometimes I feel like I'm not putting enough information into it and sometimes too much. There's always this question—is there enough or not? This is where I toss and turn: Is it important or not?
—Sherri, grade 9

Because of such concern with the ordering of ideas, we expected to see more revising of larger linguistic units (one or several sentences) in papers addressed to the teacher-as-examiner.

Table 8.2 presents the relevant data. Overall, there was a slightly higher rate of revising in the teacher–learner dialogue papers, with 6.8 revisions per 100 words compared with 5.6 per 100 words in papers written to the teacher as examiner (F [1;66] = 3.32, p < .07). Differences in kinds of revision were small, though in the predicted directions. For teacher-as-examiner, an average of 15% of the changes involved higher-level revisions (one or several sentences), compared with 7% for teacher–learner dialogue (t = 1.95, p < .03, one-tailed). For teacher–learner dialogue, 68% of the changes involved lower-level revisions

Table 8.2   Influence of audience on revising patterns

	Audience	
	Dialogue	Examiner
Totals (%)		
Surface	25.0	24.3
Lower	68.1	61.4
Higher	7.0	14.5
Total Words	335.8	451.5
Revisions per 100 words (rate)	6.8	5.6
n of papers	27	48

Significance of Audience Effects
Rate of revision:
    Univariate F (1;66) = 3.32, p < .07.
Levels of revision (%):
    Multivariate F (2;65) = 1.71, p < .19.
    Univariate Tests:
        Surface: F (1;66) = 0.02, ns.
        Lower: F (1;66) = 1.69, p < .20.
        Higher: F (1;66) = 3.82, p < .06.

(words and phrases), but this was not significantly higher than for teacher-as-examiner (61%).

Influence of Subject on Revising Patterns

Although students do some writing in most classes, the teaching of writing is usually considered the domain of the English teacher. It is in English classes that correct grammar, structure, and organization of extended writing are generally taught. Instruction in revising is also more likely to occur in English classes (Applebee, 1981).

Because of this emphasis, we would expect to find that papers would be more extensively revised for English classes than for other classes, though we made no predictions about differences in the kinds of revision that might occur.

Data from the student interviews corroborated our initial expectations. Students often reported that it was "easier" writing papers for classes other than English:

> I feel a lot more comfortable writing a paper for another class. I have to think of every single word in English. I have to think where to put it. When it's for another class I can just write 'em down.
>
> —Mark, grade 11

Table 8.3 Effects of subject on revision

	Subject	
	English	Social Science
Totals (%)		
Surface	22.9	29.4
Lower	63.8	64.1
Higher	13.5	6.8
Total Words per Paper	397.3	446.6
Revisions per 100 Words (rate)	6.3	6.1
n of papers	56	19

Significance of Subject Effects
  Rate of revision:
    Univariate $F (1;66) = 0.00$, *ns.*
  Levels of revision (%):
    Multivariate $F (2;65) = 1.17$, *ns.*
    Univariate Tests:
      Surface: $F (1;66) = 1.38$, *ns.*
      Lower: $F (1;66) = 0.00$, *ns.*
      Higher: $F (1;66) = 1.98$, $p < .17$.

> For History teachers . . . don't need drafts. As long as you get the information down and grammatically correct the paper is OK.
>
> —Wayne, grade 9

Table 8.3 compares revising patterns in analysis papers written for English and for social-science classes. Neither the rate nor the kinds of revisions differed significantly between the two subjects. We saw earlier that English papers are more likely to be revised than are papers from social science classes. However, once students have decided to revise at all, they approach the task in much the same way, regardless of the subject. Perhaps because students have no model to follow other than the one practiced in English classes, they use the same patterns when revising their social science writing.

Influence of Writer Proficiency on Revising Patterns

Previous studies (Bridwell, 1980; Faigley and Witte, 1981; Sommers, 1978) have shown that the kinds of revisions may be more important than the rate of revising in distinguishing between skilled and less skilled writers. More skilled writers tend to concentrate on higher level revisions (involving one or several sentences) while less skilled writers are more concerned with surface level changes.

The comments of our case-study students suggested similar contrasts. The more successful writers' comments often focussed on changes made at the sentence or several sentences level:

> I try to get it smaller . . . make it more concise. I put in nice sentences . . . making it sound better.
>
> —Donna, grade 11

> I look for clarity. I read it out loud to make sure it sounds right. Then . . . sentence variety. Some short ones, some long ones.
>
> —Sherri, grade 9

Less successful writers concentrated their efforts at the surface and word level, and claimed that they rarely made substantial changes between drafts. The following comments, drawn from the case-study interviews, are typical of those from less successful writers:

> [When moving from a draft to another draft] Basically what I do is copy it over. Then if I run into a spot where it doesn't sound right or it's missing something then I change it there.
>
> —Terri, grade 9

> My final draft is almost the same as the final rough copy. If you look at it, you'll see that it's almost the same as the final copy.
>
> —Jan, grade 9

ESL students have different concerns. Because they had not yet mastered the lexical and syntactic forms of written English, they often had to search for the words and the proper grammatical form to express their messages. We expected their revisions to be predominately lexical. Their comments reflected the problems they had:

> Sometimes I change some sentence, reorganize it. But I not sure some words . . . I not sure its meaning. So I'm not sure it's proper to use in this sentence so I have to look at dictionary and check it.
> —Li, grade 9

> I just do it. I write out whatever I think and go over everything after . . . for grammar.
> —Tai, grade 11

Table 8.4 displays the revisions made by the three groups of writers. As in earlier studies, the rate of revision on the revised papers did not differ significantly among the three groups of writers. Although the likelihood that each group of students would revise a paper at all was different, as reported earlier (Table 8.1), when they do revise, each group makes about the same number of changes per 100 words.

If we look at patterns of surface, lower, and higher level revisions (Table 8.4), the three levels vary as predicted among the three groups of students.

Table 8.4   Influence of writing proficiency on revising patterns

	Writing Proficiency		
	Better	Poorer	ESL
Totals (%)			
Surface	18.6	35.9	17.7
Lower	63.8	54.6	74.8
Higher	18.1	9.6	7.5
Total Words per Paper	494.6	320.4	422.6
Revisions per 100 Words (rate)	5.7	4.4	6.8
n of papers	25	27	22

Significance of Writing Proficiency Effects
  Rate of revision:
    Univariate $F(2;66) = 1.14$, ns.
  Levels of revision (%):
    Multivariate $F(4;130) = 4.18$, $p < .003$.
    Univariate Tests:
      Surface: $F(2;66) = 6.01$, $p < .004$.
      Lower: $F(2;66) = 5.04$, $p < .009$.
      Higher: $F(2;66) = 2.55$, $p < .083$.

Differences at the surface level (punctuation and parts of words) were most significant ($p < .004$), with the less successful writers paying more attention than the other groups to changes at this level. Differences in lower level revisions (words and phrases) were also significant ($p < .009$), receiving the most emphasis from the ESL students. As predicted, higher level revisions (one or several sentences) accounted for a higher percentage of the changes made by the more successful writers, though the overall differences in higher level revisions showed only a trend toward significance ($p < .08$).

The changes that Bill made to his concluding paragraph when going from the second to the third draft of a paper on *Dandelion Wine* are typical of the revisions made by the more successful writers in our sample:

> [Draft II:] The theme that runs through <u>Dandelion Wine</u> was that no matter what one does or does not do, that he is no better that anybody and that he must die eventually. This fact was realized by Doug when his friend left him and how the wine goes unchanged through the years.
> [Draft III:] The theme than runs throughout <u>Dandelion Wine</u> was that one person can not change the world and no one is better than another person because we all must die. The disappearance of John Huff and the tracking of the summer through the dandelion wine help mature Douglass Spaulding and tell him that although he is alive, he must eventually die.
> —Bill, grade 9

In contrast, the changes in Mark's paper are typical of the kinds of revisions made by the poorer writers. Spelling and punctuation errors are corrected and a word is changed, but nothing else is altered:

> When John was young, Mit~~sm~~ema, an older man at the savage reservation, taught him to mo~~a~~ld clay. While John is artistic and he is knowledgeable~~x~~ with his ~~re~~ ability to read, John is niave when about love.
> —Mark, grade 11

Finally, Lynn's drafts are typical of those made by the ESL writers. Changes within as well as between the two drafts focus on lexical items:

> [Draft I:] Because her father was too love her, ~~and~~ afraid she ~~just will can't~~
>   her
> wouldn't things by herself. And keep away from out the things might hurt her.
> [Draft II:] Amanda's father was too love her ~~afriad~~ afraid she couldn't handle by herself, so keep her away from all the things might hurt her.
> —Lynn, grade 11

The Influence of Successive Drafts

Revisions can occur either as emendations of a current draft or as changes introduced in moving from one draft to another. To examine the effect of succes-

**Table 8.5   Number of drafts for
revised papers**

	n of Papers	Percent
Better Writers		
One draft	13	40.6
Two drafts	13	40.6
Multiple drafts	6	19.8
Poorer Writers		
One draft	29	72.5
Two drafts	10	25.0
Multiple drafts	1	2.5
ESL Writers		
One draft	5	35.7
Two drafts	8	57.1
Multiple drafts	1	7.1

Chi-square = 12.80, *df* = 4, *p* < .01.

sive drafts on revising patterns, we looked first at the number of drafts students were producing, and then at the kinds of revision made in first and later drafts.

Table 8.5 summarizes the number of drafts for each of the papers in our total sample of revised papers. Three levels of drafting are indicated: papers written as first-and-final drafts, with revisions made directly on the draft (one draft); papers that were copied over, with changes between the first and second draft (two drafts); and papers with any revisions beyond the second draft (multiple drafts). From these data it is clear that poorer writers' revisions are more likely to be part of a first-and-final draft than are the revisions of either of the other groups of students. Conversely, better writers are far more likely to produce multiple drafts (three or more) than are either of the other groups.

Table 8.6 looks at the kinds of revisions made on successive drafts of our subsample of analytic writing for English or social science. Several trends are evident in these data. Overall, patterns of revising change for each group of writers when more drafts are produced. Better writers show an increased rate of revising at the surface and lower levels on later drafts. Poorer writers, who concentrate revising at the surface and lower levels on first drafts, give somewhat more attention to larger units of language when they produce second drafts. ESL writers move from focussing on lower level revising to both more surface and more higher level revisions on their second draft.

Producing more than a single draft appears to allow students to concentrate on different parts of their text. During the first (or only) draft, writers must do their revising in areas where they perceive they have the most problems in getting their

Table 8.6   Revising patterns on successive drafts

	Rate of Revising per 100 Words				n of Papers
	Surface	Lower	Higher	Total	
Better Writers					
First drafts	0.5	3.4	0.7	4.5	14
Second drafts	1.3	3.1	1.2	5.6	9
Multiple drafts	3.1	9.1	0.2	12.3	2
Poorer Writers					
First drafts	1.6	3.1	0.4	5.1	19
Second drafts	2.6	2.7	1.8	7.1	7
ESL Writers					
First drafts	0.8	5.9	0.2	7.0	13
Second drafts	1.4	4.6	1.3	7.4	9

message written down, whether it be grammar, organization, or word usage. Other drafts allow students the chance to look again at their text, and when they do, they pay attention to concerns which were perhaps neglected or over-shadowed by what they considered to be their major problems in initial text production. By encouraging and allowing time for two or more drafts, teachers may assist this change in the focus of revising. Successive drafting gives all students opportunities to practice different ways of revising their text. By having more opportunities to practice revising in different ways, students should be able to develop a more flexible set of strategies for revising.

CONCLUSION

This study describes the revising patterns of high school students on their on-going school assignments. Because our case-study students wrote a large number of papers in response to typical school tasks, the revising patterns we found should provide a useful complement to the results of more structured studies of revising of high school writing.

In our work with the case-study students, we found that fewer than half of the papers we collected were revised. The likelihood of students revising their papers was influenced by how demanding the writing task was. The more demanding the writing task (in terms of audience, function, and importance placed on writing in the subject area), the more papers were revised.

The rate and kinds of revisions that students made when they did revise were also influenced by the audience for the writing, by the proficiency of the writer, and by the number of drafts produced. Papers written as part of a teacher–learner dialogue tended to have more revisions reflecting the working out of ideas, while those written to the teacher-as-examiner had more revisions concerned with proper presentation of the material.

The proficiency of the writer influenced revisions in ways consistent with previous research: Better writers made more higher level revisions, poorer writers made more surface level changes, and ESL writers made more lower level revisions. However, the analysis of revising patterns on successive drafts suggests that these general patterns may describe initial text production, with different emphases appearing when revision is extended into second or multiple drafts.

This study leaves a number of important questions unanswered. Are later drafts produced because different revising patterns are needed? Or does the focus of revision shift naturally in moving beyond the first draft? To what extent do students feel compelled to revise? What parts do the teacher's comments play in motivating specific revisions? At what point do changes in the text become improvements in the quality of the writing? How can the learning and teaching of revision be made more effective?

Studies such as this give us a necessary base for addressing such questions, but much work remains to be done before we can answer them with any assurance.

Chapter 9
Where Problems Start: The Effects of Available Information on Responses to School Writing Tasks*

Judith A. Langer

INTRODUCTION

One of the issues to emerge from our studies of writing in the secondary school concerns the amount and nature of the informational writing students do. The case-study findings (discussed in Chapter 4) suggest that more than half the writing students do is completed in content classes; even in English, assignments emphasize informational writing. At the same time, most teachers orchestrate the use of informational writing in somewhat restricted ways, primarily to test how well students have learned the material being studied. In this context, their responses to student work tend to focus on conventions of writing or accuracy of information with little attention to the source of the problems the student may be having in dealing with the particular topic. There is little consideration of the amount of knowledge a student already has about the topic, or of the ways in which the kinds of understandings may interact with performance on the writing task.

Since informational writing (or any writing for that matter) is a function of the knowledge a writer has available in developing the piece, writing as a skill is too intertwined with knowledge of the subject matter to isolate the two without considering how one affects the other. Because topical knowledge directly helps shape a paper, the teacher's understanding of what students know about a topic can be very useful in planning writing assignments, in setting expectations for various students, and in providing pertinent in-process comments.

The influence of an individual's relevant knowledge on new learning is hardly a new concept. Research in the field of reading has reaffirmed, in systematic

---

* Originally published in a different version in *Research in the Teaching of English* 18:1 (February 1984).

ways, Polanyi's (1958) assertions that meaning is personal and context laden. Tacit knowledge focuses a reader's attention on the meaning of words, not on the words themselves. This notion of personal meaning has been particularly important in identifying specific ways in which meaning is constructed when individuals read through a text (Carey, Harste, & Smith, 1981; Goodman, 1973; Heath, 1981; Langer, in press-a).

Unfortunately, this vein of inquiry has been limited to relationships between background knowledge and reading comprehension—while the specific effects of topic knowledge on written expression have been ignored. While writing researchers have generally assumed that knowledge of a topic affects student writing, the ways in which that knowledge interacts with writing performance have remained unstudied. Does familiarity with a topic lead, for example, to a clearer organization, to a smoother, more error-free style, or to both?

Intuition and experience suggest that when students write to a topic about which they have a great deal of well integrated knowledge, their writing is more likely to be well organized and fluent; conversely, when students know little about a topic, their writing is more likely to fail. When students have few ideas about a topic, or when they are unwilling to risk stating the ideas they do have, their writing may rely on glib generalizations, unsupported by argument or enriching illustrations. At other times, when their knowledge is fragmentary, their writing may become little more than a list of vaguely associated items with few explicit connections among their ideas.

If this analysis is correct, we would expect that topic specific background knowledge would affect the general quality and local coherence of written work, and that analysis of student writing would show evidence of direct topic-knowledge influences. The studies reported in this chapter were designed to test these relationships.

THE STUDY

Two 10th-grade American history teachers (Sal and Bobby) assisted in this part of our investigation. They were both experienced teachers from a middle class school district in the San Francisco Bay area. Four classes (two per teacher) totalling 99 students were assigned two writing tasks at two points during the semester. Prior to data gathering, one researcher met with the teachers to discuss topics they were planning for class study and to discuss key concepts related to each unit of study. Together they previewed the text, discussed the unit of study about to begin, and agreed upon three major concepts considered critical for student learning. The three concepts were used as a basis for a free association measure of topic-specific knowledge. Writing assignments to follow the free-association activities were also discussed, and the teachers devised prompts to stimulate writing about the concepts. This procedure was repeated later in the semester to permit analysis of the effects of topic-specific knowledge on school writing across two separate instructional sequences for each teacher.

Measuring Topic-Specific Knowledge

Sal's units of study were about "city and frontier" and "utopian societies" while Bobby's were about "American society in the 18th and 19th centuries" and "values in the 1920s." To assess students' knowledge of these topics, Langer's (1980, 1981, 1982, in press) measure of topic-specific knowledge was administered just before each writing task. The measure elicits topic-related knowledge using free association to key concept words from a unit of study. Free association responses to the key concept words are categorized according to the kinds of knowledge they represent. These categories progress from (a) a diffuse, personal response, to (b) a concrete, functional response, to (c) an incorporation of abstract, superordinate principles. (For a complete description of the categories and how they were developed see Langer, 1981, 1982, in press-b.)

Writing Topics

This free association measure was used to assess the students' topic-related background knowledge before each writing assignment was begun. The topics and stimulus words were:

Sal
1. Write a paper comparing city and frontier life with regard to individualism and democracy.
(opportunity, democracy, individualism)
2. Write a one or two page essay on your version of a Utopian society, the kind you would like to live in.
(utopia, urban, rural)

Bobby
1. It has been stated that in the 18th and 19th centuries the South was a deferential society. In one or two paragraphs, explain why this was true. In your answer, be sure to discuss the concepts of prejudice and acquiescence and how each related to this conclusion.
(deferential society, prejudice, acquiescence)
2. Some historians refer to the 1920s as a decade in American history when sexual freedom and the pursuit of happiness flourished. At the same time, it is noted that the 1920s were characterized by harsh moralistic and antiforeign sentiments. Explain how social changes during the 1920s influenced the growth of new values that conflicted with traditional ones. (3/4 to one full page)
(fundamentalism, Americanism, materialism)

The variations in these assignments are typical of the variations in Sal's and Bobby's approaches. Topic differences are addressed in the analyses.

Measures Obtained

Standardized achievement scores for the California Test of Basic Skills were obtained for all students for whom they were available in school records.

For the prior-to-writing knowledge measure, each teacher presented the students with each of the three concept words just before distributing the writing assignment; students were asked to write everything that came to mind about those words. Two raters were trained to score the topic-specific knowledge measures following procedures outlined by Newell (1983). Three "knowledge" scores were derived for each student. The first, a simple count of total responses to the free association stimulus words, measures topic-specific fluency, or the amount of information available to the writer at the beginning of the task. The second, a score reflecting the highest level of organization attained in the responses to each of the stimulus words, measures the extent of organization imposed upon the available information. The third measure combines aspects of both fluency and organization; it is equal to the total number of responses that reflect the two most organized categories of knowledge. Analyses were based on average scores assigned by two independent raters. Interrater reliabilities ranged from .98 for fluency to .81 for organization.

Each student writing sample was scored on five separate measures: overall quality, coherence, syntactic complexity, audience, and function. As a measure of overall quality, each paper was scored holistically on a five-point scale. Interrater agreement across two independent scorings was .79. Some of the papers were also graded by the teacher; when available these marks were included in our analyses as a second measure of overall quality.

Hasan's (1980) measure of interaction among cohesive chains was used to assess the coherence of a randomly selected half of the papers. This system of analysis distinguishes three kinds of lexical tokens: relevant, peripheral, and central. The ratio of central to relevant tokens is then taken as the primary measure of text coherence. Thus, a more coherent text would not necessarily have more cohesive ties than a less coherent one, but would be expected to have more interaction among the cohesive chains. (See Chapter 5 and Appendix 3 for further details on the derivation of this measure.)

To provide a measure of the overall syntactic complexity in each sample, the mean number of words/clause was also calculated. (This measure was chosen because it is easily derivable from the calculations required for the analysis of coherence.)

Audience and function categories (as described in Chapter 2) were analyzed to determine whether these aspects of informational writing tend to differ based upon student knowledge of the topic. For example, do students who have less highly organized knowledge about the topic tend to write reports rather than analyses? Do they attempt to avoid or bypass some of the facts by engaging in instructional dialogue with the teacher instead of writing to the teacher-as-examiner?

Table 9.1   Relationships among writing measures

	Correlations (n of papers)		
	Teacher's Mark	Coherence	Words/Clause
Holistic Score	.44**	.06	.25
	(57)	(99)	(96)
Teacher's Mark		.27	−.15
		(22)	(20)
Coherence			−.10
			(96)

**p < .01.

KNOWLEDGE AND WRITING

Pearson product moment correlations were used to examine general relationships among the writing and knowledge measures. Findings suggest that while the teachers' marks and our raters' holistic score are significantly correlated ($p < .01$), these are not related to the coherence and syntactic (words per clause) measures nor are they related to each other (see Table 9.1).

Table 9.2 explores relationships among the three knowledge measures. The measures of fluency and organization are not significantly correlated with one another, although both are significantly related to the combined measure.

When the knowledge measures are correlated with the writing scores (Table 9.3), the combined knowledge measure has the strongest relationship to the holistic score ($r = .30, p < .001$). The organization score related significantly to overall quality as measured by both the holistic scores and teachers' marks. Fluency (the simple total of all responses) relates significantly to the holistic scores but not to the teachers' marks.

Findings presented in Table 9.3 also indicate a significant relationship be-

Table 9.2   Relationships among knowledge measures

	Correlations (n of papers)	
	Organization	Combined
Fluency	.15	.66***
	(193)	(193)
Organization		.37***
		(193)

***p < .001.

Table 9.3   Relationships between knowledge measures and measures of writing quality and coherence

| Knowledge Measures | Correlations (n of papers), by Measures of Writing | | | |
	Holistic Score	Teacher's Mark	Coherence	Words/Clause
Fluency	.20**	.04	.06	.09
	(144)	(59)	(99)	(96)
Organization	.26***	.34**	.02	.09
	(144)	(59)	(99)	(96)
Combined	.30***	.16	.20*	.10
	(144)	(59)	(99)	(96)
Reading Achievement	.43***	.45*	−.03	.21
	(89)	(35)	(56)	(54)
Language Achievement	.34***	.29*	−.12	.40***
	(89)	(35)	(56)	(54)

$*p < .05$, $**p < .01$, $***p < .001$.

tween the combined background knowledge measure and Hasan's (1980) measure of coherence. None of the other relationships between the knowledge measures and the writing scores are significant.

Relationships between achievement test scores and the writing measures are also displayed in Table 9.3. As we would expect, reading and language achievement scores are significantly related to the holistic score of writing quality ($r = .43$ and $.34$, respectively) and to the teachers' marks ($r = .45$ and $.29$). The relationship between language achievement and words per clause was also significant ($r = .40$). This may be because the standardized test includes many items testing syntactic knowledge at the sentence level.

Table 9.4   Partial correlations controlling for reading and language test scores

| | Writing Measures | | | |
	Holistic Score	Teacher's Mark	Coherence	Words/Clause
Knowledge Measures				
Fluency	.15	−.01	.09	.00
Organization	.17	.26	.01	.10
Combined	.25**	.09	.22*	.04
degrees of freedom	84	31	52	50

$*p < .05$, $**p < .01$.

To examine the extent to which relationships between knowledge scores and writing were simply a reflection of the effects of general academic achievement, partial correlations were calculated controlling for the reading and language subtest scores. This series of analyses reduced the size of the relationships only slightly (see Table 9.4), although the reduction in degrees of freedom (caused by missing scores on the standardized tests) sharply reduced the levels of statistical significance. This pattern of results suggests that the effects of topic-specific background knowledge are independent of, instead of overlapping with, the effects of general knowledge. These findings are similar to those reported by Langer (1982) in her work on the relationship between background knowledge and reading comprehension, where the effects of topic specific knowledge and general reading achievement were similarly independent.

TOPIC DIFFERENCES

The analyses so far have looked at relationships across topics, ignoring any differences that might emerge from the different tasks posed by the four assignments. Most school assignments specify not only the general content area to be discussed, but also the mode of argument or organization that is likely to be most appropriate in responding. Analysis of the four teacher-developed topics in the present study suggests that these assignments pose two different writing strategies as appropriate response patterns. The "City and Frontier" and "1920s" assignments prompt a compare/contrast organizational pattern, while the "Utopian Society" and "Deferential Society" assignments prompt more general thesis/support structures. In the latter, the general topic is provided by the teacher, and to respond appropriately the students must offer additional information elaborating that single concept. In the compare/contrast assignments, on the other hand, students must relate each of their ideas to the organizational framework prompted by the language of the assignment.

In our analyses, the type of argument required to respond appropriately to a prompt proved to be a more influential factor in task complexity than the amount of structure that seemed to be provided by the prompt itself. Although Bobby's "deferential society" assignment appears to be much more structured than Sal's "Utopian Society," both ask for a thesis/support structure, and both prompted similar types of writing from students. This is illustrated in the examples that follow. The first paper, written by Kam, received a high holistic score and a high mark from the teacher.

UTOPIA

In the world right now there is much love and goodwill yet hardships like violence and hunger seem to overrule this goodwill. Leaders throughout the world have been trying to change these hardships to goodwill throughout out world's history. I think that in my Utopia I would like things to be as they were a while ago when our state was more rural. Instead of cities being the norm, they would be considered rarities. Instead of one tring to "get away from it all" into the country, one would be in the country. Trees would still be standing everywhere . . . but this right now is unrealistic. If one lets his imagination to run however, this kind of society could be reached. We could have people living on the moon which would lower the density of our world. If a society was set up in outerspace our world would not be so crowded. Many say that violence is caused because people feel crowded. In this way violence would be lowered. In my Utopia people would not be excited about crime, about violence like I just viewed in our society now. There would be no question of whether women or blacks or chicanos or Japanese Americans were "equal" to white men. No difference would even be noted; no person would even notice that someone had different color hair or different color skin. In my ideal society, people would accept people with their different beliefs. A communist country could live in harmony with a democratic country without a threat of a "war" breaking out. This is my ideal society; in general to have society with absolute constitutional values of equality, liberty, freedom and the pursuit of happiness!!!

Appearence wise, I would want no change to make it more man made, instead get closer to the basics.

Kam's paper received an "A" from her teacher and a holistic score of 7. Although there were many ideas she might have included in her presentation of an ideal society, and some of them might have been more important than others, the prompt does not require such differentiation. For this reason, a free-floating, associational response such as Kam's is acceptable. Elaborations are necessary, examples might be desirable (but not required), and a larger number of ideas rather than the sophistication or conceptual organization of the ideas appears appropriate.

Elio, on the other hand, has less information available with which to elaborate on the topic of the South as a deferential society than Kam had about her vision of a Utopian society:

Well in the 18th and 19th centuries most slavery were in the South, because in the 18th and 19th centuries 99% of the white people thought they were superial because when they saw the blacks in Africa they seemed to live like animals. They brought them over to America to help them turn to (Chris) religion and (they) white man thought they were helping the black people.

Elio received a grade of 2 out of a possible 10 on this essay and a holistic score of 2. Although Elio's assignment appears to call for less personal opinion and knowledge than Kam's, both assignments essentially ask the students to list the facts they know to support a thesis presented in the assignment itself. Kam's higher score appears to be a function of the greater number of facts she included, not of a better organization of information.

In contrast, the "City and Frontier" and "1920s" assignments prompt a different type of passage structure: compare/contrast. Although these assignments differed in the extent to which the teacher elaborated upon what was expected, both provide a clue to the compare/contrast structure required for the student to write a more highly organized essay. Even if the essay points to specific ideas to be discussed (as in the question about the 1920s), the students' ability to do so will depend on on how well they can organize related knowledge around the key contrasts.

Ram's 1920s paper is an example of a well organized, high scoring paper, with a teacher grade of 11/12 and a 10 holistic score:

> In the 1920's, many changes of values took place that were not part of the traditional view of life. Sexual freedom for example came about in this era. After the war, many individuals felt that they wanted to make America a better place by making social activities more prominent. They began to think about man as a person, and what he could get out of life. Instead of focusing on what man could do to improve society, people began to inquire upon what they could do to allow themselves more freedom and pleasure. A general feeling of "individual freedom" was going around, and among other things, sexual freedom was an issue. People felt that it was time to uncover the shame of sex. Even so, many people, especially the farmers in the "traditionalist" country reacted negatively to this expanding idea. Also, people with strong religious beliefs about sex were often appalled.
>
> The pursuit of pleasure went along with many things—one being the concept of materialism—everyone wanted to make money and invest in stocks etc. Besides this, people generally wanted to be admired, to have money to partake in the pleasurable world they had just discovered . . .

Ram goes on to link the growing materialism with the stock market crash, and concludes his lengthy paper with a paragraph on equal rights, using both the suffragettes and prohibition to defend his point. Although Ram certainly knows a great deal about his topic, it is the interrelationships among ideas, the high level of organized knowledge, that makes his response not only a good one, but particularly appropriate to the assignment.

Julia's paper about city and frontier life is an example of a somewhat lower rated paper, with a holistic score of 6:

> I think the city provided more opportunity for people because it provided jobs for the poor and rich people. The cities were on the coast near harbors so they could commerce with other countries. The city provided more Democracy because the people were closer together, more people lived in cities rather than on farms. Therefore the majority (the city people) would probably get what they wanted. I think the city provided more individualism too because in the cities there were more jobs and different types of jobs. People could do what they wanted—on farms their was mainly one job: working in the fields and around the house. More opportunity was provided for city people.

Julia's paper provides an interesting contrast to Ram's in that although Julia seems to have a moderate amount of information that is relevant to her topic (reflected in our measure of fluency), she uses her paper to list her ideas instead of linking them in a comparison/contrast structure. The organizational framework she uses is one that is more appropriate for the thesis/support prompts than the one she was actually given. In her case, simple amount of knowledge is insufficient; a higher level of organization of knowledge is called for.

These examples suggest that, across assignments, background knowledge may be useful in different ways. Sometimes frequency and sometimes organization mattered. When the assignment prompted integrated knowledge, then higher level, better organized information was appropriate. When the prompt was more general and called for examples and elaborations, fluency mattered more. These interpretations would lead us to expect quite different patterns of relationships between writing quality and background knowledge for the two types of topics; Table 9.5 summarizes the relevant data.

In general, the statistical results support the impressions drawn from examining student papers. For the two topics that required compare/contrast essays, the measure of organization of background knowledge was strongly related to essay quality. For the two topics requiring details to elaborate upon a thesis statement, the amount of information available (reflected in the fluency score) was important and the organization of that information was not.

These findings imply that different assignments, given for different purposes, tap different aspects of a writer's knowledge of a topic. A low score on a particular paper might not mean that a student does not know the information, but that the knowledge that was available was not organized in a useful way for that particular assignment.

Table 9.5   Within-topic relationships between background knowledge and the quality of writing

| | Correlations with Holistic Scores | | | |
| | Thesis/Support | | Compare/Contrast | |
	Utopian Society	Deferential Society	City & Frontier	1920s Values
Knowledge Measures				
Fluency	.26*	.33*	.03	.15
Organization	.02	.04	.39***	.68**
Combined	.27	.34	.42***	.31
n of papers	39	27	59	19

*p < .05, **p < .01, ***p < .001.

Table 9.6 Relationships among background knowledge, audience, and writing quality

	Means			
	Audience Categories		MS	
	Dialogue	Examiner	Error	F (1,141)
Knowledge Measures				
Fluency	14.2	10.7	59.13	6.92**
Organization	2.1	2.0	0.18	1.10
Combined	6.0	7.3	23.66	2.44
Writing Measure				
Holistic	5.9	6.3	2.00	2.38
n of papers	57	86		

$**p < .01$.

AUDIENCE AND FUNCTION

A final analysis examined the extent to which students' choice of audience and function in their writing was related to the kinds of knowledge they brought to the task. The relevant analyses of variance are summarized in Tables 9.6 and 9.7.

Looking first at audience, students who cast their writing as part of an instructional dialogue with the teacher had significantly higher scores for overall fluency than did those who addressed their papers to the teacher-as-examiner (Table 9.6). Mean scores for the combined measure of topic knowledge, on the other hand, were somewhat higher for the papers addressed to the teacher-as-examiner ($p < .12$); so were the holistic scores of the writing that resulted ($p < .13$).

The fluency measure is based on all information the student cites as relevant, while the combined measure is limited to information that reflects some higher level organization of that information. This suggests that the students who wrote to the teacher-as-examiner limited themselves to information that they were able to organize and focus around the topic, while those who wrote as part of a teacher–learner dialogue made less of a distinction about what was relevant to the topic or how their ideas interrelated.

Table 9.7 summarizes the results of a similar analysis of differences between function categories. Here the contrast is between the majority of students who responded with analytic essays, and a much smaller proportion who relied instead upon summary. In general, it seems that the students who wrote analytic papers had more relevant knowledge available as they began the task (as re-

Table 9.7   Relationships among background knowledge, function, and writing quality

| | Means | | | |
| | Function Categories | | MS | |
	Summary	Analysis	Error	F (1,140)
Knowledge Measures				
Fluency	11.5	12.2	62.29	0.15
Organization	2.0	2.0	0.18	0.05
Combined	4.6	7.2	23.23	4.60*
Writing Measure				
Holistic	5.5	6.3	1.99	4.37*
n of papers	19	123		

*$p < .05$.

flected in the combined score for topic knowledge), and obtained a significantly higher ($p < .04$) holistic writing quality score as a result.

CONCLUSION

The analyses in this chapter had a number of purposes: (a) to examine the relationships between topic knowledge and quality of informational writing; (b) to determine ways in which the focus of an assignment interacts with topic knowledge to affect the written work; and (c) to identify aspects of student writing that might be instructionally informative for the teacher.

Not surprisingly, the data clearly suggest a strong and consistent relationship between topic-specific background knowledge and the quality of student writing. More interesting, however, is the evidence that different kinds of knowledge predict success in different writing tasks. When the assignment calls for a simple reiteration of facts, or elaborations of a given idea, a large amount of unintegrated (or loosely linked) information will suffice. However, when the student is required to present a thesis, analyze, and defend it, the degree of organization of knowledge, as opposed to simple fluency, will determine success.

These findings have some interesting implications. At the classroom level, they reemphasize the extent to which the teaching of writing is inextricably intertwined with the exploration of the topics about which students are writing. On the one hand, the results may increase our understanding of some well-established teaching techniques, including prewriting activities that seek to provide students with a wide range of relevant information, or to categorize and organize that information before beginning to write. On the other hand, these results may provide a rationale for sharpening our selections among such activities, matching the kind of information incorporated in the activity more closely with the kinds of knowledge that may be demanded by the writing task itself.

Similarly, the results may help teachers sharpen the responses they provide to work in progress, whether in writing conferences or in the remarks they put on student papers. Too often, comments about knowledge of the topic are inseparable from those about organization and surface presentation, although superficial and poorly organized knowledge bases may be largely responsible for other writing problems.

The analyses of interactions between topic knowledge and audience and function categories, though exploratory, suggest that when students have only fragmentary knowledge about a topic, they avoid engaging in writing activities that require them to say more than they know. They may resort to writing summaries when analyses would have been more appropriate, because the summary format permits them to recount facts without having to interrelate them more fully. Rather than indicating that students lack knowledge of the proper form for analytic writing, papers of this sort may indicate that they lack enough knowledge of the topic to present it in the form requested. In such a case, practice in writing an analytic paper will not be helpful; further study of the content may be.

Another coping tactic suggested in the analyses concerns the students' use of instructional dialogue when it is not called for. When students inappropriately adopt the less formal stance of a teacher–learner dialogue, it may again be because they lack sufficient knowledge of the topic to deal with it more formally. In many cases this may prove to be an effective coping strategy, one which the teacher could put to good instructional use. The student may simply be saying, indirectly, that a teaching/learning dialogue is necessary, rather than an evaluation of completed learning. With student writing of this sort, the teacher who focuses on organization of the paper will be missing the heart of the problem.

The findings reported in this chapter both parallel and complicate those found by Langer (1980, 1981, in press-b) in her work on the relationship between topic-specific background knowledge and comprehension of expository text. This body of work found that background knowledge was highly related to the comprehension and recall of a passage, and that the topic-specific knowledge measure predicted comprehension independently of either reading achievement or IQ scores. In these studies, a measure of the organization of knowledge was a better predictor of comprehension success than was a simple fluency measure (based solely on frequency of responses).

In the context of the present study, these findings suggest the possibility that having highly organized background knowledge about a topic may be more consistently helpful to readers than to writers. For some tasks, writers may need the same kinds of highly organized knowledge that readers do, but for other tasks they may also require an abundance of loosely related items of information for use in their writing. This distinction may arise from differences inherent in the two activities; writers not only need to generate and present intricately linked ideas, but also need a large body of loosely associated information that can be used to elaborate and enliven the presentation.

Chapter 10
Process and Product: Case Studies of Writing in Two Content Areas

James D. Marshall

INTRODUCTION

The studies reported in this volume have described a number of dimensions of writing in the secondary school: the instruction which shapes it, the processes students employ in creating it, and the product that results from their efforts. While much of the research has focused on typical patterns of instruction and performance within age groups, ability levels, and discipline areas, another interest has been to seek out and describe instruction that is atypical in its attempt to integrate writing into the curriculum. The present chapter reflects such interests, presenting our analysis of two content-area classrooms, chosen because of teachers' attempts to give writing activities a more prominent role.

PROCEDURES

With the help of local educators, we compiled a list of 12 content-area teachers who seemed to be making an unusual effort to expand the uses of writing in their classrooms. After preliminary interviews, the two teachers who seemed to have made the most progress in reformulating their classroom activities were selected for intensive study.

The first, Dan Phillips, is a general science and biology teacher with over 20 years of experience. For much of his teaching career, Phillips has made a special effort to employ writing in his science classes; during the last few years he has also been available as a consultant to nearby school districts, giving workshops on writing instruction to science teachers.

The second teacher selected, Doug Nelson, is a social studies teacher with over 10 years of experience. He became interested in writing instruction 3 years ago and, like Phillips, has been active in giving in-service writing workshops in

Table 10.1   Data collection for case studies of content-area writing

	Phillips (Science)	Nelson (Social Studies)	Total
Observations	26	16	40
Interviews	2 group	2 group	
	15 individual	7 individual	26
Writing Collected	118	144	262

surrounding districts. His school has supported his efforts to expand the uses of writing in social studies by granting him released time to further his work.

Each of the teachers was interviewed to gather information on background, educational philosophy, and typical approaches to writing instruction. At the same time, a series of classroom observations was initiated, extending over 7 months for Phillips and 4 months for Nelson, for a total of 40 observations in all. During each observation, notes were kept on teacher and student activities—with special emphasis given to writing activities. In addition, all handouts employed by the teacher were collected. Table 10.1 summarizes the data collection.

After several observations, 12 students (6 from each of the teachers) were selected for closer study. Each of these students was then interviewed, initially as part of a group of 3 students, and then individually. In all, a total of 4 group interviews and 22 individual interviews were conducted.

During the interviews, students were asked to describe their writing behaviors as specifically as possible. How did they write for science class or social studies class? How did that writing differ from the writing they did in English? What was expected in science and social studies? What kind of instruction had they received? The interviews were tape-recorded for later analysis.

Students were asked to save and bring to the interviews all of the writing that they had completed for Phillips or Nelson. These pieces became the focus for discussion during the interviews. How long did they work on a particular piece? What steps did they take? What gave them the most difficulty? At the end of 7 months, 262 pieces of writing had been collected, 118 from the 6 students in Phillips' class and 144 from the 6 in Nelson's.

WRITING ASSIGNMENTS: RATIONALE AND ORGANIZATION

At least two rationales can be constructed for the inclusion of writing instruction in content-area classrooms. On the one hand, Martin (1976), Emig (1977), and others have argued persuasively that writing can enhance students' learning of information. On the other hand, concern for the quality of students' written products has led to increasingly numerous calls for the extension of writing instruction beyond the doors of the English classroom.

Phillips and Nelson subscribe to both arguments and have designed their instruction accordingly. First, they wish to encourage learning within their disciplines, and they see writing as a means of enhancing the process. They have been convinced that the construction of extended text encourages students to think through a body of material with more depth and thoroughness than other classroom activities. In the process of shaping information, students make that information their own. But the process is crucial. The final written product, while important as a goal, must be preceded by an ordered series of steps in which students use writing informally to clarify their thoughts. Thus Nelson speaks of personal writing as a "way of thinking in social studies" and Phillips argues that:

> Expressive writing can help students think through the problems they meet in science. They are free to think on paper without fear of the teacher as examiner.

Writing can be used as a tool for thought in classrooms, but only if the formal constraints usually operative in school writing are temporarily removed. The students must be free to explore a problem, to bring their own perceptions and their own language to bear on it, without fear of correction or evaluation. Only in this way will risks be taken and new learning encouraged.

But Phillips and Nelson are not only interested in using writing as an instructional tool. They also wish to improve their students' written products so that the information that has been learned can be presented clearly and persuasively. Here too, a process model is invoked. The first steps in the process are tentative and informal. Only after students have discovered what they want to say can they successfully shape their message for another audience. Yet the goal is always to reach a point where the message can be so shaped.

These two objectives, the enhancement of learning and the improvement of writing, are inarguably attractive in the abstract. But it is at the level of implementation that they must be studied, for it is only at that level that specific successes and problems are encountered. After a brief survey of the assignments Phillips and Nelson have designed to meet their objectives, we will turn to issues related to the way these assignments are implemented.

Both Phillips and Nelson have structured their sequence of assignments to correspond to their perception of the writing process itself. First, information must be explored and understood; only then can it be shaped into a coherent piece of writing. Thus early assignments in both classrooms are informal and personal. Students are asked only to generate ideas or summarize information, to ask questions, to risk mistakes, leaving a concern for form and accuracy until a later stage in the process.

Yet "early" and "late" take on somewhat different meanings in the two classrooms. In Nelson's class, all of the assignments given during the first half of the school year are informal. Only towards the end of the year are students asked to construct formal arguments and submit their writing to an examining audience. In Phillips' biology class, on the other hand, students compose tentative, exploratory pieces throughout the year, but they are likewise assigned formal reports and essay examinations. The informal assignments are intended to encourage students' learning of the material while the formal assignments test their success.

Typical assignments in Phillips' class include reading logs in which students are instructed to maintain a kind of running commentary with their textbook, asking questions and summarizing information in their own language.

Reading Log

Does the tape worm really know what it is doing to whomever or whatever it is feeding off of? Why do scientists make up all of the rules for modern day society and who is to say they're always correct in the answers they give us?
—Grade 10, Biology

In addition, students are typically asked to construct learning logs in which they summarize, again in their own words, a concept that has recently been covered in class.

Learning Log

Paramecium are round like torpedoes. All along their sides are tiny, hairlike things called "cilia." These cilia propel them through the water . . . Paramecia have a definite front and rear end. Along one side there is an oral groove. Cilia beat food into the groove where it is disgested and changed into a food vacuole.
—Grade 10, Biology

Phillips checks these assignments, but grades neither. Their purpose is to allow students to connect given information with their prior knowledge and personal concerns, without fear that their knowledge is incomplete or their language inappropriate.

The next series of assignments within a given unit asks students to begin pulling drafts of essays together for presentation to an audience other than themselves. The students do not face this task alone, however, for these assignments are structured so that support is available from both teacher and peers. For these tasks—writing to a specific audience, practice essays, and group essays—students are given a topic or question and asked to construct lists of ideas and rough drafts, to share these in groups, and to present the drafts to Phillips for formative evaluation. Only after students have received some response from their peers and from Phillips do they compose a final draft which is submitted for a grade.

Finally, toward the end of a unit, Phillips assigns formal essays ("Discuss the evidence that DNA controls heredity") and constructs essay exams ("Describe, in as much detail as you can, how a food vacuole digests food'') for which the audience is clearly the teacher-as-examiner and for which no process supports are provided. These final assignments are designed to elicit responses to issues that students have already written about in a variety of forms. In any given sequence of assignments, the same material is processed through writing, not once, but several times. In this way, Phillips feels, students learn the material more thoroughly, gaining a purchase on information that would be lost if formal writing only were assigned.

In addition to its effect on student learning, Phillips feels his sequence of assignments provides a supportive model for the writing process itself. Students are encouraged to perceive writing about scientific issues as at least a three-stage process which begins with tentative exploration, moves through a period of refinement, and ends with a formal presentation. Phillips hopes that students will employ a version of the model, in microcosm, when they write on their own.

Doug Nelson is similarly concerned with providing his students with a working model of the composing process, and like Phillips he sees that process as moving from tentative, personal drafts to more formal work. Yet Nelson has taken an even more structured approach. At its center is the student journal in which students write at least once a week on a topic Nelson sets. The journal itself is structured in that students are instructed to number its pages 1A, 1B, 1C, 2A, 2B, 2C, and so on. The "A" page, they are told, is to be used for prewriting: listing, brainstorming, outlining. The "B" page is to be used for the first draft of the assignments they are given, and the "C" page is to be used for a final version. The layout of the journals themselves, in other words, encourages students to think of writing as a three-stage process. When journals are collected, students are aware that Nelson expects to see each page filled, each step taken.

Yet if individual assignments call for an ordered series of steps, Nelson's sequence of assignments also moves in a discernable direction. Early in the year students do a number of 10-minute free-writing exercises on topics of current interest. Also early come assignments in which students are to write personal analyses of social issues, such as dominance within their own friendship groups, adolescent behavior, or the role of racism in their school. Every three weeks Nelson collects the journals, checks to see that the three steps have been completed, reads final drafts, and offers generally positive comments on the content—rarely the form—of the writing.

About midyear, Nelson begins to make more demands in terms of the form the writing is to take. Having reached a point where students can generate text for themselves, Nelson now wants to help students construct arguments that will persuade an audience. The transition is eased by the fact that students are to present their arguments, not as formal essays to be submitted for a grade, but as letters written to a specific audience within the structured format of the journal. The audience might include the students' parents, a friend who has not studied the issue at hand, a fictional acquaintance, or Nelson himself, addressed personally as an individual whose views must be taken into account. Nelson believes that the shape of the letter is more familiar to students than the formal, five-paragraph essay, and that students' positive attitude toward the journal, encouraged by a full semester of writing within its structure, allows them to see the arguments as a natural extension of earlier writing tasks.

Toward the end of the second semester Nelson begins assigning formal argumentative essays. Students understand that these are to be graded for organization and persuasiveness, but by this time, Nelson feels, they have built a repertoire of skills and a range of writing habits that will allow them to meet the constraints of the task with greater confidence and a higher rate of success.

Both Phillips and Nelson, then, have built their assignments around a model of the writing and learning process. In general, their tasks call for students to write for themselves before writing for an examining audience, and to use writing to think through a body of information before presenting that information in final form. Yet despite the similarity of their intentions and their assignments, different patterns appear as each teacher attempts to realize his objectives in the classroom. It is to the problems inherent in implementation that we will now turn.

IMPLEMENTATION: THE PROBLEM OF SUPPORT

We have seen in earlier chapters that the typical school-writing task is limited in its purpose and its form. Produced largely for a single audience—the teacher-as-examiner—such writing cannot readily serve the learning functions for which Phillips and Nelson have argued. In fact, with its emphasis on product over process, typical instruction may well interfere with the goals Phillips and Nelson have set. No matter how thoughtful their procedures nor how intelligent their teaching, both represent only a portion of the writing instruction their students have received and are receiving in school. In this sense, their goals may be compromised by the context in which they must operate.

In his biology classroom, for example, Phillips assigns exploratory writing before formal pieces in order to encourage students' personal manipulation of information. While these assignments may encourage learning, it is the formal writing—the tests and final drafts—which count in the determination of grades, and it is the formal writing which receives most of the students' attention. Because they are ungraded—and must be to serve their purpose—the informal assignments have less value in students' eyes, representing an interesting and sometimes engaging break from the routine. But the real agenda remains the product that can be evaluated.

The students' attention to product over process was evident in the ways they went about some of their writing tasks in Phillips' classroom. One lab session, typical of several, ran like this:

Phillips wrote on the board:

1) Observe and dissect the flower.
2) Make a drawing, label the parts.
3) With a razor blade, slice open the ovary and describe what you observe.
4) Make a list of everything you see, use it to write a paragraph.
5) Explain in as much detail as you can how pollination takes place.

The assignment, as given, provides a structured opportunity for students to engage personally in observing, reporting, and explaining a phenomenon. Moreover Phillips cautioned his students not to worry about form when answering Questions 4 and 5, stressing that "Content is important, not spelling or neatness. I simply want to know what you've discovered." Yet as soon as the students began the task, an interest in observing was displaced by an interest in reporting the "right" discovery, and reporting it in the "right" way.

The students quickly gathered in their lab groups and set up the microscopes. When the slides were in position, each student looked briefly in the microscopes—the average seemed about 3–5 seconds—and then, as if on cue, one student in each group opened the text to look for a picture of what they were supposed to see. In three of the groups, one student began copying the text's version of the flower. Students from other groups began to gravitate toward "better" students, and to ask for advice on what was supposed to be under the microscope. In only one of the groups did students spend more than the initial few seconds actually looking at the slide. In fact, it was only in this group that the first three steps of the lab were followed with any care. Within 10 minutes, the rest of the class was constructing lists, based on the text and the quickly circulated answers of the better students. Though students were to address Questions 4 and 5 for homework, a substantial portion of the students left class with a rough draft of the lab completed. They copied these over in ink, and turned them in for a grade the next day.

Throughout the class, Phillips was moving about the room, drawing students back to the microscopes, answering questions, in one case telling a student to close his textbook and construct his list from what was observed directly. Whenever Phillips was working with a small group, the lesson went as he had planned it. Yet when left to their own resources—and Phillips could not be everywhere at once—the students stopped relying on their own observations and fell back on the text and their peers. It was as if students needed to be told, almost constantly, that their personal observations could form the basis of a response. In the absence of such support, their primary concern was to complete the assignment as quickly and as correctly as possible.

The intention here is to fault neither Phillips nor his students, but to describe one, perhaps basic, feature of school writing. It is the final product, in this case the lab report, that will be evaluated, not the steps one has taken to arrive at this product. Students are aware of this, which may undermine Phillips' efforts.

Nelson has taken a more direct approach to the problem of instructional support. As we have seen, his sequence of assignments provides a highly structured support system early in the year, and then slowly removes the support so that students must meet task demands through their own resources. The process allows students to build on what they already know, developing new skills with supportive guidance, eventually mastering the skills so that guidance is no longer necessary. Care must be taken in implementing such a program, however, for the support must be appropriate to the task and to the level of skill students already possess. The task should be one that the students could not have done on their own, but can learn to do with the support provided by the teacher. If a task is too heavily structured, the opportunity for students to stretch their present abilities may be lost.

A description of one of Nelson's classes, typical of several, illustrates how this can occur. Nelson's students had, for six weeks, been working on a unit on Russia, using Henrick Smith's *The Russians* as a text. The current assignment was to write a letter to an American businessman "ignorant of the Russian factory system." Students were to convince the businessman that the factory system is or is not productive, using information they had drawn from their reading and class discussion. The assignment itself specifically guides students as to the approach they should take:

> As you are describing the Soviet factory system to your friend [the businessman] do two things: first, write with your friend in mind. Use definitions, analogies, and concrete examples. And also, use each of the following terms in your paper. You may use them in any order you choose.

Following the assignment itself was a list of 14 terms including "storming," "bottlenecks," and "Russian nature."

Students were given a week for the assignment. In that time, they organized their thoughts and wrote a draft in their journals. On the day this class was observed, they were to share their work with other students in the class and receive written responses to it. As he passed out the evaluation sheets on which students were to place their responses, Nelson explained:

> You should each take three of these . . . Now, here's what we're going to do. I suggest you clear your desk of everything except the evaluation sheet and your paper. We're going to set this up so that at least two other people have a chance to look at your writing. [Here Nelson reads the evaluation sheet.] "What do you like best about this paper? Pick the four terms that are used most effectively in this paper. In each case, give the term, then describe what makes the writing effective. Weaknesses. Of the terms that are used, pick the four that are least effectively described and developed. Explain why and offer suggestions for improvement . . ." Your job is to help the writer re-see the paper. OK, pass your paper to the person behind you. People in the last seat pass your paper to

the person at the front of your row. I'm thinking about 15 minutes for each. OK, go.

For the rest of the period, students quietly read their peers' papers and filled out the evaluation sheet, exchanging papers on cue every 15 minutes while Nelson graded work at the front of the room. At the end of the period, Nelson collected the papers, told the students that they could see the evaluations after he had checked them over, and dismissed the class.

Two observations seem relevant here. First, the assignment itself is so highly structured—even to the specific terms which must be included—that the direction of the students' arguments has been virtually predetermined. Even though Nelson, through the journal's layout, has encouraged students to prewrite and to construct a rough draft, the purposes which might motivate such steps have been largely eliminated. There is no need to generate information or find a provisional form: both have been established by the assignment.

Second, the peer-evaluation task, while formatted in a way that might well help students get started, provides little scope for student-shaped responses. The best students can do, in the time allowed, is to slot four positive comments and four negative comments within the form provided. There is neither room nor time for thinking.

Again, the intention here is not to criticize Phillips and Nelson, but to describe some of the complexities involved in insuring that such programs function as intended. In implementing their programs, Phillips and Nelson seem to face the problem of an excluded middle. If insufficient instructional support is provided for students, the initial steps necessary to make writing a mode of learning are abbreviated, if taken at all. If too much support is provided, students may take the steps, but lose their reason for doing so. At the center of the problem, of course, are the students themselves. How do they respond to the instruction they are receiving in these classes? The next section will consider this issue by looking at students' written products and at the processes they employ when writing for school.

RESPONSE: PRODUCT

The writing collected from the 12 students studied in depth reflects the instructional patterns discussed thus far. Results from an analysis of the functions represented are presented in Table 10.2 (for a summary of the categories, see Chapter 2). As can be seen in Table 10.2, the writing in Phillips' and Nelson's classes was largely informational in character (96% for Phillips' students and 98% for Nelson's students). Only 4% of the writing from Phillips' students and only 2% from Nelson's students was primarily personal; imaginative writing occurred in neither sample.

Within the informational mode, writing in both classes was dominated by

Table 10.2.   Content-area case studies: writing
function

	Percent of Papers	
	Phillips (Science)	Nelson (Social Studies)
Informational		
Notes	1.7	0.0
Record	0.8	2.8
Report	12.7	1.4
Summary	53.4	7.6
Analysis	23.7	82.6
Theory	3.4	4.2
Persuade	0.0	0.0
Personal	4.2	1.4
Imaginative	0.0	0.0
n of papers	118	144

summary and analysis. Such pieces represented 77% of the writing collected
from Phillips' students and 91% of the writing from Nelson's.

Figure 10.1 compares these samples with the writing collected from the larger
case-study sample (Chapter 4). As the graph illustrates, there is little difference
in function between the writing collected from Phillips' students and the science
writing collected in the larger case study. Phillips' students wrote slightly more
frequently in the personal mode (4% vs. 0%), but overall, the uses to which
writing was put were largely the same.

The writing collected from Nelson's social-studies class shows more devia-
tion. While the pieces here were still largely informational in character, there
was a higher frequency of analytical pieces in the Nelson sample (83%) than in
the larger case-study sample (63%). This difference may be explained in terms of
the kinds of assignments Nelson gave.

Writing from both classes was also coded for intended audience, following
the procedures described in Chapter 2. Results are presented in Table 10.3.

The audience for writing in Phillips' class was most frequently the teacher-as-
examiner (85%). Only 6% was written for the students themselves; another 9%
was written within a teacher–learner dialogue. None of the writing collected was
addressed to a wider audience.

In Nelson's class a very different pattern emerges. Here, only 44% of the
writing collected was written for the teacher-as-examiner, while 54% was written
within a teacher–learner dialogue. As in Phillips' class, however, only a small

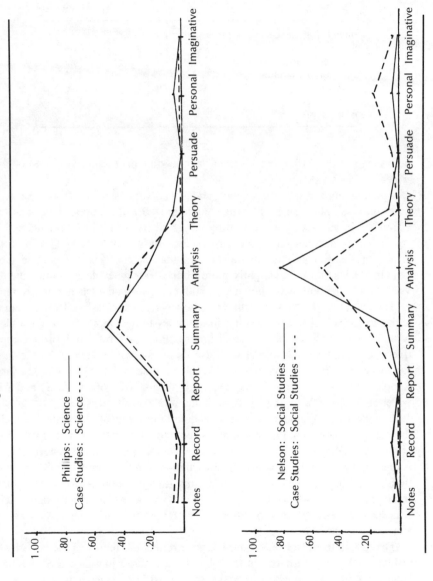

Figure 10.1 Content Areas: Writing Functions

Phillips: Science ——————
Case Studies: Science - - - - -

Notes Record Report Summary Analysis Theory Persuade Personal Imaginative

Nelson: Social Studies ——————
Case Studies: Social Studies - - - - -

Notes Record Report Summary Analysis Theory Persuade Personal Imaginative

Table 10.3   Content-area case studies: intended audience

	Percent of Papers	
	Phillips (Science)	Nelson (Social Studies)
Intended Audience		
Self	5.9	1.4
Teacher–Learner Dialogue	9.3	54.2
Teacher as Examiner	84.7	43.8
Wider	0.0	0.7
n of papers	118	144

percentage of the writing was written for the students themselves (1%) or for a wider audience (1%).

Again, comparison with science and social-studies results from the larger case-study sample may be helpful. As Figure 10.2 illustrates, there was little difference in audience for the writing collected from Phillips' students and the science writing collected in the larger case study. Students in Phillips' class wrote for themselves slightly more often than science students in the larger sample (6% vs. 1%), and slightly more often in a teacher–learner dialogue (9% vs. 1%), but the dominant audience in both groups was the teacher-as-examiner.

The audience for Nelson's students, however, was clearly different than the audience for social science writing in the case-study sample. Nelson's students wrote primarily within the teacher–learner dialogue—a reflection of the supportive role played by the journal in Nelson's class—while students in the larger sample wrote primarily for the teacher-as-examiner. Yet students in the larger sample wrote slightly more frequently for themselves (6% vs. 1%) and for a wider audience (6% vs. 1%) than students in Nelson's class.

In spite of assignments aimed at encouraging students to write for and to themselves, students in Phillips' classes seem to have difficulty doing so. Only a relatively small percentage of the writing collected in his class was written for an audience other than the teacher-as-examiner—an indication that Phillips' intentions are perhaps being crowded out by his students' concern for the evaluated final product. As we saw in the description of classroom activities, such a concern may lead students to abbreviate or ignore the early steps of the writing and learning process.

The results from Nelson's class likewise reflect the nature of the tasks he has provided. Writing primarily in their highly structured journals, the students in Nelson's class feel free to take risks and to explore issues—most often in an analytical frame—without fear of formal evaluation. The question, of course, is whether the processes they employ with the support of the journal, and the

Figure 10.2   Content Areas: Intended Audience

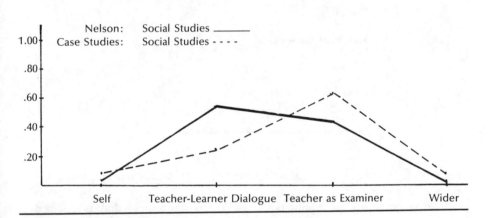

teacher–learner dialogue that motivates it, can be carried over to other school-writing tasks. This question can best be answered with reference to the processes these students report using when they write for school.

RESULTS: PROCESS

Interviews with students from both classes were analyzed for reports of the steps taken when writing for their respective teachers and for the knowledge students were drawing upon when producing the writing. Results from Phillips' science students are presented in Table 10.4.

The three steps most frequently reported by Phillips' students were reading, taking notes, and composing a rough draft of their work. Reading, in fact, seemed central, in that it was included in 74% of the discussions of writing process. Somewhat less frequently, Phillips' students reported exploratory writ-

Table 10.4   Characteristics of the
writing process in Phillips' biology
class

	Percent of Student Reports
Steps in the Process	
Read	73.9
Quotations	4.3
Incubate	13.0
Thesis	0.0
Notes	52.2
Explore	26.1
Reread	17.4
Rough draft	56.5
Outline	21.7
$n = 23$	
Knowledge Drawn Upon	
Text	83.3
Teacher	20.8
Self	4.2
Other	45.8
$n = 50$	

ing (26%), outlining (22%), rereading their notes (17%), or thinking through a piece (incubation: 13%).

The pattern of reading, taking notes, and composing a rough draft is reflected in the sources of information students reported using while writing for science. Here students indicated that they relied on the text to provide relevant information some 80% of the time, and on their teacher approximately 20% of the time. Other sources of information, reported 46% of the time, largely represented information from other students—a function of the group work which Phillips encourages. But the most telling result, given Phillips' objectives for the class, was that students reported using their own knowledge and observations less than 5% of the time when writing for science.

These results can be explained, at least in part, by the difficulty students had in following Phillips' procedures for writing. As Jenny, a 10th grader, noted, "It's easier to paraphrase things from the book than to write from observation notes." The task of observing, translating observations into language, and shaping that language into a coherent piece of writing is eased—if not eliminated—when the language has already been shaped by a text. Yet it is only when the task is completed step-by-step that Phillips' objectives can be fully met.

Concern for the final product often led Phillips' students to short-circuit the steps. Michele, for example, spoke of her unwillingness to organize her thoughts before beginning to write. Asked to construct a piece comparing meiosis and mitosis, she remarked:

> You put the definitions of meiosis and mitosis first. He likes us to write out little notes so you have something to start with, but I don't like to do that . . . . It's easier for me just to write it. I don't like to write little words out. I just like to write the whole thing out.

Another student, Susan, likewise reported difficulty with prewriting:

> Phillips wants us to write something down and then to write down the first thing that comes to our mind. Me, I just organize it right away.

When students "organize right away," rather than following Phillips' suggestions, the text from which the information is drawn tends to provide the organization and the language of the piece. The following is a portion of a first draft from Elizabeth on an essay entitled "Platyhelminthes":

> Platyhelminthes is a phylum of flatworms.
> One familiar member of the platyhelminthes phylum is the planaria. These are often called 'the cross-eyed worm' because of the eyespots on the dorsal side of this flatworm. Aside from having an ectoderm and endoderm on the dorsal and ventral sides of the worm, it also has a mesoderm—a third layer of cells.

The formal tone and technical language of the piece make it likely that Elizabeth has—at best—paraphrased the information from a textbook. She has more-or-less passively reported the information rather than in any sense engaging with it on a personal level. She is "right" in that her information and organization are correct, but it is not apparent that she has used her writing as a tool for thinking and learning.

Students are not often encouraged to take risks, to shape information in their own terms and in their own language. Even in Phillips' class, such risks have a price. As Terry, another 10th grader, put it, "In science you can be wrong, and most of the time I am." Her feelings were echoed by Jenny: "In science, if you don't know what you're talking about, you can't do it. Like that last test." There is an irony here in that Phillips' assignments have been designed precisely so that students will reach a point where they "know what they're talking about." But students' concern with being "wrong," and with being graded accordingly, interferes with Phillips' agenda.

We have seen that students in Nelson's social studies classroom have been, to some extent, protected from such a concern. Their frequent use of journals eliminates formal evaluation, allowing them to write more frequently as part of a teacher–learner dialogue. How do they go about their writing tasks? As with Phillips' students, interviews with Nelson's students were analyzed for the steps taken and the sources of information used when writing. Results are presented in Table 10.5.

Nelson's students described a very different writing process than did Phillips'. Rather than a pattern dominated by reading, taking notes, and composing a rough draft, Nelson's students most often reported writing an exploratory piece (57%), sometimes thinking about the issus (24%), outlining (33%), rereading what they had written (24%), or composing a rough draft (29%).

These steps students reported taking are reflected in the sources of information they reported using when writing for social studies. Some 50% of the time, students drew on personal knowledge derived from their own observations and reflections. Only about 33% of the time did students draw their ideas from a text, and only about 16% of the time from their teacher or other sources. The journal—and the nature of the assignments Nelson makes in it—apparently encouraged students to draw on their own resources when writing for social studies and to write in a more-or-less exploratory fashion.

Table 10.5   Characteristics of the writing process in Nelson's social-studies class

	Percent of Student Reports
Steps in the Process	
Read	0.0
Quotations	0.0
Incubate	23.8
Thesis	19.0
Notes	9.5
Explore	57.1
Reread	23.8
Rough Draft	28.6
Outline	33.3
n = 21	
Knowledge Drawn Upon	
Text	33.3
Teacher	16.7
Self	50.0
Other	16.7
n = 7	

The support provided by the journal eased the process of writing in social studies. Janet, a 9th grader, suggested how this occurred:

> I didn't like [the journal] at first. I thought it would be boring. It seemed like so much work to me. But writing for Mr. Nelson has gotten easier now. I can sit down more easily and write something out. Before I would sit down and I would want to come up with the perfect sentence to start with, and just write a perfect paper without having to do anything. That's why it seemed like so much work, because I could never do that. Now it's shorter, but it's longer. There's more steps involved, but it's easier to sit down and write down anything and then organize it. Before I used to put so much pressure on myself.

By following the three-stage process Nelson has laid out in the journal, Janet, and the other students in Nelson's class, were able to discover their message before giving it final form. The sense that writing can serve such a function often led to the kind of exhilaration expressed by Len:

> You've sort of had the shackles lifted from you. You're freer and you can work within your own limits. It's kind of like you're in your own space. You can really put your personality down on the paper without putting down what they want on the paper.

Students often contrasted their writing for social studies with other school-sponsored writing. When writing for English, for example, the sense of exhilaration and exploration are absent. Len again:

> In English, I have to go through a rough draft, but it has to be more highly polished, and [the process] is more cumbersome. I get less of a feeling of freedom. It changes my style, because you have to fit these guidelines. What I'm doing is looking to write something that will fit these guidelines. Like if I have this really great idea, but it doesn't fit with their idea and their guidelines, then I can't write it. Whereas, with Mr. Nelson, if he gives us a topic to write on, and I come up with this idea that doesn't fit with the lines, I can make the lines change.

Len's feelings were echoed by Carolyn:

> In social studies, I feel more free to write whatever I want. In English, you have to be, I don't know, more mechanical. You have to write what the teacher wants.

Students' contrasting attitudes and approaches to writing in English and social studies can be understood by looking closely at the writing they must produce for each. The following two efforts were written by Sam during the same month. The first, a social-studies assignment, was an attempt to reflect on the problem of deviance, after class discussion of an article by Robert Merton.

Deviance

My first example of deviance is not a particular incident, but rather about a deviant boy in my eight years of Grammar School. Jim had the bad luck to be different physically as well as mentally. Jim was very fat, and was unable to do many things he wanted to. An example would be sports. He wanted to be a good athlete, but as a result of his weight, he was a louse at everything he tried. Jim was also a bit spoiled at home, his parents gave him a lot of material goods as well as telling him he was god's gift to the world. Robert Merton says, "People are deviant because society tells them how to act, but does not provide them with the tools to act accordingly." Well, Jim was just the opposite, because he was "over-equipped." As a result of his disabilities, Jim made up lies about himself as an athlete, and bragged about them. At the time we called him other things, but now I would call his actions deviant, and he was always very unpopular. He tried to make friends then by more lying, as well as bragging about the material goods he had been spoiled about. This dug Jim into a deeper hole, and soon everybody hated Jim.

The paper goes on to explain how Jim became a scapegoat for Sam's class, bringing the class together in their loathing for Jim.

Before writing this draft, Sam had generated ideas on the "A" page of his journal and had decided on a provisional form. He clearly felt free both to draw on his personal knowledge and to write in a personal fashion, using "I" and a good deal of informal language ("he was a louse at everything he tried"; "his parents gave him a lot of material goods as well as telling him he was god's gift to the world"). He embeds text-based information (the quotation from Merton and the concept of "scapegoat") within a context that supports it, integrating that information grammatically and conceptually with his prior experience. The only evaluation Sam received on the paper was positive. Nelson jotted "good writing" next to Sam's use of Merton's quotation, and "perceptive and interesting discussion" at the end of the piece.

The second effort was written for English class, and also deals with a character who can be construed as "deviant." Here, however, the approach is very different.

Holden's Dilemma: An Analysis in Relation to Myth

J. D. Salinger's novel, The Catcher in the Rye is the confessions of a seventeen-year old boy caught on the threshold between childhood and adulthood. Holden Caulfield, the cather in the rye, was sent to boarding school by his parents during his adolescent years. He no longer has his parents to guide him nor the protection of being a child. He lacks the knowledge and experience of an adult to guide himself. He is also deeply troubled by the unjustified death of his kid-brother, Allie, whom he loved and admired greatly. Holden needs an influence to guide him across the threshold without becoming unglued. The fact that Holden had a breakdown, does become unglued, can be explained as being a result of the disintegration of the meaning of myth. This can be shown in three ways. First is that Holden has to make up his own religion because he lacks a formal one. Second, is that Holden is confused as to the rites of passage from childhood to adulthood. And third is that Holden has to make up his own myths because in his generation the old myths are no longer meaningful.

In this piece, Sam was clearly using language in a more formal (and also more awkward) fashion. There are no personal reflections and no personal voice. The knowledge shaping the piece came from the text and from the teacher, through lectures on the function of myth. The organization has been set (the now familiar three examples) and the thesis carefully stated. The teacher's response was to circle three commas as being unnecessary, to circle the verb "has" in the third sentence, and to remark in the margin: "Shift in verb tense—be consistent." At no point in the piece was Sam allowed to integrate his own experience into the writing. In fact, such a move was actively discouraged by the formal constraints in which he had to work. Sam's writing for English seems to offer little scope for the strategies learned in Nelson's class.

In general, none of the students in Nelson's class reported carrying over the processes they had learned to their work in other school writing. The journal assignments were so different from other writing tasks that they called for a completely different set of strategies. In fact, students reported using exploratory writing 57% of the time when writing for social studies, but only 20% of the time when writing for English. As Janet put it:

> In English, I get really worried about how I should say it. I think of it more as writing for perfection. This [journal writing] is more like writing a letter. You sit down and you write and you just explain the situation.

The concern for a final and formal written product, absent when writing for Nelson, dominated students' discussion of this writing for English class. In the latter, students felt constrained not to employ the personal and exploratory strategies Nelson encouraged. Donald stated it strongly:

> In social studies, it's more like you're putting yourself on the paper. In English, it's more you're putting an act on the paper. You're giving them what they want. It's just like you're playing a role in English, while in social studies, you can put more of what you are.

The support Nelson provides has allowed his students to use writing to generate and process information on a personal level. On some tasks, as we have seen, that support can be too structured, closing out opportunities for student-shaped responses. Yet in general his procedures have affected the way his students go about their writing tasks in his classroom. Unfortunately, it is apparently only in his classroom that this shift has taken place. Outside the rather safe confines of the journal, students face assignments which do not call for—and do not seem to allow—the level of personal engagement Nelson has encouraged. Like Phillips, he has brought his objectives and his procedures into a context which may moderate his level of success.

CONCLUSION

How successful were Nelson and Phillips in meeting their objectives? One of the best indicators may be the reports of the students themselves. In spite of her problems in following Phillips' writing procedures, Jenny argued that:

> If you write about it, you learn without wanting to. You don't have to sit there and study it. Phillips has you write down everything you know about a subject and that way you learn what you don't know. Then, when you look at somebody else's, you see that they know different parts of it, so you learn without trying. On multiple-choice tests, you could guess. When you have to write, you have to think.

Phillips and Nelson would agree, and yet Jenny, like other students in the sample, cannot always act on these thoughts. She has been schooled—and, for the most part, continues to be schooled—to consider writing, not as a tool to be used for her own purposes, but as a task to be completed for her teacher. If Phillips' and Nelson's objectives are to be met, they themselves will need support from their colleagues in implementing writing programs which are consistent in the strategies they ask students to employ. When this occurs, writing may well become a powerful and readily available resource for shaping students' learning across the curriculum.

Chapter 11
Language, Learning, and Interaction:
A Framework for Improving the Teaching of Writing

Judith A. Langer
Arthur N. Applebee

INTRODUCTION

Writing is above all else a means of communication, one of the many forms of interaction that we have developed in our exchanges with one another. Occasions for writing can be analyzed in terms of their characteristics as communication events—the roles of the participants, the topics discussed, and the forms and conventions that mediate what takes place.

If we construe writing in this way, our various studies of writing in school contexts suggest that most such writing events are flawed in some rather fundamental ways. In this chapter, we will use the results from the study to highlight the most instructionally inhibiting of those flaws, and will suggest an alternative view of the role of teacher and student.

The Failure of Interaction

The studies we have been reporting in this volume focussed on situations where we expected to find instruction at its best. The 15 students whose growth and development we traced attended a school selected for its advantages: a well trained and dedicated teaching staff, a highly academic orientation, and a supportive community. The textbooks whose lessons we analyzed were among the most popular in the nation, chosen for use presumably because they offered the most helpful materials. The individual content-area teachers whose classrooms we sought out and studied were chosen because writing activities seemed to play an unusually extensive and positive role within their classrooms. Yet as we look back over our analyses, the most consistent interpretation is that there is a systematic and pervasive failure in the quality of the instructional interaction between teacher and student.

Some aspects of this failure are obvious and easy to document. An earlier report from this study (Applebee, 1981) described typical patterns of instruction in American high schools. In that report, we found that most writing assignments were truncated, involving little more than the presentation of a topic, a length, and a due date. Instruction, to the extent that it occurred at all, occurred after the writing was complete, in the extensive comments and editing that teachers offered in response to students' work. Though English teachers differed in their emphases from teachers of other subject areas, all used their writing assignments as a way to evaluate previous learning, whether of English skills or of the information and concepts presented in other subjects. Partly as a result of this emphasis, much of the writing that students were asked to do was totally framed by language provided as part of the instruction. Rather than construct text, students were more often asked simply to complete it, by supplying missing items of information that would in turn demonstrate their learning. Word- and sentence-level skills were exercised in most tasks (occurring indeed in some 42% of class time), but text-level skills, the kinds needed to construct a coherent paragraph, were needed much less often (some 3% of the time in class or for homework).

The studies reported in the current volume present a more complex picture. We continued to find many instructional situations that fit the national pattern; the textbook analyses in particular reinforced our earlier description of emphases and approaches, but so did much of the writing that our case-study students were completing. As had been the case in the national samples, their writing for school was narrow in scope and emphasis, driven by the need to demonstrate their mastery of subject-area material. They too wrote relatively infrequently, engaged at best trivially in a composing process, and saw little point or relevance in many of the tasks they were asked to do. Yet much of this pattern of activities was emerging out of instructional contexts that appeared on the surface to be more promising, that indeed appeared to be based on exactly the sorts of approaches we might most enthusiastically recommend.

All teachers in our earlier, as well as present, study meant to "teach" and wanted their students to "learn." Some used more dynamic instructional approaches focussing on process, while others were more concerned with presentation and form. However, in some real way, most of their attempts fell short of being effective; the writing experiences became relatively trivial exercises in which students polished content or form the teacher had selected as the focus of instruction. Absent in almost all instances was a reason for writing—beyond simple obedience.

The exceptions to this pattern can help us understand the causes. One exception that we have explored in some detail is the writing that took place in Nelson's social studies classroom (see Chapter 10). Much of the writing in his classroom assumed that the students might indeed have something of interest to share with Nelson and with other students. These interests gave purpose and direction to their writing, and in turn the students reported a new found involvement and control in exploring their own ideas and seeing them grow. Their sense that they were shaping their own work was markedly different from the reactions of students in most classrooms.

If we compare the reactions of Nelson's students with those of others we have studied, one of the most important differences turns out to be the roles adopted by teacher and student within the general framework of the writing event. Though Nelson is very much a teacher, controlling the syllabus and the activities that form the context for the writing that occurs, his students are allowed to take an active role in determining what will be said. Just as happens in most out-of-school contexts of communication, the meaning that develops is negotiated among all participants, teacher and student alike. In contrast, the more typical writing assignment that serves primarily to evaluate student performance is one-sided; rather than a negotiation of meaning, the teacher's purposes are preemptive. To perform adequately in such contexts, the student must follow the pattern provided (whether of content or of form); any further exploration must take place outside of the central parameters of the assignment.

THE PURPOSES FOR SCHOOL WRITING

We have come to see the nature of the communicative situation as the fundamental factor shaping the success of instruction. When there is room for students to develop purposes of their own within the context of their school writing, teachers have a natural opportunity to provide structured help where such assistance is needed. When the tasks have a clear and overall purpose, the usefulness of any separate activity the students engage in can be judged in terms of what it contributes to the whole task, and evaluation of how well the students "did" can be based on what each set out to accomplish in the first place. The focus, from start to end, for students and teacher, is on the development and elaboration of meaning within the context of the instructional event. No matter how well intended, when the meaning is preempted by the teacher rather than more naturally negotiated, the structure of the interaction inevitably breaks down and the instructional goals are subverted.

We will use two examples to illustrate in more detail how the best intentioned of approaches breaks down when the teacher's goals leave too little scope for the students to develop their own purposes. Consider first Emily, writing an essay on *All Quiet on the Western Front* for her 12th-grade English class. The assignment itself was typical of many she completed that year, and reflected, at least on the surface, the teacher's efforts to adopt a process-oriented approach to writing instruction. The assignment began by giving Emily considerable choice in what she would write about. Rather than simply presenting a topic, the teacher offered nine "questions and ideas regarding the book." These suggestions ranged from the broad ("Select an idea developed in the book and show how that idea is presented and how it contributes to the book as a whole") to the very specific

("Discuss Paul's attitude toward the death of two or three other characters and relate them to his philosophy of war"). Emily chose a third option: "Paul Baumer uses such adjectives as 'superfluous,' 'lost,' 'crude,' and 'insensible' to describe himself and his comrades. Explain and discuss the reasons for their change from the 'Iron Youth' to alienated and hopeless 'automata.'"

To lead the students through the task, Emily's teacher organized it around a series of stages: (a) the development of a focussed thesis; (b) elaboration of the thesis in an opening paragraph; (c) a rough draft of the whole; (d) peer response; and (e) a final, graded essay. The concern with writing process is evident in several aspects of this assignment, including the attempt to provide some choice of topic, the division of the writing itself into several stages, and the careful inclusion of peer response along the way (complete with a response guide to insure that the comments would be constructive).

Yet the teacher's concern with process rides somewhat uncomfortably with the goals which drive this writing episode. There are two explicitly stated: (a) "to write an organized essay that reveals your knowledge and understanding of an aspect of the book"; and (b) "to practice certain writing techniques." The latter reflected the concern with "an organized essay," and included developing a thesis statement, supporting that thesis with specific evidence from the book, and writing an appropriate conclusion. These are formal concerns, and in this context the steps in the writing process become little more than opportunities to check that the form has been properly executed. Content is peripheral, though not irrelevant; in the course of executing the proper form, the students are also expected to "reveal" their "knowledge and understanding" of the book they have studied. (The wording, though casual, is itself revealing; the emphasis is on demonstrating previous learning, not on extending understanding of the book in the process of exploring new themes.)

Emily has considerable difficulty with this assignment, for it forces her to sharpen her thesis in isolation from the process of developing an argument to support it. Her first attempt at a thesis statement is simple: "The war changed the youth of Germany from Iron Youth to unquestioning automata." The teacher's response tried to carry the argument further, as well as to provide a more general strategy for sharpening a thesis:

> So what? What, then, is Remarque saying? This is always a useful question to apply to a potential thesis . . .

In moving to the second part of the assignment, Emily simply abandoned her thesis without trying to answer the question her teacher has posed. She heads her draft "The change from Iron Youth to automata," and struggles through six versions of her first sentence before finally focussing on the changes the war had brought to the lives of German youth, leading them either to die or to become automata as "the only way to be to survive."

The teacher's response to this paragraph is again concerned with providing Emily with appropriate strategies for examining the form of her writing; this time she asks:

> Does the material in your paragraph really show the assertion in the topic sentence to be true? Have you given any specific examples? Rewrite.

The questions are of course rhetorical, though the advice they contain is probably more appropriate to an essay as a whole than to an opening paragraph. Emily's solution is in fact to ignore the advice, emerging in her draft of the essay as a whole with an even more general opening paragraph, about war rather than about Germany: "War, no matter what role a person plays in it, changes everyone in some way. . . . In the book *All Quiet on the Western Front,* Maria Remarque showed the situations and changes the youth of Germany had to adapt to in World War I." This solution seems to satisfy her teacher, whose only reaction to the paragraph is some sentence-level editing.

Before the teacher read the final draft, however, there was one more stage in the process: a peer editing session, guided by an essay-evaluation worksheet. The worksheet was carefully constructed to reflect the teacher's goals. Its six items asked the reader to identify the writer's thesis and accompanying evidence, to suggest ways to strengthen the evidence presented, to comment on organization, to give at least one specific suggestion for improvement, and to end by saying "something encouraging." In reacting to Emily's work, her classmate Maya also had trouble finding her thesis ("not totally clear . . ."), though Emily's evidence was easy to isolate. In keeping with their teacher's emphases, Maya's advice focusses on form: "The essay is pretty organized, but there are too many ideas in the thesis paragraph, and it gets jumbled."

Emily's response to the whole sequence is a mixture of irritation and frustration, stemming in large part from the demands to know "where the essay is going" before she has had a chance to work through the material:

> In an English essay . . . I have to think in advance, and that's something I don't like doing. I like to have some surprise in my writing.

It would be easy to read Emily's comments as a rejection of having to think carefully about what she will write, a plea for undisciplined and undefended argument. But our experience with her writing makes it clear that this is not the case. Her writing for other classes, where formal features of the writing receive less direct emphasis, is often particularly thoughtful and well written. Her difficulties with the structure of this assignment seem to come from the need to be consciously aware of formal constraints at the same time that she is discovering her content:

> As long as I don't know where I'm going, I'm OK. But as soon as I have
> something in my head, I begin to doubt where I am now.

The discovery part of writing is something she enjoys, but in her English essays
she feels constantly pulled back because her teacher's goals for their writing do
not leave her any scope to develop her own thoughts.

Because Emily seemed to have so much trouble in writing about *All Quiet on
the Western Front,* we asked her what she would have written if her teacher had
simply asked her to write three pages about the book. Her reaction was surprisingly close to the options her teacher had offered:

> I'd just say what the book was about. I'd talk about the changes Paul goes
> through. And I'd talk about why Remarque wrote the book.

Emily recognized how close this was to the teacher's task, but insisted that
there was a fundamental difference: she would be in control of where the essay
was going, and the form would derive from what she felt it important to say.
From the perspective we have adopted, her role within the interaction would
have shifted to allow a more balanced negotiation of meaning, instead of depending entirely upon the teacher's prescription.

This example reminds us that language events are driven by their purposes,
not simply by their forms. We cannot reform instruction simply by changing
classroom activities, without attention to the purposes those activities serve.
Emily's teacher was familiar with recent recommendations for more process-
oriented instruction, and was making a conscious and careful effort to incorporate these recommendations into her teaching. But the changes she had made in
her approaches were ultimately trivial; the focus in instruction remained on the
formal devices of English essay writing, and those devices continued, as in less
process-oriented classrooms, to obstruct her students' efforts to learn to write.

If Emily's classroom shows us how process-oriented instruction in English
can go awry by ignoring the shared intentions underlying the writing activity, our
second example illustrates similar difficulties in broadening the range of writing
in content-area classrooms. Dan Phillips, whose 10th-grade biology classroom
was the focus of the studies reported in Chapter 10, believes that writing about
new material is an important part of his students' learning in science. Familiar
with recent studies of the writing process, Phillips explicitly argues the value of
leading students through a series of process-oriented activities, "without fear of
the teacher-as-examiner."

Phillips' concerns find expression in two sets of activities that run throughout
the school year. To help students sort through and make sense of new experiences in science, he emphasizes learning logs in which they record their reactions
and tentative explorations. To help them learn to shape their discussions of
science concepts toward a broader audience, he provides essay-writing assign-

ments structured around a series of process-oriented steps: (a) selection of a topic; (b) exploration of the topic through listing of ideas and free-writing; (c) sharing of drafts in peer-response groups; (d) formative rather than evaluative response from the teacher; and (e) submission of a final draft for a grade.

Though Phillips' approaches are firmly grounded in the current literature on writing instruction, our analyses suggest that in his classroom, too, the best of intentions have gone somewhat awry. Rather than embracing the opportunity to explore what they are learning, Phillips' students concentrate on getting the answers right. As we heard Jenny, a tenth grader, explain in Chapter 10, "It's easier to paraphrase things from the book than to write from observation notes."

Jenny's comment points toward the problem in the approaches Phillips has adopted: the work he assigns has a right and wrong version, and the rewards he gives, the grades at the end of it all, reward correct performance. In that context, the simplest and safest approach is to *find* the right answer in the textbook (or in the notes of the best students), rather than to *discover* it through the steps of a writing process. To the students, much that Phillips' wants them to do on their own belabors the obvious, as Susan pointed out in discussing prewriting activities:

> Phillips wants us to write something down and then to write down the first thing that comes to our mind. Me, I just organize it right away.

To the extent that she can "organize it right away," of course, Susan's approach is a reasonable one. Phillips would claim, and we would agree, that most of the time the organization she achieves is a passive one, reflecting the structures ready at hand in the textbook rather than her own knowledge and understanding. But those structures ready at hand are enough for successful performance; the answers will be right, and will be rewarded with a grade. The labors recorded in the students' learning logs and exploratory writing, on the other hand, are filed away unacknowledged.

Knowing where the rewards will ultimately be, the students twist even these assignments toward their own ends. In the samples we collected from Phillips' classroom, fully 85% of the writing assumed a teacher in the role of examiner, even when it was written in response to assignments meant to be supportive and flexible. Implemented to help students understand the material they are drawing from their textbooks, Phillips' assignments are co-opted by that content, in much the same way that Emily's work in English was co-opted by her teacher's concern with the proper form for students' essays. The driving purpose for the activity remains the teacher's, leaving the students with too little room to develop their own ideas.

At the core of effective instructional interaction there is a shared exchange of ideas between teacher and student—and a more balanced role for all participants. Though the teacher will usually initiate classroom activities, these activities should provide scope for the students' to develop their own purposes, rather than simply to demonstrate their knowledge and skill within the teacher's preemptive framework. When students are allowed scope to develop their own purposes, there is little room for activities that emphasize practice of new skills in isolation from broader purposes; nor is there room for drill in new concepts or information drawn from a content-area curriculum. We must turn instead to a different model of effective instruction, one that is adapted more clearly to the nature of instruction as a communicative event.

SUPPORT OF STUDENT LEARNING THROUGH INSTRUCTIONAL SCAFFOLDING

Young children learn language in the process of using it in supportive contexts. Adults rarely set out to teach their children new linguistic structures through drill and practice. Rather they listen to them, ask appropriate questions about what they are saying, and expand upon their children's beginnings to build a fuller meaning. These various activities of the adult language-user provide a variety of supports for the language tasks being undertaken by the child, and this process can itself be taken as a model for the instructional interaction of the classroom. The teacher's role becomes one of providing instructional support or *scaffolding* (Applebee and Langer, 1983; Bruner, 1978; Cazden, 1980) that will allow the student to undertake new and more difficult tasks. These tasks are purposeful for the student because they grow out of what the student wants to do, but cannot do without the teacher's help.

With Vygotsky (1962, 1978), we believe that individuals gain access to the store of cultural knowledge through the social process of interaction, and during that process gradually make that knowledge their own. From this perspective, the role of instructional scaffolding is to provide students with appropriate models and strategies for addressing new problems; these are in turn internalized by the students, providing them with the resources to eventually undertake similar tasks on their own.

Such processes are at work in any instructional situation, whether or not its emphases are compatible with those we have been discussing. Five-paragraph themes, the "funnel" organization of individual paragraphs, an emphasis on "vivid verbs" or "colorful adjectives"—when students define good writing against such criteria of form rather than of meaning it is because they have internalized their teachers' models of what matters. When they rely on lectures or textbooks for the arguments they make, rather than formulating their own analyses and opinions, they are again internalizing the principles underlying what their teachers have set for them to do.

We can organize our instruction around this process of internalization, helping students learn to complete on their own the kinds of tasks which, at first, they can only approach collaboratively. As this happens, we must be sure that our instructional approaches reflect their new competence, rather than allowing ourselves to become complacent with methods that "worked." Good scaffolds, erected to support students efforts, must be dissolved when they are no longer needed. Once the pattern has been internalized, our "help" may simply be an intrusion.

To illustrate how students can learn new strategies by completing writing tasks which allow them to develop their own purposes, let us look at Sherri, a 10th grader struggling with an essay for an advanced-placement American history course. Sherri had written many successful summaries and essays, but lacked a clear model of an analytic research paper. Faced with the task of analyzing Susan B. Anthony's influence in furthering the goal of women's rights, she did not know how much opinion she could include, and was concerned that she would sound too biased. Even after having completed extensive research (complete with 30 index cards of references and quotations), she was unconvinced that she could prove Anthony's "influence."

During a conference on her writing, Jim (a member of our research team) tried to help Sherri articulate the questions she could answer based on the information she had collected, and then to place an organization around those questions. The discussion helped her shape her ideas and organize her paper to convey her own emerging thesis. In the following selections from the conference, Sherri (S) and Jim (J) began by discussing the unfocussed concerns that were preventing her from getting started. To move beyond this writer's block, Jim helped her to reflect on what she knew about her topic:

> S: In the first paragraph, the more I think about what I'm writing the less I think it's a significant thing to write about. Is influence significant?

> J: What do you mean by influence?

> S: It's basically a matter of opinion. It's something that's great for English, but for research papers you're not supposed to have a matter of opinion. . . . For research papers, you're supposed to have cold facts.

> J: Leaving influence aside for a while, what questions do you think you could answer based on the materials you've gathered?

> S: Who was she and what did she do? What did other people think of her? What were her ideas?

After Sherri and Jim found that she knew a good deal about Susan B. Anthony, and that that information was organized around at least three major issues (Sherri posed the three important topics herself), Jim's task was to help Sherri think about her point, what she wanted to say in the paper:

> J: Why don't you want to write the paper based on three questions?

S: Because I want to make her important. Significant. My teacher told us not to make it just a biography.

J: What could you do to make her seem special?

[Sherri here listed several things Susan B. Anthony had done, including becoming a noted leader in the women's movement.]

J: What were things like when Susan B. Anthony began her career?

[Sherri has several points to make here, including some well chosen quotations from her notes.]

At this point Sherri was clear about her writing goals, but she was still not certain whether she knew enough. She was aware that she was unclear about how to establish ''proof'' of someone's importance:

J: Then you have a lot of material about what Susan B. Anthony did and what other people thought of what she did. What were things like when she finished her career? Were there any important changes for women?

[Sherri was less clear here. She kept leaping ahead to the current movement instead of staying within Susan B. Anthony's period.]

J: If you could show that specific things were different because of what Susan B. Anthony did, you might be able to prove some influence.

S: That's what I wanted to do, but again it seems like a lot of opinion.

J: If you stick as closely as you can to the facts you have on the index cards, you'll be backing up those opinions with facts.

By the end of this conference, Sherri was able to begin her paper.

While this is only one of many forms that instructional scaffolding can take, it is a clear example of how well staged questions can help the student think through the problems encountered in a specific writing task while also serving to model strategies that can be used in other similar situations. The support needs to be structured in a manner that reflects the steps that students need to go through to complete the tasks, rather than to work backwards from the logic of the final essay. Presented in this way, the students learn how to develop an argument on their own. Emily, struggling with her essay on *All Quiet on the Western Front*, did not have the benefit of such support for her own efforts, contending instead with the need to demonstrate skill in a particular organizational format. Neither did Phillips offer the kind of instructional support we are suggesting. Somehow, in planning their instructional activities, both got sidetracked; Emily's teacher focussed almost entirely on form and Phillips almost entirely on subject-area information. In each case, the writer's "message" itself was overlooked.

Because writing is a communicative act, its very essence is the writer's message; that message embodies what the writer wishes to say to a particular audience for a particular purpose. Even as the content of the message comes together and begins to make sense in the mind of the writer, it does so within some organized form. The forms within which writers integrate their messages are internally logical and purposeful; they grow with the integrating ideas a writer expresses and become whole as the message has been logically conveyed. Although content and form are sometimes artificially separated for purposes of research, they do not occur separately in the mind of the writer—unless molded to do so as a result of inappropriate instruction. Such a separation, we found, was a major flaw in even the best of the writing instruction examined during the course of our studies.

Although support is needed whenever a specific task poses a problem, not every such experience leads to learning. Sometimes the student already knows how to accomplish the task and just needs some help getting started. At other times, the skills and strategies needed for successful completion of the task are too far removed from what the student can reasonably do alone. To be instructional, tasks must be appropriate to the skills the students bring to them; they should help students learn to use skills or strategies they cannot yet manage, but are almost ready to undertake on their own—tasks that are within what Vygotsky (1962, 1978) has called the students' "zone of proximal development."

Even after her particularly supportive conference, Sherri was unable to switch from the summary mode with which she was most familiar to the analytic forms that she felt she needed for her own more complex purposes in this essay. As is the case in many instructional activities, a number of supportive experiences may be necessary before a student will be able to do the task alone. The teacher must strike a balance here, between providing too little scaffolding for difficult tasks, and providing so much that the student has little opportunity to assume control.

In discussing the purposes that underlie classroom activities, we emphasized the need to base instructional interaction around more broadly construed goals than simply the desire to evaluate student learning. The role of the teacher must shift, from an evaluator of what has already been learned to a collaborator who can help the student accomplish more complicated or sophisticated purposes.

In earlier chapters, we have seen what happens when such a shift does not occur. Fundamentally, when the teacher adopts the role of evaluator rather than collaborator the whole purpose of the interaction shifts, for teacher and student alike. All of the linguistic conventions which govern well formed interactions take their focus around this altered purpose. Grice's (1975) analyses of the maxims governing well formed conversation, for example, require each participant to make a contribution that is as informative as, but not more informative than, is required. Much that we have seen students do can be interpreted as a simple application of this maxim. In Phillips' classroom, what was "required" was, finally, the recitation of science information; students who went directly to their textbooks for a simple framework for presenting that information were adopting an efficient conversational strategy. (In fact, for that particular goal, their strategy was more efficient than the process-oriented alternative that Phillips preferred.) In other situations, students who present "well written" essays void of interest or commitment (the type of writing Macrorie, 1970, has called "Engfish") are also following an efficient strategy; the mastery of form that they are demonstrating is indeed what is required.

CONCLUSION

We concluded the first report from this project with three recommendations for improving writing instruction: (a) more situations are needed in which writing can serve as a tool for learning rather than as a means to display acquired knowledge; (b) recent work on the nature of the composing process needs to be brought to the attention of a broader spectrum of teachers; and (c) school writing must be motivated by a need to communicate and must be valued as an expression of something the writer wants to say (Applebee, 1981).

From our present perspective, these recommendations seem not so much wrong as incomplete; they represent a response to the surface of the problem, and mix fundamental questions about the nature of learning with more superficial concerns with the structure of the task. In this chapter, we have tried to untangle some of these concerns, placing the roles of teacher and student in the center of our analysis, and using the notion of scaffolding to begin to explore the dimensions of effective instruction within the context of a more balanced interaction.

We can take our analysis of instructional scaffolding one step further, and posit a set of questions that can be used to examine the interactions that make a difference in student learning (Applebee and Langer, 1983). These questions apply to all aspects of instructional interaction, the language of textbooks and worksheets as well as the language of classrooms:

1. Does the task permit students to develop their own meanings rather than simply following the dictates of the teacher or text? Do they have room to take ownership for what they are doing?
2. Is the task sufficiently difficult to permit new learnings to occur, but not so difficult as to preclude new learnings?
3. Is the instructional support structured in a manner that models appropriate approaches to the task and leads to a natural sequence of thought and language?
4. Is the teacher's role collaborative rather than evaluative?

5. Is the external scaffolding removed as the student internalizes the patterns and approaches needed?

When bringing such questions to our analysis of teaching, the answers we find are not particularly encouraging. In most classrooms, the teacher's goals still preempt the students' purposes. Even in classrooms where there is a concerted effort to implement process-oriented activities, the emphasis in instruction usually remains firmly on the subject matter, as the teacher sees it, rather than on helping students extend their skills while grappling with problems that they have made their own. Although the answers will not come easily, by asking such questions we hope teachers will become more aware of how the kinds of instructional interactions they establish directly affect the nature of their students' lea ing.

Chapter 12
Conclusion

Arthur N. Applebee

INTRODUCTION

This volume represents the completion of a series of studies that sought to illuminate the contexts and conditions under which high-school students were learning to write. We began with a few simple questions, and ended with many new ones. This final chapter will serve to highlight the findings that seem to us of most interest, and to suggest the questions that seem most important for further exploration.

PATTERNS OF INSTRUCTION

The first report from this project (Applebee, 1981) was primarily concerned with describing typical patterns of writing instruction in schools across the country. In the present report, the analyses of popular textbooks, as well as our studies of the cumulative experience of individual students, represent further explorations of the same basic issues. From these various lines of evidence, several conclusions seem well justified:

1. Students' writing experiences are distributed across their high-school classes. Though English classes are the place where students are most likely to receive formal instruction in how to write, their experiences in other classes have a powerful influence on their writing skills and their attitudes toward writing. To study the contexts in which students are learning to write, it is thus necessary to include the full range of school (and out-of-school) writing experiences.
2. The majority of school assignments provide little room for writing of even

paragraph length. All of the major school contexts—classwork, home-work, teachers' assignments, and textbook suggestions—are dominated by activities in which students provide information without constructing text. The favored exercise material varies from subject area to subject area, but all subjects seem to share the emphasis on relatively mechanical tasks. In the composition/grammar textbooks studied, for example, only 12% of the exercises required writing of even paragraph length—though all of these textbooks claimed that their primary purpose was to teach writing.

3. When more extended writing is required, it still tends to be rather limited in scope. The typical assignment is a first-and-final draft, completed in class, and requiring a page or less of writing. Topics for these assignments are usually constructed to test previous learning of information or skills; hence the students' task is to get the answer "right," rather than to convince, inform, or entertain a naive audience. In this respect, the de-mands of the typical extended writing activity are similar to those of more restricted tasks: the focus is on the accuracy of the information to be presented, rather than on skill in a communicative context. Again the composition/grammar textbooks highlight the extent of the problem; 95% of the extended writing tasks they suggested were designed to test previous learning.

4. The types of writing that students do during the high-school years narrow rather sharply around summarizing and analyzing tasks. Personal uses of writing, to explore new topics or to share ideas with close friends, have virtually no place in most classrooms. Literary uses have similarly dropped out of school writing experiences, though literary selections dom-inate in the reading that students do for their English classes.

5. In part because of these limited uses of writing, writing is more likely to be assessed than to be taught. The most effective instruction that most stu-dents receive comes after their writing tasks are complete—in detailed comments and corrections of their written work. Although prewriting ac-tivities play an important role in some classrooms, the relevance of such activities is limited by the pervasive emphasis on testing previous learning. Help during writing is even less frequent; when they need it, most students have to turn to friends or family members, rather than finding it in instruc-tional contexts.

6. The one exception to the general pattern occurs for poorer writers. Com-pared with other groups of students, they are more likely to be given personal or imaginative writing tasks, as well as informational writing tasks that draw on their personal experiences rather than on textbook material. They are also, however, less likely than their peers to have well developed strategies for approaching their writing tasks, and are no more likely to receive help.

PATTERNS OF DEVELOPMENT

If patterns of instruction seem limited, there are nonetheless clear patterns of development in students' writing skills during the high school years. A sense of these patterns can help teachers respond appropriately to student work, focussing attention on the major areas of development rather than on the surface errors that are usually obvious but not always instructionally important.

For school writing, the high school years are a time of transition from reliance on primarily time-ordered or descriptive modes of presentation toward more analytic methods of organization. In our studies, we have described a number of characteristics of this transition:

1. Each subject area seems to have its own characteristic patterns of organization, but across this diversity students adopt similar strategies for coping
   with new structures. The lab report in science, the book report in English,
   and the research report in social science each has its own formulaic pattern
   of organization, but students show similar patterns of development as they
   learn to cope with these formats.
2. Most students seem able to write fluent narratives by the time they reach
   high school. Rather than abandoning narrative patterns of organization
   when confronted with analytic writing tasks, they begin by embedding
   long stretches of narration within a global analytic frame. Though these
   stretches of narrative are often inappropriate to the analytic task, they help
   the writer maintain fluency and coherence in an otherwise very difficult
   situation.
3. Another characteristic of students' early attempts at analytic writing is a
   lack of intermediate levels of structure in their essays. Whereas more
   fluent writers will build an argument around a small number of major
   points, each of which is elaborated, the less experienced writer is likely to
   provide a long list of points without organizing them into groups of related
   ideas.
4. Closely related to the lack of intermediate levels of structure is a tendency
   to produce unbalanced arguments, in which some parts will be elaborated
   at great length while others will remain (inappropriately) unexplicated. As
   with their embedding of narratives in other analytic contexts, the lack of
   balance here allows the students to establish an overall analytic framework
   while maintaining the fluency of their writing through the ability to elaborate around a single topic.
5. Holistic judgments of writing ability seem to be more sensitive to this
   ability to maintain fluency within specific rhetorical contexts, than they
   are to a student's mastery of the constraints of more difficult writing tasks.
   A student who makes a real, but unsuccessful, attempt at a more difficult

task is likely to be penalized more harshly than one who avoids the task and reverts to a more familiar pattern.

6. High school students are efficient language learners, developing the writing styles and habits necessary for them to survive in school contexts. Their sense of the demands of their teacher-audiences is acute and sophisticated. To the extent that their writing skills are limited, we suspect it is because we do not demand enough of them, not because they are unable to do better.

THE WRITING PROCESS

Studies of the writing process have proliferated since Emig's (1971) classic investigation of how four 12th-grade students approached their writing tasks. In our studies, we have looked at a number of aspects of the writing process, as it is embedded in the context of real instructional situations. Our most important findings here should not be surprising, but they are surprisingly often overlooked:

1. The writing process varies with the context within which it is embedded. Students vary their approaches to school writing to meet the demands of particular teachers, particular subject areas, and particular topics.

2. The revisions students make in their papers provide particularly concrete evidence of these variations in process. As the writing becomes more demanding (whether in terms of the audience, the function, or the importance of writing to the subject), the proportion of papers with revisions increases. The kinds of revisions that are made show less variation with rhetorical context, and more with the proficiency of the individual writer and the place in the process where they occur. Revisions of later drafts seem to be motivated by different concerns than are revisions of first drafts, though the specific differences again vary with the proficiency of the writer.

3. The topic-specific knowledge that a writer brings to a writing task has a particularly strong influence on the writing process. Tasks seem to differ in their demands on knowledge, however. On some writing tasks, students do best if they have a wide variety of loosely organized associations that they can draw upon in elaborating on the topic; on other tasks, they do better if they start the task with a well-organized (even if smaller) body of topic-related knowledge.

4. Writing processes are learned, either through direct instruction in how to go about a task, or through accumulated experience of what works or doesn't work for a particular problem. Studies of the writing process are as much studies of past experience and instruction as they are of the ability or level of development of a particular writer.

5. Because writing processes are a function of context and task, the current research emphasis on process may ultimately be as fruitless as the earlier emphasis on product. The most rewarding approaches to the study of writing may be those which include writing processes as strategies that are orchestrated in the course of a particular communicative event, with its own network of purposes and outcomes. Our studies of the interaction of the organization of individual students' topic-relevant knowlege with their responses to particular writing prompts represent one beginning in this area; our studies of how students respond to process-oriented assignments in individual classrooms represent another, quite different approach.

THE FAILURE OF THE PROCESS APPROACH TO WRITING INSTRUCTION

The shifting research interest in the composing process has been paralleled by a concern to develop process-oriented writing activities. Prewriting activities, the use of multiple drafts, and the incorporation of peer response groups into instructional sequences have been among the most frequently recommended process-oriented activities. Our studies suggest, however, that the process approach to writing instruction is presently failing. Two very different problems have prevented process-oriented instruction from having the influence that the journal literature might suggest it should be having. The first stems from a lack of fit between such activities and teachers' current goals; the other is a result of the way in which process instruction has been conceptualized and discussed:

1. Process-oriented activities are not appropriate to the typical uses of writing in the high school classroom. Process instruction is oriented toward work-in-progress and the development of new skills. In school contexts, on the other hand, writing tasks are usually used for evaluative purposes, to assess the extent of previous learning. The introduction of process-oriented instruction is thus more complicated than simply the substitution of a new approach for an earlier alternative; it requires a reassessment of the purposes for asking students to write at all.

   Several other factors work against the ready acceptance of uses of writing that might be more amenable to process approaches. The most obvious are the extra time that process activities would take, and the lack of expertise that most teachers (particularly those in subjects other than English) feel in setting and responding to written work. Less obviously but more importantly, process-oriented activities can pose a real threat to the teachers' conception of their instructional role. To implement such activities effectively, the teacher must shift from a position of knowing what the students' response should be, to a less secure position in which there are no clear right or wrong answers. This shift may pose too much of a threat to some teachers, particularly those who are uncomfortable as writers themselves.

2. The process approach to writing instruction has been inadequately and improperly conceptualized, as a series of activities or steps in the writing process. Incorporated into instructional programs, such process activities become just as pointless and irrelevant to student learning as the skill-and-drill activities they were initially meant to replace.

This problem is similar to the one that plagues research on process: the processes are trivialized when they are divorced from the purposes they serve. Sometimes students are ready to write without completing a prewriting activity; sometimes they can complete a draft without having the task broken up into more manageable stages; sometimes a topic isn't worth, or doesn't need, the effort required to prepare a revision. Although most proponents of process-oriented activities would certainly agree that such activities are meant to be a means to an end, not an end in themselves, instructional applications have lacked a framework for integrating process-oriented activities with an analysis of the demands that particular contexts for writing pose for particular students. Without such a framework, process-oriented instruction may be no more successful than the exercises it was meant to replace.

INSTRUCTIONAL SCAFFOLDING

In the course of our work, the concept of *scaffolding* has been most helpful in bringing together our instructional concerns with our understanding of writing processes. In our first report (Applebee 1981), we used the term tentatively, worried both about the introduction of yet more jargon into the already cluttered educational arena, and about some of the more mechanistic implications of the image that scaffolding may suggest. In the present report we use it less self-consciously, convinced both of its explanatory power and of its usefulness as a metaphor in reforming instructional practice. It is nonetheless still a concept very much in evolution, as we formalize our use of it and explore its implications in real classroom contexts. Properly conceptualized, we see it as a way to restore the balance in classroom communication; but as Harste, Burke, and Woodward (1983, pp. 21–23) have pointed out, a more mechanistic application can reduce the concept to another way to structure a series of predetermined, teacher-centered activities.

AN END

This volume marks the close of the National Study of Writing in the Secondary School. We began the study at a time when we knew very little about the state of writing instruction, with the intention of providing as rich a portrait as possible of the contexts within which American secondary school children were learning how to write. To build that portrait, we were eclectic in our methodolgies and our focus, drawing as it seemed relevant on survey data, classroom observations, analyses of writing samples, and case studies of individual students and teachers. The one constraint that we placed upon our studies was that they were all based in naturally occurring instructional contexts; we sought a portrait that would illuminate the strengths and weaknesses of current practice, rather than a test of our own instructional suggestions and interventions.

We refrained from intervention not because we disagree with attempts to reform current practice, but because effective reform requires a thorough understanding of the practices we wish to change. For all of the criticisms we may make of current practice, schools and classrooms are orderly and sensible places; the activities that fill them have their own purposes, whether social, pedagogical, or managerial. To attempt to displace such activities without understanding what we are displacing will be at best an exercise in futility. Unfortunately, the attempt to introduce process-oriented instructional models seems in danger of becoming just such an exercise.

The problems with which we end this study are different from those with which we began, and the research methodologies that will be most appropriate to them will differ as well. Because we have limited ourselves to the range of naturally occurring variation, several important issues have been highlighted without being pursued. These include the effect of varied audience on students' writing performance; the short- and long-term effects of instructional scaffolding; the role of writing (as opposed to other activities) in promoting mastery of new material; and the willingness and ability of teachers to incorporate new models of writing instruction into their teaching repertoire. Such issues shape our continuing research agenda.

Appendix 1
Coding Sense of Audience*

DESCRIPTION OF CATEGORIES

Explanation of Audience

In any piece of writing, the writer expresses a relationship with the reader in respect to the topic. We want to classify pieces of writing according to the reader relationship expressed. The categories of audience refer to the implied reader, that is, the relationship the implied reader has to the writer.

Four Categories of Audience

Below are the four audience categories and a brief definition of each:

1. SELF
2. TEACHER–LEARNER DIALOGUE
3. TEACHER-AS-EXAMINER
4. WIDER AUDIENCE

1. Self. The writer writes to or for him or herself without considering the intelligibility of the writing to any other reader. Kinds of writing which are usually coded as SELF are diary or journal entries, notes either taken in class or from a book which are for the student's own use, preparatory notes for an assigned task or paper. Other types of writing which may be coded as SELF are pieces regarded by the writer as private or pieces where the exploration of an idea or emotion is so difficult or tentative that the writer probably did not have a

---

* This coding manual is a revision of the system of analysis proposed by Britton et al. (1975), as elaborated in Applebee (1980).

reader in mind. In general, whenever a piece of writing is written in a personal context, and does not use language which would inform the reader of the context and the interpretation, the writing should be coded as SELF.

Examples

I. I'm thinking about how stupid these people act when ask to do something and I think it is dumb because they talk about everything epesically Cariloyn, Becky & Tammy. Shhhhh!!!! I can't concentrate.
10 min sure is a long time I wonder if it is over yet, I doubt it because I still wound'nt be writing if the 10 min. was up, so I guess it is not up so I will keep on writing till I'm trough.
I'm thinking about what I'm am going to do tonight like (go out and drink refer and smoke beer).

II. If I think about what I would really like to do, I feel as if I want to curl into a ball and let everything go on without me. Knowing about it. Whichever way I turn, I feel trapped. College doesn't seem a release, it seems a new trap, another place where I have to conform to something . . .

2. Teacher–Learner Dialogue. The writer writes to the teacher as a trusted adult, assuming that the teacher will be a good listener. In this writing, the language reflects an ongoing process, an interaction or dialogue between the writer and the teacher (who is the reader). The writer feels less pressured to be "right" and more willing to take risks because the reader is not a judge but an aid who seeks to understand and clarify. Students write for a response from the teacher. The context of the writing is shared between writer and reader. The writer knows that the reader is informed and will use the text to extend the ideas rather than assess the ideas.

Examples

I. The first thing that I would like to mention about leaves is their colour. It is the first thing that really stands out, when you look at a leaf. The colour of a leaf can vary from a greeny yellow to a dark bronze. The colour can change by the different seasons they go through. For example in Spring the leaf is a lightish green, in Summer a full green, in Autumn, any colour varying from orange to dark brown, and in Winter there are no leaves at all. Of course it all depends on what sort of tree it is. Anyway the colour of the leaf can make a great difference.

II. Some of the kids in the class are craze but I don't think I could make it threw the day without them. They make you laught even when your down and they seem to make the day go fast.
I think I've learn a lot in this class even if I can't do all the work but I try and that what I think counts.

3. Teacher-as-Examiner. The writer writes to the teacher-as-examiner to demonstrate what he or she knows. In this kind of writing, the writer may make little effort to make personal interpretations of the material being written about. The writer makes an effort to "slot in" the correct information or to demonstrate mastery of requisite skills (e.g., thesis statement and supporting detail in an English essay). These pieces of writing may be in response to an explicit demand (as a quiz or test) or an implicit demand (as in a writing task which must include certain information). The writer avoids any risk-taking in this kind of writing. Often this writing is a regurgitation of what has been learned in class or from a textbook.

Examples

I. Aircraft
The biggest Aircraft company in america is the Northrop corporation trade name Beoing it is based at Beverly hills, California, perhaps the most famous plane they have built is the 707 which was sold to many leading Airlines encluding, Saudi Arabian Airlines, Etheopian Airways, Arance, Continental Western, El A4, Northwest Orient, Lofthansa, PIA, and pan am, Also beoing have had great sucesses with there 720, 727, 737 and 170 And now there is the 747 Gumbo Jet and the first to carry passengers.

II. The Yankee's previous opinion of the king was that he was no more than a lummox. He held this thought until in the poxhouse when the King carried a dying girl to her mother. The Yankee then saw him as heroic.
   As they were peregrinating, the Yankee decided that the king's polliation was that he was harmless, however proud he was. For example, as they were being sold, the Yankee had to assuage Arthur, who was demurring that he was the King.

4. Wider audience. Code this category when the writer addresses an audience beyond that of the teacher. The relationship between writer and reader can be of 3 general kinds: (a) experts to novices; (b) student to peer group; (c) writers to their readers. Each of these is discussed below.

Expert to novice: The writer adjusts the presentation so that a novice could understand it. The writer is comfortable and knowledgeable about the topic.

Student to peer group: The writer adjusts the language to that of the peer group. The writer may take into account the views and attitudes of the group.

Writers to their readers: This general category includes pieces marked by a context wide enough to bring in readers whose sophistication, interests, and experience can only be estimated. The writer strives to make an impression on the readers.

Examples

I. [expert to novice] Both the motives and methods of scientific researh have undergone a profound change. Today, they bear little resemblance to those of the previous half century, still less to those of the previous two centuries.

For centuries, scientific research has been the concern of men with an almost eccentric curiosity. The researchers of the past were often amateurs who had had no scientific training, for example the Dutch microscopist Leeuwenhoek. Leeuwenhoek was obsessed with the visual powers that a lens could give him. He knew nothing of lens manufacture and had to learn this trade, starting at the beginning. When he mounted his carefully ground lenses in metal, Leeuwenhoek had first had to lern from alchemists, the business of metal extraction and fashioning. He was partof no vast research laboratory and was a layman. He was merely a man with no idle curiosity and a desire to find out more about the structure of the organisms, by which he was surrounded.

II. [student to peer group] The rooms were changed a lot and so also was Mr. Comer. The way the rooms were changed was. The benches were in different orders and Mr Comers desk was pushed back to the blackboard. . . . Mr Comer was changed a lot two. The ways he was changed were, there was no "are you at your bench." Mr Comer also was going round giveing more of a helping hand than usual. The boys talked to Mr Comer about the job and he wasn't the usual old cross looking black patch, He was happy took a joke and listend to a joke. If any-body was doing anything wrong he didn't catch them by the ear and blow his top, instead he told them where they were wrong and explined how to do it. Thes effects weren't of him on the following Monday.

III. [writers to their readers] The snow was falling up in the mountains where the hawks were flying above in the distance. Down below the wind was whistling through the cracks in the log walls of the cabin. The river was frozen from snowbank to snowbank. On the other side of the river a large buck was chewing on the bark of a tree. Off in the distance I heard a noise, a loud gunshot. The buck suddenly ran off swiftly but quietly in the snow. There was no sound at all as I watched the snow being kicked up behind the buck. The next thing I heard was a scratchy loud voice that said, "Damn . . . How could I a missed that?"

Rules for Coding

[Note: The coding of audience and function will be done separately for student writing. Do not consider function while you are coding audience.]

1. Letters. Disregard the salutation and closing. Categorize the text as you would other texts. Do not automatically code WIDER AUDIENCE.

2. Quality. Do not code up or down (i.e., from SELF to WIDER AUDIENCE) based on the quality of the writing. Remember—base your decision on the type of reader the writer had in mind.

3. Multiple audiences. When the writing slides between different audiences, read the text as a whole and decide which audience is dominant.

Appendix 2
Coding Functions of Writing*

DESCRIPTION OF CATEGORIES

Explanation of Function

In any piece of writing, the writer uses the language to perform a particular function. Language can be used to inform, persuade, or subjectively interpret an event. As the function of different pieces of writing differs, so does the language used in the writing. The categories of function refer to the way the language is used in a piece of writing.

Three main categories of function

Below are the three main categories of function and a brief description of each.

20. INFORMATIONAL. Language used to convey information, advise, instruct or persuade. It can be used to record facts, explain ideas, exchange opinions, transact business.
30. PERSONAL. Language used is close to self, unstructured, assumes a shared context between reader and writer. Demands for the language to do or make something are at a minimum. Typically an oral rather than a written function.
40. IMAGINATIVE. Language used to make a construct, an arrangement, a formal pattern. Language is used as an art medium.

---

*This coding manual is based on the system developed by Britton et al. (1975), as extended in Applebee (1980).

FUNCTION CATEGORIES

Main Categories and Subcategories

20. INFORMATIONAL
    21. Note taking
    22. Record
    23. Report
    24. Summary
    25. Analysis
    26. Theory
    27. Persuade or regulate
    28. Other
30. PERSONAL
    31. Journal or diary
    32. Notes or personal letters
    33. Other
40. IMAGINATIVE
    41. Stories
    42. Poems
    43. Play scripts
    44. Other

FUNCTION CATEGORIES

Subcategories: Informational

The subcategories of informational all convey information, arguments or opinions. These categories grow more and more abstract in the language which is used as they go from record to theory. One way to think about this change in abstractness is that the writer and the writing get further and further away from immediate experience.

21. Note taking. Code this category when the writing is notes for the writer to use. Study notes, laboratory notes, organizing notes made to prepare for another task are all examples of this category.

Examples

I. Combo CHARACTERS
   Estella and Miss H.
      Estella = "jewel likeness of his L.E.'s"
      Miss H = "falsehood and degeneracy"

Joe and Arlick
Extreme opposites of spiritual possibility
Edmund Wilson "can't get good and bad into one"

22. Record. Code this category when writers write about how their world is at that moment. The language used in the writing is like that of a play-by-play sports commentary and is frequently in the present tense. The writer is recording what is immediately present in the environment.

Example

I. Suddenly the top of the tree starts to break up and fall. The guy is terrified and very confused. The top of the tree is swaying wildly like a kite in the wind. It's meraculous that it hasn't fallen yet. He is despertly tring to get down but the tree is like a pendulum on a clock. Finally he is descending. The tree starts to break. The top of the tree is coming right down on top of him. It looks like he's going to be killed. The tree grabs him and pins him 30 feet in the air. He staggers to his feet almost falling on to the ground below. He gathers a little strength and begins chopping some branches off. He climbs down on the stubs of the branches. The ground welcomes him as he reaches it.

23. Report. Code this category when writers write about past experiences or observations. Reporting deals with observable events and scenes but does not include generalizations drawn from such observation. Writing of this type is often the retelling of one incident in the past, and usually uses the past tense, although some descriptive passages may not always follow this rule.

Examples

I. My favorite vacation was when I went to Yellow Stone International Park in July of 1980.
I went there with my whole family for three weeks to enjoy the beauty of the park. It was great. We went to the Old Faithful Geyser and the Geyser Valley. We also went on a few trails in the forest which sometimes lead us to mud pots and steam holes.

II. The story begins on the side steps of the Notre Dame Cathedral in Paris in the year fourteen hundred and forty-eight years six month and nineteen day. That historic day that the boy Quasimodo or Hunchback or the the religious people Beelezebub was found by Monk Claude Frollo.
After caring for Quasimodo in his own room Claude Frollo made him a room in the cellar of the cathedral. Though he was an extremely ugly creature Claude Frollo was very fond of him and he was a great source of joy to him.

24. Summary. Code this category when writers generalize from a number of events, procedures, or situations in order to tell in a concrete way how things are done or how they occur or what they are like. Summary functions to tell the reader "this is what always happens." Writing of this type is often the retelling of recurrent events or noting the steps in a procedure. The use of the present tense or words like "always," "every time," or "usually" in the language may point to this category although this is not a hard and fast rule. Whenever the writer detects a pattern of repetition in events, the writing is summary.

Examples

I. You have two liquids and must heat them sufficiently to vapor and you have some type of tube system that takes the vapors to a new chamber to condense, then boil them, as you do this over and over your amount of liquid grows smaller, and so does your increse in % of gain. This is why pure substances are so expensive.

II. Building a window frame can be a hard job. The first step in building a window frame is getting the right supplies. Wood and nails are the two supplies needed. First you cut out the wood. Then you take the pieces and put them in the order they should be put together. When getting pieces of wood in order take small finishing nails and nail frame together. Finally get piece of glass and slide in frame and make secure and your job is through.

25. Analysis. Writing in this category involves classification and categorization. Whenever the writer tries to explain the reasons for an idea or emotion, code analysis. Most writing in this category orders ideas and makes a case for them, makes logical or hierarchical connections between generalizations, or explains causality, motivation, or relationships of people or events.

Examples

I. The reason I think summer is hear is that I see the birds nesting and all the baby animals are out anouther reason is that it is getting warm out and the lakes are warming up and all the trees bushes and grass is turning green, plus I know summer is hear because of the thunderstorms and bad weather that is being thrown at us.

II. Martin only become more determined after his rejection. He soon became a highly respected and well-paid author. Ruth found this out and went back to him only for his money. Martin soon found this out and killed himself. However, he did not kill himself just because of Ruth. He had other problems also. One of Martin's other problems was his struggle against the bourgeois society.

As you can see Martin's main reason for living was Ruth, and when he lost her, he couldn't handle it. Anybody with conviction and dedication to his profession would have been able to handle the situation better than Martin did.

26. Theory. Code this category when the writer speculates about events or relationships using a generalization as a basis for prediction and extrapolation. The writing should have hypotheses and deductions from them. In order to qualify for theory, the writing must speculate about general principles.

Examples

I. I have 3 generationa of cats which will be the basis of my problem. I am attempting to determine how the F1 and F2 generations inherited their coat colors and also determine the parents' phenotypes and genotypes. I am dealing with dominant and recessive genes, genes that are neither dominant or recessive to each other, and sex-linked genes.

My hypotheses were that the yillow tabby tome cat was the father of the first litter of the F1 generation, and the F2 generation; and that the grey tabby ton cat was the father of the 2nd and 3rd litters of the F1 generation.

My research has shown that by the way the genes were inherited, these most likely were the correct fathers. . . .

II. By using an analogy of rope waves which are transverse, the phenomenen may be explained. Suppose a rope is threaded through a type of grid, and a second grid through which it is threaded, is placed further along the rope. If both slits are parallel, the wave will pass all the way along the rope and emerge at the other side of the second slit. If however the second slit is placed perpendicular to the first, the wave is blocked or cut off.

In the rope wave before it reaches the first grid, transverse vibrations of the rope particles occur in every plane, but the vibrations are restricted to those moving up and down in a plane parallel to the grid, when the rope wave has passed through the first grid or slit. Hence if a second slit is placed parallel to the first, the wave due to these transverse vibrations in one plane will pass through. In the second case, where the next slit is placed perpendicular to the first the transverse vibrations cannot occur due to the position of the slit which cuts them off.

If the analogy is applied to light waves, which must now be assumed to be transverse, the polarisation phenomenen can be explained. The crystals must have the power of restricting light to one plane. Hence polarised light is obtained when the light is passed through the first crystal which is called the polariser and continues polarised through the second crystal—the analyser—if placed with axis parallel to the first. If placed so that it is perpendicular to the first, the polarised light is cut off & darkness is seen. This experiment shows how polarised light differs from ordinary light.

27. Persuade or Regulate. Code persuade when there is an explicit attempt in the piece of writing to persuade or instruct. The attempt must be deliberate and a recognizable assault on other people's behavior in order to qualify for this category. Examples of this type of writing are political speeches or advertisements. (School writing which gives reasons why or why not a position should be held are not usually coded persuade; they are usually coded analysis.) The language used in this writing overtly commands, urges or persuades; and the reader acknowledges the writing is manipulative.

(*Note:* Virtually all writing attempts to persuade in the sense of being convincing or making a point; but persuade should be coded only if persuasion overrides all other purposes.)

Code regulate when the writing tells what should be done and how to do it in situations where the rules must be obeyed. There is a direct attempt to regulate actions and behaviors without any need to persuade or convince. Examples of this type of writing are rules (where there is an obligation to obey them) or statements of what to do. Regulative writing carries consequences if it is not obeyed; the other informative categories do not.

Example

I. Is Christianity Fighting a Losing Battle Against Pop-Groups?

The question of numbers is the first thing to turn to in any discussion of popularity. Obviously it cannot be denied that those who follow the fortunes of the raucous singers are more in number than the more sober-minded fellows who try to live a Christ-like life. Indeed, it appears that the foremost "Beatle" John Lennon quite admitted (some sources suggest that he was dismayed) that some of the worship which ordinarily would be attributed to God is being whole-heartedly proffered to otherwise untalented pop-groups. This can only result in harm both for the worshipped and worshippers. The former is bound to decline in the popular view, and he becomes disillusioned, thinking that the adulation afforded him is all he will ever need; the latter may become too enthusiastic in the belief that their "idol" is an infallible "God", and thus their world collapses when the career of their "idol" crashes, as it is bound to do.

Now, the Bible itself has condemned the worship of idols, since it presumably takes away the worship due to the creator. But even in the Christian Church itself, this can happen. In a Church, the central theme is Christ. But are there not those within the church who idolize their own eloquence in committee meetings, or their skill in playing, singing, or accompanying? Indeed, some worship is accorded to the vicar or minister himself.

But in all these adversities, the true Christian knows one thing: if the all-powerful God exists and supports his church, then the church cannot fail; and that, while everyone should make an almost superhuman effort in seeing that good and right have a clear way in the world, God will even make use of tragic circumstances and (in this case) loss of priority, to bend and fabricate these wrong things into instruments by which the world may be saved.

Subcategories: Personal

31. *Journal or diary entries.* Code this category of personal writing when the writing is the kind of diary or journal entry that attempts to record and explore the writer's feelings, mood, opinions, and preoccupations of the moment. This kind of writing often looks like "thinking aloud" on paper.

Examples

I. I'm thinking about our new house that we are going to move into tonight on Jan. 25. I like the house because it is sharp.

What I am doing now is not usually because I have to write speeches all the time for drama class, I have been in it for 3 years.

I wish I were at home with a coke and some sort of a snack and watching t.v.

This is all right writing about what you are doing. I just thinging about what Becky said "Dennis you creep."

II. I would enjoy wearing this dress [accompanying picture] for partys, dances & outings. The colour I would choose would be blue and I would like it in crimpleen material, white for the collar. With it I would wear a gold watch like this [picture].

I would enjoy wearing these shoes [picture] with the dress and watch. They have got a nice shape front. I like the style very much and I would like them in white black bointant.

32. *Notes or personal letters.* Writing coded in this category includes note-making activities when the writing is being used to "think aloud" or brainstorm. Also included are letters written for the purpose of maintaining contact with friends or relatives.

Subcategories: Imaginative

41. *Stories.* Code this category of imaginative writing when the genre of the piece of writing is a story. Remember that in order to qualify as imaginative, the story must have value as a verbal construct and not be used as a means to an end. Narratives based on personal experience are coded here if the major purpose is the imaginative reconstruction of experience, rather than providing information about "what happened."

Example

I. George Peabody embrassed his wife Anna and with a perfunctory nod, began his journey to Norfolk House and the interview. For fourteen years, George had prayed for the position of a Chief Clerk, now it was within his grasp, if only he could contain his weaknesses.

Arriving at Norfolk House, George was directed by the porter to the green-room, which was ten floors up. George preceded with a brisk and athletic movement, that is until the tenth floor, then for no reason at all, his legs collapsed to sticks of rubber. Before entering the waiting-room, George examined his appearance and feeling satisfied, with a sudden jerk swung open the door of the room, releasing it to crash agaist the wall. Immediately, all eyes were upon him. George gave a weak smile and seeing through the corner of his eye a vacant seat, advanced towards it. Once seated George was at liberty to examine the room and its contents. The room, itself was pleasantly decorated with pastel shades, which soothed his eyes if not his nerves. Apart from a few chairs the only other articles in the room were three gentlemen of identical dress, a little older than himself and all having an air of experience. George clutched his umbrella for support, but seeing a pile of magazines, released it and with a rather ungainly movement lurched out and grabbed the nearest book, to his dismay the pile collapsed before his eyes. As George was in the process of re-organizing the pile, his name was called over the loud speaker to enter the green-room.

42. Poems. Writing coded in this category must be in the form of a poem. It may or may not have the formal elements of a poem (i.e., rhyme scheme, meter, etc.) but it must have an arrangement of the phonic substance of the language itself to qualify as a poem.

Example

I. Pirates
One year I went to Skeggness
I had a happy week.
On Wednesday night I walked two miles
Along the sandy beach to Skeggness
When I got there,
I did what I wanted to do.
I hired a canoo for half an hour.
I cast it of I ramed a boat.
I grounded once again.
I cast it of I got the hang of it.
I ramed a pile of boats
And then I lerned to Stear
I speed along like a big dolfin.
I went around a small island
And pulled into the side
but as I was just climbling in I fell back
    In my boat.
A whistle went my time was up.
Home I had to go
But I always rember I am a hazard to the sea.

43. Play Scripts. Code this category when the imaginative writing is in the form of dialogue as scripted for a dramatic play.

GENERAL RULES FOR CODING FUNCTION

1. *Business Letters.* Code the content of the letter. Simple sharing of information, making an appointment, or ordering materials are coded as REPORT. Providing general information about a company, a product, or the skills of a job applicant is coded as SUMMARY. Making a case for a particular course of action or policy is usually coded as ANALYSIS, though it may occasionally involve THEORY or be completely taken over by PERSUADE.

2. *Quality.* Do not code up or down (i.e., from RECORD to THEORY) based on the quality of the writing. Remember—base your decision on the function or use of the writing; whether or not the writing is successful at achieving it is irrelevant.

3. *Multiple Functions.* In pieces of writing where one function is used to support another (e.g., summary to support analysis, or analysis to support theorizing) the overall effect of the piece is the determining factor in deciding function. How much of the paper is support versus how much is statement of position or opinion is not a determining factor. Always code up to the highest level of abstraction when more than one subcategory occurs in a piece of writing.

[If, especially in a poorly written paper or in a lengthy paper, the function shifts without one section supporting another, code this 50. *Mixed function.*]

[Note: The coding of function will be done separately for student writing. Do not consider audience while coding function.]

SPECIFIC RULES FOR DECIDING
BETWEEN CATEGORIES IN FUNCTION

A. Personal narrative or writing about a personal experience should not automatically be coded PERSONAL. Personal experience can be the basis for INFORMATIVE writing such as REPORT or IMAGINATIVE writing such as STORY. In order to qualify for PERSONAL, the writing is likely to have strong emotive content, will be written only for the writer's benefit, and the context of the writing will not be clear to the general reader. Personal experience coded as REPORT will be detached and objective with a sense of trying to get the facts "straight" and understandable to the reader.

B. Discussion of processes should not automatically be coded SUMMARY. When the described process is used to support a general statement about types of processes, the paper should be coded ANALYSIS. Remember—look at the function of the description: if it is an end to itself it is probably SUMMARY; if it is a means to an end, it is probably ANALYSIS.

C. Writing which is a modern version or a paraphrasing of a set piece (like a famous poem or play) should not automatically be coded INFORMATIONAL. Such pieces may be coded IMAGINATIVE if the resulting piece of writing is also a formal arrangement of language rather than merely an attempt to inform.

EXAMPLES OF SUBCATEGORIES IN THE SUBJECT AREAS

I. Social Studies

Often writing in this area is a chronological sequence of historical events. When this kind of writing is used to "reproduce" events as they might have looked to an onlooker, the writing is probably REPORT. When the writing is more generalized and the writer is moving away from the immediate events, it is probably coded as SUMMARY. If the writing gives reasons for the events, code ANALYSIS.

Examples

I.a. Marie Antoinette stepped on the scaffold. She looked at the crowd. All who saw the event would remember the expression on her face, and the impact she was to have on history. Code: REPORT.

I.b. The day Marie Antoinette stepped on the scaffold history changed because of the repercussions the event had in other countries. Code: ANALYSIS.

I.c. Hitler refused to see the British Envoy. Then a British ship was torpedoed in the North Atlantic. Britain went to war with Germany. Code: REPORT.

I.d. Germany attempted a blockade of British seaports and when this proved inconclusive, made preparations for an invasion by sea and air. Britain went to war with Germany. Code: SUMMARY.

II. Literature

Sometimes writing in this area is a retelling or a synopsis of the story or book which was read. If the writing reproduces the events in the story much as they appeared originally without an attempt to summarize or categorize, code REPORT. When the writing generalizes and summarizes characters and events, code SUMMARY. If the writing gives reasons for events or characters' behaviors, code ANALYSIS.

Examples

II.a. Alec lead the Black off of the ship. Henry could not take his eyes off the horse and the boy. The horse was surely a wild desert animal; but in Alec's presence he seemed docile. Code: REPORT.

II.b. Somehow Alec had a quieting effect on the Black. When he lead the wild horse off the ship, he had no trouble. And again, when the horse got loose in the streets of New York, Alec's presense calmed him in the midst of a rage. Code: SUMMARY.

II.c. Alec could quiet the seemingly wild Black because of the bond of trustingness they had built up during the time they spent on the island. Code: ANALYSIS.

Appendix 3
Coding Manual for Cohesive Chain
Interaction

1. The first step in the analysis is to break the text down into the individual clauses.

2. Next a lexical rendering of the text is carried out. This involves replacing all implicit lexical items in the text with the word or words which they stand for. Implicit lexical items include such linguistic markers as pronouns, demonstratives, and other words or phrases which stand for an item or items used earlier in the text. For example:

> I had known <u>Georgene</u> for years.
> <u>She</u> once danced professionally with the Rockettes.

Here "Georgene" and "she" refer to the same person; therefore, in the lexical rendering the pronoun is changed to its original references:

> I had known <u>Georgene</u> for years.
> <u>Georgene</u> once danced professionally with the Rockettes.

In the following example, there is a substitution which refers back to an earlier item in the text:

> I <u>play cello.</u>
> My wife <u>does</u> too.

Some words and phrases which often in discourse function as substitutes are *do, has, any, one,* and *the same.*

Ellipses also refer to previously mentioned items in a text, as in the following:

I really need to borrow your <u>pen</u>.
You see, I can't find <u>mine</u>.

Here "mine" stands for "my pen," as reflected in this lexical rendering:

I really need to borrow your <u>pen</u>.
You see, I can't find my <u>pen</u>.

3. When the lexical rendering has been completed, the search for cohesive chains begins. Cohesive chains are threads of continuity which run through a text, but which are not necessarily contiguous. Once found, all chains should be listed (see example passage). A chain is formed by a set of at least two items which may be related to each other in one of the following two ways:

a. *Identity Chains.* This is where every member of a chain refers to the same person, object, or event. For instance a piece of discourse on the life of De Gaulle might well have many references to De Gaulle; these would constitute an identity chain. Or, multiple references in a text to a *particular* chair, or to a *specific* World Series, would each form an identity chain. Multiple reference to places also constitutes an identity chain, whether the reference is to a specific room or, at a somewhat more abstract level, to a city or country. In addition, a specific university, company, or other type of institution, when mentioned more than once in a text, constitutes an identity chain. Concreteness is a prime criterion here. Concepts such as "sincerity" or "nationalism" cannot form identity chains, nor can references to, for example, the "British" or "left-handed people." However, these kinds of referents are equally important in this system, as they combine with certain others to form the second and larger category of cohesive chains, which is discussed below.

b. *Similarity Chains.* Typically, most cohesive chains in a text will fall into this category. Similarity chains consist of lexical items which refer to either nonidentical members of the same class of people, places, objects, events, or concepts, or to members of nonidentical but related (in specific, formally prescribed ways) classes. An example of nonidentical members of the same class (the former) is:

I <u>play cello</u>.
Bill <u>plays violin</u>.

Here, "cello" and "violin" are both members of a class of musical instruments, and thus constitute a similarity chain. In addition, the verb "play" in both sentences also forms a similarity chain. Correspondingly, the verbs in the following sentences also form a similarity chain:

Bill <u>strolled</u> home.
Then he <u>walked</u> to the store.

These verbs are both members of the class of verbs of locomotion or travel. As a rule, judgements of this nature about similarity chains should be made explicitly. The analyst should be able to state clearly what class the particular lexical items in question belong to. Moreover, it must be kept in mind that these strands can appear at different points in the text, and there can be any number of members of a certain class present in the discourse. Therefore, the analyst needs to keep a sharp eye out for these types of relationships.

Concerning members of nonidentical but related classes of lexical items, there are five relations which may obtain. The first is *reiteration,* where either the same lexical item is repeated in the text (as we have seen above in several examples, e.g., the verb "play") or where the words with the same root appear in the text, as in the following example:

The committee <u>suggested</u> that sexist language be removed from the regulations.
If this <u>suggestion</u> is adopted, words such as "he" and "his" will have to be avoided.

Here a tie is formed through the reiteration of the same root (suggest) in "suggestion" and "suggested." A closely related category to *reiteration* is *synonymy,* where there is an almost total overlap of meaning between lexical items. This includes such pairs as "woman, lady," "buy, purchase," or "smile, grin."

Another common relation is *antonymy,* or oppositeness of meaning. Pairs such as "question, answers," "clean, dirty," or "atheist, believer" (when the context makes it clear that "believer" means "believer in God") fall into this category.

A somewhat trickier sense relation is that of *hyponymy,* where the meaning of one member of a pair subsumes that of the other. If one member of the relationship refers to a class "x", then the other refers to a subclass "y"; "x" subsumes "y". For example:

Bert loved <u>pasta</u>.
<u>Linguine</u> was his favorite.

The class is *pasta,* of which *linguine* is a subset. Another instance of this relation is:

Kenya has a great deal of <u>wildlife</u>.
<u>Elephants</u>, <u>lions</u>, and <u>gazelles</u> are especially common.

The three types of animals listed in the second sentence are members of the class of "wildlife." In the category of *hyponymy,* there are differing degrees, or gradations, of generality, as in "food, fruit, berry, blueberry." The rule of thumb in searching for hyponymy relations in a text is that the analyst should be able to characterize explicitly the particular class or set in question, in a way that is intuitively plausible to native speakers of English. Overgenerality should be avoided: a great many things can be characterized as "objects on earth," but this is not a useful classification.

The final relation to be discussed is called *meronymy,* and refers to part–whole relationships. For example, "chassis" and "car" or "petal" and "flower" both stand in this relation to one another.

In finding similarity chains in a text, individual chains may contain only one of the above mentioned relations. The text should be examined thoroughly, until the analyst is reasonably certain that all nouns, verbs, adjectives, and adverbs have been characterized as either belonging, or not belonging, to a chain. Lexical items can belong to only one chain. When identity and similarity chains have been isolated, numbered, and clearly listed (one page should be sufficient for listing all chains, not one page for each chain), then the next stage of the analysis begins.

4. *Cohesive Chain Interaction Analysis.* Here the analyst must look at the relationships between the members of the various chains. For two chains to interact, at least two members of chain x must stand in the same semantic relation to at least two members of chain y. The aim is to find out how any one chain makes contact with any other: what is the nature of the relation which brings two chains into contact. The relations to check for include: doer/doing, doing/ affected by doing, location/located, number/enumerated, action/time of action, action/manner of action, and attribute/items being described. Some examples follow. Remember, however, that in an actual text, interaction may not occur only in contiguous sentences; the entire text must be examined. Wherever a member of one chain comes into contact with a member of another, one of the types of interaction that have been outlined above may well obtain. If there are two or more occurrences of that type of relation between two chains, then interaction is said to occur. For example: doer/doing, location/located:

> Judy went to the drug store.
> Then, she walked to the grocery store.

Here there are two references to "Judy," and two verbs of travel, "walked" and "went." These form an identity and a similarity chain, respectively, and these chains interact in a doer/doing relation. Moreover, the two instances of "Judy" are in a location/located relation with "drug store" and "grocery store," two members of the class of "store types." Subsumed under the broad heading of doer/doing are such relations as sayer/saying, builder/building, thinker/thinking, etc.

Doer/doing; doing/affected by doing; action/manner of action; action/time of action.

First, James scrubbed the pots lethargically.
Next, he lazily washed the dishes.

We have three instances of cohesive chain interaction here. "James" forms an identity chain, "pots" and "dishes" form a similarity chain, and "washed" and "scrubbed" also form a similarity chain. The two instances of "James" are in a *doer/doing* relation with "scrubbed" and "washed," which are in a *doing/affected by doing* relation with "pots" and "dishes." In addition, "scrubbed" and "washed" are in an *action/manner of action* relation with "lethargically" and "lazily." Moreover, "scrubbed" and "washed" are also in an *action/time of action* relation with "First" and "next."

Figure A3.1

Joseph Priestly, Scientist (Summary/Science)

1. Priestly discovered oxygen.
2. Joseph Priestly, an English scientist, is usually given credit for the discovery of oxygen.
3. Priestly was the first scientist to publish the results of Priestly's experiments with oxygen.
4. As recently as 200 years ago, people did not know that there were different gases in the air.
5. People thought air was made up of only one gas.
6. The nature of burning, rusting, and other processes was a mystery.
7. Mystery challenged many scientists of that day, including Priestly.

Identity Chain	1. Priestly (7)
Similarity Chains	1. A mystery; mystery
	2. Oxygen (3)
	3. Discovered, discovery, experiments
	4. 200 years ago, that day
	5. Gases, gas
	6. Air, the air
	7. Know, thought
	8. People (2)

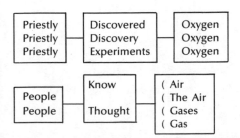

Describing/described.

> Jane was beautiful that day.
> Her hair was particularly lovely.

"Jane" and "Jane's hair" ("her hair" goes to "Jane's hair" in the lexical rendering) form an identity chain, while "lovely" and "beautiful" form a similarity chain, as near synonyms. These chains interact in the manner described above, with the adjectives describing and Jane being described.

The final relation, *number/enumerated,* refers to a situation in which number words, either actual numbers or terms such as "many," "most," "few," etc., are used to modify nouns which form a cohesive chain. If two or more such relations exist in a text, then these constitute cohesive chain interaction.

These are the types of cohesive chain interaction that this analysis is concerned with. When the analyst has thoroughly studied the text, then a diagram is created indicating which members of which cohesive chains interact in the text. An example of the process is presented in Figure A3.1. This text has already been lexically rendered.

Finally, tabulate the number of lexical items which are in cohesive chains. These are called *relevant tokens*. Next, tabulate the number of relevant tokens which enter into cohesive chain interaction. These are known as *central tokens*. Dividing *central tokens* by *relevant tokens* yields a measure of coherence.

References

Applebee, A. N. (1974). *Tradition and reform in the teaching of English: A history*. Urbana, IL.: National Council of Teachers of English.

Applebee, A. N. (1978). *The child's concept of story*. Chicago, IL: University of Chicago Press.

Applebee, A. N. (1980). *A Study of Writing in the Secondary School*. Final Report. NIE-G-79-0174. Urbana, IL: National Council of Teachers of English. ERIC Document No. ED 197 347.

Applebee, A. N. (1981). *Writing in the secondary school*. Research Monograph No. 21. Urbana, IL: National Council of Teachers of English.

Applebee, A. N. (1982). Writing and learning in school settings. In M. Nystrand (Ed.), *What writers know*. New York: Academic Press.

Applebee, A. N., & Langer, J. A. (1983). Instructional scaffolding: Reading and writing as natural language activities. *Language Arts, 60*, 2, 168–175.

Baker, S. (1977). *The practical stylist*. New York: Thomas Y. Crowell.

Barnes, D. (1974). *From Communication to Curriculum*. Harmondsworth, England: Penguin Books.

Bissex, G. L. (1980). *Gnys at wrk*. Cambridge, MA: Harvard University Press.

Bridwell, L. (1980). Revising strategies in twelfth grade students' transactional writing. *Research in the Teaching of English, 14*, 3, 197–222.

Britton, J., Burgess, T., Martin, N., McLeod, A., & Rosen, H. (1975). *The development of writing abilities (11–18)*. London: Macmillan.

Bruner, J. (1978). The role of dialogue in language acquisition. In A. Sinclair, et al. (Eds.), *The child's conception of language*. New York: Springer-Verlag.

Carey, R., Harste, J., & Smith, S. (1981). Contextual constraints and discourse processes: A replication study. *Reading Research Quarterly, XVI*, 2, 201–212.

Cazden, C. (1980). Peek-a-boo as an instructional model: Discourse development at home and school. *Papers and Reports of Child Language Development, 17*, 1–29.

Educational Products Information Exchange Institute. (EPIE) (no date). *Report No. 76*. New York: Educational Products Information Exchange Institute.

Elbow, P. (1973). *Writing without teachers*. New York: Oxford University Press.

Emig, J. (1971). *The composing processes of twelfth graders*. Research Report No. 13. Urbana, IL: National Council of Teachers of English.

Emig, J. (1977, May). Writing as a mode of learning. *College Composition and Communication*, 122–127.

Faigley, L., & Witte, S. (1981, December). Analyzing revision. *College Composition and Communication, 32.*

Flower, L., & Hayes, J. (1978, March 31). Protocol analysis of writing processes. Paper presented at the annual meeting of the American Educational Research Association.

Flower, L., & Hayes, J. (1980). The cognition of discovery: Defining a rhetorical problem. *College Composition and Communication, 31,* 21–32.

Goodman, K. (1973). Theoretically based studies of patterns of miscues in oral reading performance. Final Report. Washington DC: U.S. Office of Education, Bureau of Research.

Goodman, K., & Goodman, Y. (1978). Reading of American children whose language is a stable rural dialect or a language other than English. Final Report. Washington, DC: National Institute of Education.

Graves, D. (1975). An examination of the writing processes of seven-year old children. *Research in the Teaching of English, 9,* 227–241.

Grice, P. (1975). Logic in conversation. In P. Cole & J. Morgan (Eds.), *Syntax and semantics III: Speech acts.* New York: Academic Press.

Halliday, M. A. K., & Hasan, R. (1976). *Cohesion in English.* London: Longmans.

Harste, J. C., Burke, C. L., & Woodward, V. A. (1983). *Child as Writer/Reader, and Informant.* Final Report, NIE-G-80-0121. Bloomington, IN: Indiana University.

Hasan, R. (1980). The texture of a text. Unpublished manuscript, Sophia University, Tokyo, Japan.

Hayes, J. R., & Flower, L. S. (1980). Identifying the organization of writing processes. In Gregg, L. W. & Steinberg, E. R. (Eds.), *Cognitive processes in writing.* Hillsdale, NJ: Lawrence Erl aum, Associates.

Heath, S. B. (1981). What no bedtime story means: Narrative skills at home and school. *Language and Society, II,* 49–76.

Helgeson, S. L., Blosser, P. E., & Howe, R. W. (1977). The status of pre-college science, mathematics, and social science education: 1955–1975. Vol I. Science Education. Columbus, OH: Center for Science and Mathematics Education.

Langer, J. A. (1980). Relation between levels of prior knowledge and the organization of recall. In M. Kamil and A. J. Moe (Eds.), *Perspectives in reading research and instruction.* Washington, DC: National Reading Conference.

Langer, J. A. (1981). From theory to practice: A pre-reading plan. *Journal of Reading, 25,* 2, 152–156.

Langer, J. A. (1982). Facilitating text processing: The elaboration of prior knowledge. In J. A. Langer and M. Smith-Burke (Eds.), *Reader meets author/bridging the gap: A psycholinguistic and sociolinguistic perspective.* Newark, DE: International Reading Association.

Langer, J. A. (in press–a). How readers construct meaning: An analysis of performance on standardized test items. In R. Freedle (Ed.), *Cognitive and linguistic analyses of standardized test performance.* Norwood, NJ: Ablex.

Langer, J. A. (in press–b). Examining background knowledge and test comprehension. *Reading Research Quarterly.*

Langer, J. A., & Nicolich, M. (1981). Prior knowledge and its effect on comprehension. *Journal of Reading Behavior, 13,* 4, 373–379.

Macrorie, K. (1970). *Telling writing.* Rochelle Park, NJ: Hayden.

Martin, J. (1976). *Writing and learning across the curriculum.* London: Ward Lock Education.

Matsuhashi, A. (1979). Producing written discourse. Unpublished doctoral dissertation, State University of New York at Buffalo.

Matsuhashi, A. (1981). Pausing and planning: The tempo of written discourse production. *Research in the Teaching of English, 2,* 113–134.

McCrimmon, J. H. (1980). *Writing with a purpose.* Boston, MA: Houghton Mifflin.

Meyer, B. (1975). *The organization of prose and its effects on memory.* New York: Elsevier.

Meyer, B. (1981, Spring). Prose analysis: Procedures, purposes, and problems. Department of Educational Psychology, College of Education, Arizona State University.

Mischel, T. (1974). A case study of a twelfth grade writer. *Research in the Teaching of English, 8,* 303–314.

Murray, D. M. (1978). Internal revision: A process of discovery. In Cooper, C. R. & Odell, L. (Eds.), *Research on Composing.* Urbana: IL: National Council of Teachers of English.

Murray, D. M. (1978). Teach the motivating force of revision. *English Journal, 67,* 7, 56–60.

National Assessment of Educational Progress. (NAEP). (1977). *Write/rewrite: An assessment of revision skills; selected results from the second national assessment of writing.* Denver, CO: Education Commission of the States.

Newell, G. (1983). A case study-protocol analysis of writing to learn in two content areas. Unpublished doctoral dissertation Stanford University, Stanford, CA.

Odell, L. (1977). Measuring changes in intellectual processes as one dimension of growth in writing. In C. Cooper and L. Odell (Eds.), *Evaluating writing.* Urbana, IL: National Council of Teachers of English.

Osterdorf, L. (1975). Summary of offerings and enrollments in public secondary schools, 1972–1973. Washington, DC: National Center for Education Statistics.

Perl, S. (1979). The composing processes of unskilled college writers, *Research in the Teaching of English, 13,* 4, 317–336.

Pianko, S. (1979). A description of the composing processes of college freshmen writers. *Research in the Teaching of English, 13,* 5–22.

Polanyi, M. (1958). *Personal knowledge.* London: Routledge & Kegan Paul.

Rumelhart, D. (1975). Notes on a schema for stories. In Bobrow, D. G. & Collins, A. M. (Eds.), *Representation and understanding: studies in cognitive science.* New York: Academic Press.

Rumelhart, D. (1977). Toward an interactive model of reading. In S. Dornic (Ed.), *Attention and Performance VI.* New York: Academic Press.

Sawkins, M. W. (1975). What children say about writing. *The writing processes of students: Report of the first annual conference on language arts.* Buffalo, NY: State University of New York.

Scardamalia, M., Bereiter, C., & Goelman, H. (1982). The role of production factors in writing ability. In P. M. Nystrand (Ed.), *What Writers Know.* New York: Academic Press.

Sommers, N. (1978). Revision in the composing process: A case study of college freshmen and experienced adult writers. Unpublished doctoral dissertation, Boston University, Boston, MA.

Sommers, N. (1980, December). Revision strategies of student writers and experienced adult writers. *College Composition and Communication. 31,* 4, 378–388.

Stallard, C. K. (1974). An analysis of the writing behavior of good student writers. *Research in the Teaching of English, 8,* 206–218.

Suydam, M. N., & Osborne, A. (1977). The status of pre-college science, mathematics, and social science education: 1955–1975. Vol. II. Mathematics education. Columbus, OH: Center for Science and Mathematics Education.

Vygotsky, L. S. (1962). *Thought and Language.* Cambridge, MA: MIT Press.

Vygotsky, L. S. (1978). *Mind in society.* Cambridge, MA: Harvard University Press.

Weiss, I. R. (1978). Report of the 1977 national survey of science, mathematics and social science education: Final report. Durham, NC: Center for Educational Research and Evaluation.

Wiley, K. B., & Race, J. (1977). The status of pre-college science, mathematics and social science education: 1955–1975. Vol. III. Social science education. Boulder, CO: Social Science Education Consortium.

Yost, M. (1973). Similarity of science textbooks: A content analysis. *Journal of Research in Science Teaching, 10,* 4, 317–322.

Zimet, S. G., et al. (1971). Attitudes and values in primers from the United States and twelve other countries. *Journal of Social Psychology, 84,* 167–174.

Author Index

Pages in italics indicate complete bibliographic citations.

Subject Index